Patterns That Remain

Patterns That Remain

A Guide to Healing for Asian Children of Immigrants

STACEY DIANE ARAÑEZ LITAM

OXFORD

UNIVERSITY PRESS

OXFORD
UNIVERSITY PRESS

Oxford University Press is a department of the University of Oxford. It furthers the University's objective of excellence in research, scholarship, and education by publishing worldwide. Oxford is a registered trade mark of Oxford University Press in the UK and certain other countries.

Published in the United States of America by Oxford University Press
198 Madison Avenue, New York, NY 10016, United States of America.

Library of Congress Cataloging-in-Publication Data
Names: Arañez Litam, Stacey Diane, author.
Title: Patterns that remain : a guide to healing for Asian children of immigrants / Stacey Diane Arañez Litam.
Description: New York, NY : Oxford University Press, [2025] |
Includes bibliographical references.
Identifiers: LCCN 2024023749 | ISBN 9780197762677 (hardback) |
ISBN 9780197762691 (epub) | ISBN 9780197762684 (updf) | ISBN 9780197762707 (online)
Subjects: LCSH: Asian Americans—Mental health. |
Asian Americans—Psychology. | Adult children of immigrants—Mental
health—United States. | Adult children of immigrants—United States—Psychology.
Classification: LCC RC451.5.A75 .A827 2025 |
DDC 616.890089/95073—dc23/eng/20240909
LC record available at https://lccn.loc.gov/2024023749

DOI: 10.1093/oso/9780197762677.001.0001

Printed by Sheridan Books, Inc., United States of America

To my sweet boys Kit Anthony and Chaston Patrick.
You are now, and will always be, my greatest teachers.

Contents

Foreword by Kevin Leo Yabut Nadal, PhD   ix
Preface   xiii

1. Breaking the Silence About Unhelpful Patterns and Mental Health   1

2. Understanding Historical Trauma and Scarcity Mindsets   15

3. Patterns That Remain Among Asian Americans   24

4. Childhood Attachment Wounds in Adult Relationships   40

5. Insecure Attachment Styles Among Asian Americans   51

6. Identifying and Challenging Sexual Scripts   59

7. Becoming Balanced People: How Patterns Impact Our Well-Being   77

8. Wholehearted Acceptance: Toward a Healing Orientation   100

9. Pattern-Breaking Strategies for Self-Nourishment   117

10. On Parenting and Healing Diasporic Wounds   136

Conclusion: Final Thoughts and Takeaways   155

Acknowledgments   157
Appendix 1: The Healing Orientation Model Elements (HOME)
   Assessment   161
Appendix 2: Participant Demographics   165
Notes   167
Resources   175
Bibliography   177
Index   185
About the Author   193

Foreword

Growing up as a Filipino American and a child of immigrants, there were many experiences that made me feel different than my non-Filipino peers. My parents spoke with accents and typically said English words incorrectly; because they were not educated in the American school system, I learned how to fill out my own parental forms and to correct my own homework. At Thanksgiving dinner, the turkey was merely one of many main entrees—competing alongside savory Filipino dishes like *lechon, kare kare,* and *dinuguan.* Regarding food in general, we were taught to never be wasteful—which often meant eating everything on your plate (even though your stomach was already at full capacity) or disregarding expiration dates altogether.

Having grown up in a large Filipino American extended family—with at least 50 kids who I considered my cousins, regardless of our actual blood relation— I felt at ease when I was with other people who looked like me. There was no need to explain (or even talk about) the odd things that our families did; it was just understood. However, once I exited my front door and walked onto schoolgrounds (or any other space in which I was in the minority), that ease typically transformed to anxiety or embarrassment. I desperately wanted to fit in. I did not want anyone commenting on my parents' accents or word choices. I did not want anyone questioning the food I brought for lunch. I did not want anyone to notice any differences between us. I was just as American as anyone else—a kid who liked watching cartoons on Saturday mornings and *Solid Gold* on Saturday nights (if my parents let me stay up that late).

During my adolescence, these feelings of "otherness" lingered, with experiences of racial microaggressions and homophobic bullying becoming common occurrences. Yet, such encounters were rarely discussed, mostly because there weren't any outlets to do so. With full-time jobs, my parents did not have the capacity to know about everything going on in my life. Well-intentioned teachers were not equipped to have conversations about racial dynamics, heteronormativity, or even mental health issues. And the rest of my peers—especially other young people of color and children of immigrants—were just doing our best to succeed. Consequently, I just internalized all negative emotions and hoped that things would get better—while occasionally engaging in teenage angst, parental defiance, and behavioral issues that could have (and statistically *should* have) resulted in a less happy ending than what actually transpired.

While these formative experiences became early motivators that shaped my career trajectory (as a psychologist and scholar who studies and writes about racial identity, queer identity, mental health, and intersectionalities), I often wonder about what would have been possible if I had had more people or resources who validated my experiences. If I had had someone to normalize that being queer was something to be celebrated, would I have spent so many years agonizing in the closet alone? If I had had someone who acknowledged how my ability to successfully codeswitch as well as I did was an extraordinary talent and skill, would I have ever developed the imposter feelings that haunted me well into my adulthood? And if I had had someone to explain to me that my parents being so distant or unavailable was more about systemic oppression than it was about their own limitations, would I have learned to appreciate them way earlier than I did?

These are the questions that consistently emerged and re-emerged when I first read *Patterns That Remain: A Guide to Healing for Asian Children of Immigrants* by Dr. Stacey Diane Arañez Litam. My initial thought was about how helpful such a resource would have been for me as a young person. Perhaps it could have been something that helped me feel more part of a collective, instead of feeling like I was the only one. My second thought was about how useful this book will be for the Asian Americans who read it. While I feel privileged that my personal journey with psychotherapy, my experiences as a psychologist, and my strong support system led me to wellness and success, I know that there are so many people who spend their whole lifetimes searching for healing and validation. Because of this, I have no doubt that this book can be a stepping point for so many people to begin (or continue) their journeys toward self-discovery, self-recovery, and self-acceptance.

Each chapter felt like it was personally speaking to me—with the author effortlessly integrating anecdotes from her own family and personal history while also sharing relatable content from the dozens of other Asian Americans she interviewed. What felt most compelling for me is knowing that although Dr. Litam and I grew up in different generations and geographic locations, our experiences were so similar. In this way, we learn about the power of culture—that even though our families are not related in any way, grew up in different parts of the Philippines, migrated to different parts of the United States, and have never crossed paths before, they instilled similar values into their children and grandchildren.

Relatedly, when we think about the diversity of the Asian American umbrella group—which consists of over four dozen ethnicities, as well as hundreds of languages, religions, and cultural identities—we know that they also encounter similar yet nuanced experiences in the United States. Because of systemic oppression, white supremacy, U.S. imperialism, and more, Asian Americans become racialized in a way in which they are taught to be silently invisible. Yet, Dr. Litam's work in centering their voices—especially representing a vast spectrum of South Asian, Southeast Asian, and East Asian Americans—assists readers in embracing their role in a collective and empowers them to want to be louder and more visible.

What I most appreciated about the text was Dr. Litam's ability to present an array of psychological concepts in accessible ways. She describes concepts like historical trauma, mental health, and attachment, offering both general definitions and relatable examples that are typically not provided for Asian Americans. For example, because most of the academic literature on historical trauma has traditionally focused on the Holocaust and Jewish people, the enslavement of Black people, or the genocide of Indigenous peoples, Asian Americans are often left out of the conversation. However, by telling her family's own history with war and violence, Dr. Litam encourages her readers to examine the ways that their own families may have been affected by historical oppression and how that trauma has been passed down to future generations.

Finally, the author is successful at ensuring that not only readers are introduced to (and validated by) various concepts, but that they also learn practical methods to assist in their healing journeys. Readers are asked to reflect on their own self-concepts and their own relationships—alluding to their need to work both internally (i.e., interrogating their own thoughts and emotions) and externally (i.e., challenging their impact towards, and needs from, others). The Healing Orientation Model Elements (HOME) Assessment is especially valuable in helping couples to communicate with each other about their needs and desires—particularly for those who may struggle with recognizing how their foundational experiences influence their current relationships.

Patterns That Remain: A Guide to Healing for Asian Children of Immigrants should be required reading for all Asian Americans, especially for those who are interested in understanding how our collective histories of trauma and oppression affect our individual lives. I am confident that this text can be a reliable resource for jumpstarting Asian Americans' journeys toward wellness and healing, especially when used concurrently with psychotherapy and other mental health treatment. As Asian Americans and other communities of color continue to navigate a world in which they are silenced or violently targeted, this book can serve as a guide to validate, normalize, and celebrate our strengths and resilience. Kudos to Dr. Litam for facilitating this conversation and for equipping the next generation with the toolbox that many of us wish we had had.

Kevin Leo Yabut Nadal, PhD
Distinguished Professor
City University of New York

Preface

It is winter break in the 2021–2022 academic year. I am sitting in the playroom with my six-month-old son, and we are reading *The Very Hungry Caterpillar* for what feels like the hundredth time. The snow is gently falling just beyond our big bay windows, and although everything on the outside feels peaceful and quiet, I am overwhelmed by an internal sense of chaos.

My mind is racing at the thought of all the emails I haven't answered since this morning.

"What if a student needs something over break?"

"What if a clinical supervisee is experiencing a client emergency and they need my help to resolve a crisis?"

"What if a company needs a speaker for a fabulous opportunity and time is of the essence?"

I am distracted and desperately waiting for the slightest indication of a "sleepy sign" so I can put my baby down for a nap and get back to work. I am watching his chubby little hands, willing them to slowly rise up to his face and rub his tired eyes.

I am convinced that future opportunities, contracts, and good news await me in my inbox.

Without warning, something unfamiliar snaps me back into the present moment. My son has picked up his book and plopped himself into my lap. The weight of him fills me with comfort, joy, and gratitude. He has never done this before, and I am in awe at his new ability.

I've been racking my brain, trying to find ways to give my son a wonderful life, yet his heart is full just sitting here with me in the present moment. He already knows he is enough.

At this moment, I realize I have a pattern.

For as long as I can remember, I've been a chaser, forever pursuing the next great accomplishment, award, or opportunity. Once I achieve it, I don't even allow myself time to feel satisfaction. There is no pride, no gratitude, no peace. The moment I receive good news, I am already looking ahead, ready to chase the next thing.

Somewhere along the line, I had internalized the belief that *I will never have enough money, and money is what will keep my family safe.*

This scarcity mindset is one that many Asian Americans and children of Asian immigrants internalize from a very early age. We have swallowed this cultural script whole without stopping to reflect on the extent to which it serves us or harms us.

We fear that we will never have enough—enough love, enough connection, enough money, enough time, enough resources, enough food. We are forever chasing, gathering, harvesting, working in frenzied states to achieve an ambiguous goal that we can never accomplish.

Rest, psychological and emotional well-being, connection and belonging, unconditional love and acceptance: We want these things desperately, and yet we have internalized cultural scripts from our ancestors that fundamentally prevent us from achieving what we desire deep inside.

When I was a child, I believed my parents were there for me in all the ways they thought mattered, but not emotionally. They attended my sporting events, cheered me on when I won awards, and ensured I had the resources to succeed. Although I attended (and they paid for) the most prestigious educational programs, I never truly felt seen or valued. Any award or accomplishment I earned was met with statements like, "Of course you did that, you've always been so smart" or "You earned that because I prayed for you" or "I gave up my career to raise you right and make sure you would be successful."

In these moments, I felt dismissed. I began to believe I was not enough, nor had I achieved enough. I needed to accomplish more.

As Asian Americans and children of Asian immigrants, many of us are wounded. We are fragmented pieces of ourselves who were not given permission to fully feel, fully experience, or fully grow. When our parents immigrated to the United States, they made the ultimate sacrifice: They left their families, their culture, and their language. They encouraged us to assimilate, to let go of our language and culture to fit into Western society. They taught us to behave in ways that would make them proud and avoid bringing shame to our families. They taught us not to rock the boat or make waves.

My parents believed that because they had sacrificed so much to come to America, my successes were an extension of their own. My identity was not mine, but something they could leverage as social capital when they were in community among other Asian Americans, all of whom would speak about their children's accomplishments as if they were going to battle. Whose child was attending which university? Which sibling had attracted the most eligible partner? Whose child had accomplished the most prestigious professional accolade? The endless comparisons would pit us against one another like pieces on a chessboard. Our accomplishments were carried like points of pride that could be thrown alongside the tiles of a Mahjong table.

Sitting with my son in the playroom, I realized that enough was enough. How much longer would I drive myself into the ground to earn my parents' approval of *me-apart-from-them*? How much longer would I keep my head down and work endless hours to strive for more financial security when, objectively, we had enough? Most importantly, how do these mindsets keep me from focusing on my legacy? My relationships? My husband? My family?

I knew that letting go of this scarcity mindset and cultivating a perspective of abundance would require me to critically reflect on the cultural scripts I had inherited from my parents, my ancestors, and society at large. I knew that in doing so, I needed to obtain a deeper understanding of my parents' struggles. I needed to untangle the complex and nuanced messages, beliefs, and values of my family of origin to unlock a greater sense of connection, belonging, and emotional well-being. *I believe we can contextualize our ancestors' stories in ways that will empower us to move beyond these limiting narratives, begin to heal our attachment wounds, and become better parents, partners, and people.*

I also knew I needed to begin processing the internalized shame and sexualization I had been carrying as an Asian American woman living in the United States. I was becoming more aware of the ways in which media and cultural portrayals of Asian Americans had impacted my personal, professional, and sexual development. I am no longer willing to let those limiting internalized perceptions embody a presence in my day-to-day life. I refuse to allow these harmful representations to continue paying rent in my mind.

I watch my son grow more and more each day. I am in constant awe of how he does things in his own time, in his own way. He eats, he laughs, he lives as though he is already in a world of abundance. Nobody taught him how to do that; he just inherently knows.

Ultimately, parenthood is a practice in mindfulness. When I am with my son, I must continue pulling my mind away from thoughts about work, emails, and academe. Those will always be present, a never-ending process. Meanwhile, the time I have with my son is fleeting. Today as I write this, and in the future as I read this, he is older than he's ever been and he's as young as he will ever be.

Now that I am learning to separate myself from the bind of my parents' sacrifice and recreating a new sense of identity, I can focus on my legacy. As Asian Americans, our legacies do not have to be limited to the accomplishments we've made through work to prove our value, establish ourselves as worthy of happiness, or satisfy our parents' wishes. Instead, our legacies can consist of the people whom we've touched along life's journey. The more we can let go of the cultural scripts that scream, "We are not enough!" the more successful we will be on our journeys toward greater mental well-being, secure attachment, and an integrated identity for our children, our partner, and ourselves.

Until we have labels that describe our experiences, those experiences remain invisible. I am writing this book to aggregate the stories, experiences, and realities that many Asian Americans and children of Asian immigrants have carried for years, possibly decades, but did not have the language to capture. I believe there is power in our stories and that reflecting on our histories represents an important first step toward healing. Before we can clearly see where we are going, we need to understand where we have been—and where our families have been. We must reflect on our parents' stories as well as our own childhood experiences to inform our futures.

I hope to connect with each of you by leveraging the power of Asian American stories, both my own and those of our communities. I believe that hearing similar stories from others cultivates a greater sense of universality, community, and understanding, and a recognition that we are not alone. In preparation for this book, I spoke with 30 Asian American thought leaders, content experts, and community members to capture their experiences, challenges, and strategies toward healing.

In addition to leveraging the diverse voices of Asian American community members, I sprinkled in a few other features that make this book unique. Each chapter culminates with a quick-and-dirty TLDR (Too Long, Didn't Read) that provides a comprehensive overview of major takeaways. You will also find a Questions to Ponder section that is designed to spark juicy moments of self-reflection, introspection, and curiosity. These questions are best explored while embodying self-compassion, feelings of love and kindness toward our families of origin, and an openness to learn more about our patterns. Some chapters include another section, Questions to Bridge the Gap with Parents, which is offered to begin broaching intergenerational dialogues. Finally, I include the Healing Orientation Model Elements (HOME) Assessment in Appendix 1. The HOME Assessment is an engaging, fun, and interesting self-survey that offers insight and awareness about specific elements of our relationships. Though the HOME Assessment emerged from conversations with Asian American storytellers, it has not been psychometrically tested or validated as a psychological assessment; in other words, don't use it to "diagnose" a failed relationship! Instead, I hope it emboldens deeper levels of self-reflection and encourages dynamic conversations with your partner, or even your therapist.

At some point throughout these first pages, you may have wondered, "Who is this person?", "What does she know?", and "Why should I listen to her?"

I am, first and foremost, a mother, a wife, and the daughter of Filipino immigrants. Extending beyond these core identities, I am a professor in a graduate counselor education program, a clinical mental health counselor and supervisor, a clinical sexologist, a researcher, a public speaker, and a business owner. My clinical, pedagogical, and research areas are focused on helping Black,

Indigenous, and People of Color (BIPOC) access healing by embracing strength-based, trauma-sensitive, culturally responsive, and decolonized mindsets. I know in my heart that storytelling represents both a healing process and a means of transferring knowledge. My hope is to leverage what I have learned as a mother, partner, daughter, researcher, counselor, content expert, and educator to help others begin their journeys toward greater self-awareness and overall well-being. I hope that sharing my story, as well as the stories of many others, will help future generations move beyond the limiting narratives inherited from their families of origin and society as a whole to heal attachment wounds and become better parents, partners, and people. Although I have made great progress throughout my own journey, I know that unlearning these cultural scripts represents a lifelong process. New challenges, objects of awareness, and complex dynamics will undoubtedly arise as our lives unfold. And when they do, I hope this book provides the language and foundation necessary to meet each experience with humility, grace, and curiosity.

I wrote this book with the experiences of Asian Americans and children of Asian immigrants in mind. Many of the challenges we face today echo centuries of oppression and are deeply intertwined with our ancestry and culture. Though the experiences, challenges, and constructs explored in this book are primarily grounded and contextualized within a distinctly Asian American framework, I recognize that they extend well beyond our narratives. In reality, insecure attachments, emotional childhood wounds, scarcity mindsets, and limiting cultural scripts can impact anyone, regardless of ethnic identity. As a result, this book has the potential to benefit anyone, including BIPOC, biracial, multiethnic, and multiracial individuals who have internalized unhelpful cultural scripts and find themselves emotionally wounded, striving to feel more attached, and wanting to operate from places of abundance. Beyond that, this book is for individuals who see themselves in these stories and who recognize the importance of breaking unhelpful generational patterns.

If you have noticed feelings of resentment and ambivalence about your upbringing, this book is for you.

If you have been told that you need to work twice as hard to get half as far and have historically denied yourself rest and the belief in abundance, this book is for you.

If you are curious about how cultivating greater empathy and understanding toward your parents and ancestors can unlock opportunities to heal generational diasporic wounds, this book is for you.

If you are a parent or a caregiver, either currently or in your heart, and you want to intentionally break unhelpful cycles for your family and for your child(ren), this book is for you.

If you have struggled with vulnerability in relationships and have engaged in problematic coping skills when conflict arises between you and your partner, this book is for you.

By the end of this book, I hope you will take away new cultural scripts about your inherent worth, value, and light as a whole person who is worthy of love, belonging, and healthy relationships. I also hope you obtain the knowledge, awareness, and skills to begin cultivating empathy for your parents, your wounded inner child, and your adult self to begin healing from diasporic wounds. Ultimately, I hope that beginning your healing journey will help you unlock greater well-being, balance, and joy as a person, partner, and parent.

This book is not a substitute for professional mental health counseling services. Instead, I hope you will use this book as a resource to broach topics and enhance conversations about healing, growth, and attachment with a trusted licensed mental health professional.

At times throughout this process, things may feel daunting. You may experience complex feelings, put down this book to take a break, and notice emotional flashbacks. Emotional flashbacks, or moments that remind us of previous challenging experiences, can identify specific events in our lives that we need to understand and reframe rather than *to get over*. When emotional flashbacks occur, they can be signs that you have stumbled upon parts of your childhood, and yourself, that are worthy of healing. I hope you rise to the challenge. *You are deserving of breaks, and you are deserving of rest.* Healing follows discomfort, and it is time to allocate the same compassion to yourself that you extend so freely to others.

I am thrilled at the idea of untangling these experiences with you. A future characterized by abundance, joy, and connection awaits you between these pages.

It's time to rock the boat.

1

Breaking the Silence About Unhelpful Patterns and Mental Health

How do we begin the monumental task of understanding how unhelpful patterns and cultural scripts may be keeping us from unlocking joy, achieving optimal mental health, and enjoying secure relationships? How do we arrive at places of collective healing when so many of us have been carrying around these deep childhood wounds for years? To explore the answers to these questions and so much more, we need to establish some background.

Although Asian Americans are often grouped together as one monolithic entity, the term *Asian American* encompasses over 50 distinct subgroups, each of whom demonstrate heterogeneity across language, educational background, religion, immigration and migration histories, beliefs about mental health, and attitudes toward help-seeking behaviors. Though we cannot aggregate the stories, experiences, and challenges of all Asian American families, based on my interviews, areas of research, and anecdotal evidence, it seems as though our communities tend to share a few overlapping commonalities. These include values related to collectivism, filial piety, saving face, and promoting interpersonal harmony.

Collectivism refers to a mentality where individuals prioritize one's community as a whole rather than the individual members. Examples of communities can include families of origin, extended family, and one's ethnic subgroup on broader levels (the Filipino American community, the Korean American community, etc.) The presence of collectivistic values among Asian American communities often overlaps with other traditional values, including *filial piety* (respect for one's parents and ancestors), *saving face* (avoiding embarrassment or shame), and promoting interpersonal harmony to avoid conflict.

What happens when these values are embodied so deeply that we prioritize the comfort, happiness, and well-being of those around us, even at the expense of ourselves? Many of us have focused on preserving the comfort of others for so long that we haven't stopped to think about how these cultural values create barriers to our well-being. Children of Asian immigrants often feel a great sense of indebtedness to our ancestors and carry the cultural scripts of filial piety, saving face, and collectivism as a means of honoring our parents and demonstrating respect for their sacrifices. We internalize beliefs that the best way to convey gratitude to our parents is by honoring their wishes and accomplishing their dreams without stopping to reflect on our own aspirations.

It is difficult to comprehend the challenges our immigrant parents faced when they abandoned the comfort and familiarity of their homes and arrived in a new country where everything seemed foreign. For many Asian immigrant families, the idea of achieving the American Dream was an enticing aspiration. Some parents became enchanted with ideas of providing a greater set of educational and occupational opportunities for their children. They worked long hours and endured countless sacrifices to better position their children for success. Others sought to flee oppressive countries of origin where they feared their children would be unable to thrive—or even survive. Indeed, our Asian American community carries histories that include imperialism, colonialism, and colonization. Our ancestral stories have chapters characterized by war, political upheaval, violence, and resource scarcity that have driven waves of migration from Asian countries to the United States.[1] Regardless of their origin story, it seems as though all immigrant parents are bound by several powerful concepts and values: *Work hard, be obedient, and sacrifice for family.* Values are passed down through stories, and I knew it was time to come to a reckoning with mine.

My Origin Stories

My ancestral story parallels the experiences of countless other Filipinos and Filipino Americans. My Lola (Tagalog for grandmother) Dory was born in Batangas, Philippines, in 1932. When the Japanese army invaded Manila in December 1941, she was only nine years old. Lola Dory recounts how the Japanese army occupied the first floor of our ancestral home while her father, sisters, and caregivers were relocated on the second floor. One morning, her father was awakened by the sounds of yelling below. He quickly packed up his daughters and fled to the foothills of the Luzon Mountains before taking residence in the Taal Volcano Island for four years. My Lola remembers the smell of our ancestral home, which burned for nearly one week after Japanese forces reduced everything in the town to ashes. When recounting her trauma narrative, she emphasizes the importance of obedience, endurance, and sacrifice. Without these values, she may not have survived such harrowing experiences.

I never met my great-uncle, Lolo (Tagalog for grandfather) Cecilio. Lolo Cecilio was the older brother, or *kuya*, to my grandfather Lolo José. When the Philippine army requested that civilians join the fight against Japanese forces, my Lolo José and his brother Cecilio were among the first in line for the draft.

Because my Lolo José was too young, the Philippine army did not allow him to enlist. While Lolo José stayed home to care for his younger siblings, Lolo Cecilio went on to enlist in the Philippine army and fought bravely alongside Filipino and American soldiers. After months of intense battle, few resources, and no reinforcements, the American and Filipino soldiers stationed on the Bataan Peninsula were forced to surrender to the Japanese army on April 9, 1942. What followed was the *Bataan Death March*, an event that is still largely considered one of the worst human rights atrocities to have ever occurred. The captured American and Filipino soldiers were lined up and forced to march approximately 65 miles in over-100-degree weather without food, water, or rest. Over the span of seven days, thousands of troops died from starvation, dehydration, malaria, and gratuitous violence. By the end of the war, an estimated 527,000 Filipino soldiers and civilians had been killed. In total, between 131,000 and 164,000 Filipinos were killed in 72 war crimes.[2]

Lolo Cecilio was described as a caring, compassionate, and law-abiding man. Though he miraculously managed to survive the Bataan Death March, he died of malaria before the labor camp liberation in 1945. His body was never recovered or returned to our family. Lolo Cecilio likely survived the brutal treatment of the Bataan Death March by keeping his head down, not challenging those in authority, and not being too loud or calling attention to himself. Relatives who share his story revere his ability to embody these important values, especially given the challenges he faced. Lolo José went on to marry Lola Dory and together they had five children. He earned a master's degree in reproductive pathology from Cornell University and became a doctor of veterinary medicine in 1946. After a life well lived, Lolo José died in 2017 at the age of 96. To this day, my family lauds his devotion toward family, hard work, and duty.

The origin of my values only came to light upon reflection of my ancestral heritage. My values of obedience, endurance, sacrifice, and compassion had been imparted through the stories passed down across generations. I had not chosen them; I had inherited them.

Cultural Scripts and Conspiracies of Silence

How is it that so many of our immigrant parents and ancestors carry the same or similar cultural scripts and values espousing the importance of hard work, obedience, and sacrifice despite our varying histories, experiences, and challenges? To unlock the power of our stories, we must contextualize how our ancestors' experiences may have contributed to their cultural scripts.

In 1989, my father immigrated to the United States from the Philippines. Although he was already a physician in our home country, he was forced to complete an oncology residency and fellowship once more in the States. He rented small spaces and endured many freezing months without heat in the brutal winters of New York and Ohio. When possible, he would take additional night shifts at the hospital because working residents were given access to hot meals and open cots. On one occasion, my father chipped a tooth while eating *champoy* (a dried plum) and could not afford to get it fixed.

My mother's sacrifices seem equally insurmountable. Once my father was settled as a resident in the United States, she flew across the Pacific Ocean with my brother and me. At the time, we were four and two years old. I cannot imagine the fear, worry, and concern she must have quietly held in her heart as she moved across an ocean alone with two small children. Our family quickly grew to include my two younger brothers, whom she raised without the help of *yayas* (Tagalog for nannies) in our Houston, Texas, home. When my father accepted a position in Ohio, my mom stayed back with four young children for seven months so we could finish out the school year.

Looking back, I don't remember picking up on my mother's fear. Like many immigrant parents, my mother does not discuss the details of her experiences often. When I ask how she managed to raise my brothers and me alone, she says *she just did it; she had no choice.* Like countless other immigrant parents with children, there is simply no other option *but* to survive.

Perhaps she had internalized the historical cultural scripts passed down from my Lola, which emphasize the importance of sacrifice for one's family. Maybe she manifested the strength and endurance of my Lolo Cecilio, who survived the Bataan Death March against all odds. Perhaps she embodied the hard work and resilience of my Lolo José, who quietly published nearly 40 academic articles despite facing countless instances of racial discrimination in the United States. It seems the cultural scripts in my family include messages such as "Don't act in ways that draw too much attention," "Don't be too loud or cause trouble," "Don't rock the boat," "Do whatever it takes to survive," "Endure under pressure and discomfort," and "Follow the rules and honor your commitments." Both of my parents carried these messages deeply and leveraged them without question in ways that undoubtedly contributed to their success as they adjusted to life in a new country.

My parents were magicians at feeding four children and creating childhoods that never hinted at their deeper struggles. I never learned of their sacrifices until much later in life. Many Asian Americans with whom I have spoken share similar experiences. Our immigrant parents avoid discussing the details of their historical trauma and immigration stress because they want to protect their children or avoid burdening others. Within the extant body of literature, this collective experience is commonly referred to as *a conspiracy of silence.*[3] The conspiracy-of-silence phenomenon occurs when historical trauma narratives, such as the stories left unspoken among Asian American families, remain unaddressed; parents avoid discussing it and children avoid asking about it.

Though our parents' intentions are admirable, ignoring these historical trauma narratives can combine with internalized social and cultural scripts in ways that impact our abilities to form secure attachments, cultivate empathy for our parents' struggles, access joy in our relationships, and achieve optimal psychological health. When parents avoid communicating openly about their trauma experiences, these stories remain unprocessed, and access to healing becomes difficult. In many cases, our immigrant parents simply did not have the luxury or language to share their stories, pursue greater meaning, or facilitate personal reflection because they were solely focused on survival and assimilation. Ultimately, the conspiracy of silence among Asian American families contributes to a lack of understanding across Asian American generations and can result in relationship challenges as well as attachment wounds between parents and children. The conspiracy of silence has also been identified in research as a significant mechanism in the continued transmission of trauma from generation to generation.[4] When it comes to inheriting aspects of historical trauma and intergenerational patterns, what remains unspoken can be just as powerful as what is openly shared.

The Power of Cultural Scripts

The lack of communication between parents and children about historical trauma is one way that limiting cultural messages and harmful cultural scripts persist across generations and contribute to attachment wounds. Covert messages weigh heavily on the hearts and minds of Asian Americans and children of Asian immigrants. It is not what is said but what is *not said* that children notice from an early age. If you ask teachers, child-focused mental health professionals, and even parents of young children, each of them will tell you that children have an uncanny ability to make meaning out of ambiguous circumstances They can't help it; it is their superpower. When parents avoid sharing personal challenges with their children because they believe they are *protecting them*, children tend to internalize different beliefs associated with this silence. Their young minds immediately go to work in an attempt to put the pieces of a complex puzzle together.

Depending on the child, beliefs may include:

Our family story is one I must be ashamed of because we don't talk about the past.
My parents do not explicitly verbalize their love for me, so I must not be lovable.
My parents emphasize the importance of hard work, so that must be the only way to prove my value.

I am indebted to my parents and must adhere to their wishes and honor their sacrifices at the expense of my own well-being.
My personal problems and emotions do not matter; I should feel more grateful.

The overt and covert messages that previous generations convey about who we are and who we are meant to become can impact our parenting styles and behaviors; our relationships with partners and children; our worldviews about ourselves, others, and society; and our abilities to be successful, motivated, and creative in workplace settings. Regardless of our countries of origin, Asian Americans and children of Asian immigrants often believe we must work twice as hard to get half as far. We carry cultural scripts that emphasize obedience, rule following, and assimilation. These messages are typically grounded within the framework of historical trauma narratives and limiting cultural scripts wherein individuals who deviated from these behavioral expectations faced dire consequences. These consequences included false imprisonment, political backlash, physical violence, verbal harassment, threats, racial discrimination, and in some cases murder. Other limiting cultural messages have been perpetuated through media, stereotypes, and socially embedded interactions that reinforce behaviors aimed at achieving white proximity while denigrating other behaviors perceived to be "too ethnic." This form of intra-ethnic othering is where terms such as "fresh off the boat" and "whitewashed" originated.[5]

We are taught to care for others and prioritize family above all else to honor and respect the hard work and sacrifice of our parents and ancestors who chased the American Dream. We are raised to believe the only path to success is to become a doctor, lawyer, or engineer. We are told that getting married and starting a family represents an all-important endeavor. We are expected to achieve these milestones without question through hard work, grit, and resilience. We accept this path of success from an early age and uphold it as the formula for happiness in Western society. Those of us who deviate are faced with the possibility of ridicule and ostracization from our families.

Dr. Valli, a first-generation Indian American woman, educator, and mental health professional in her mid-30s, shares how cultural messages about career and collectivism intersect in complex and nuanced ways:

I found myself in much trepidation as I charted out my career plan. Knowing I would never become an engineer, doctor, or lawyer meant I was willing to kiss my father's approval goodbye. I would never be the cousin who was praised in family gatherings. If anything, I would be the niece whose "poor career choices" were used as an example to warn others.

Dr. Valli's story echoes an all-too-familiar challenge for many Asian Americans and children of Asian immigrants: Who will we become and how will our family relationships change if we deviate from our parents' ideas of success? On one hand, covert messages of silence and overt messages espousing values of collectivism, conflict avoidance, hard work, and obedience seem to have paid off as more and more Asian families settle into American society in pursuit of the American Dream.

On the other hand, the building blocks to the American Dream represent the same core foundations that maintain the presence of the *model minority myth*. The model minority myth is the false belief that portrays all Asian Americans, especially East Asian–presenting individuals, as universally successful, highly educated, and law-abiding citizens. The phrase was coined in 1966 by California sociologist William Petersen, who described how Japanese Americans had achieved success after World War II. Years later, *Time* magazine published a 1987 issue that featured Asian American youth alongside the headline, "Those Asian American WHIZ KIDS." The feature firmly planted the model minority myth into the American zeitgeist.

In reality, wide disparities in income and education exist among Asians in the United States. According to the Pew Research Center, although Asian households had higher median annual incomes ($85,800) in 2019 compared to all U.S. households ($61,800), only two Asian groups (Indians and Filipinos) had household incomes that exceeded the median for Asian Americans overall, while Mongolian and Burmese groups reported poverty rates at twice the national average. Educational attainment also varies greatly among Asian Americans: Although 54 percent of U.S. Asians aged 25 and older earned a bachelor's degree or more, fewer than one in five Laotians and Bhutanese earned at least a bachelor's degree in 2019. Portraying Asian Americans as universally successful overlooks the wide disparities of income, education, and experiences that exist among our community and prevents access to important resources. The model minority myth is also especially harmful because it invalidates experiences of racial oppression faced by other communities of color while rendering Asian American challenges invisible. Even worse, it is used to overlook the ways in which racism and systemic oppression perpetuate disadvantages for Latine and African American communities while creating a false dichotomy that weaponizes Asian American identities. In other words, endorsing Asian Americans as *model minorities* positions other communities of color as *problem minorities*.

Depicting Asian Americans as exceptionally high-achieving also comes at a great cost to our emotional, psychological, and physical well-being. When society's narrative about Asian Americans is one that does not recognize our struggle, then addressing barriers to accessing professional mental health services, promoting overall health and physical well-being, and advocating for our culturally embedded needs become even more challenging. Portraying Asian Americans as a community without problems invalidates our great need for resources and contributes to disbelief when we ask for help. In other words, if nobody sees an Asian American weep in H Mart, did they really shed a tear?

Between the positive reinforcement of material success and the perpetuation of cultural scripts by our families and communities, many Asian American individuals and children of Asian immigrants are left to suffer emotional and mental health challenges in silence. For those of us who were raised in households that discouraged conversations about emotions and vulnerability, the very idea of expressing feelings of anxiety, sadness, anger, and depression can elicit deep, visceral feelings of shame. Discussing our emotions, feelings, and challenges can be weaponized against us as evidence of our lack of gratitude. As Asian Americans and Asian children of immigrants, we may internalize messages that demonstrating emotional vulnerability is one way to rock the boat and instill discomfort within the household. What we often fail to realize is that the discomfort occurs not because of our emotional expression, but because many of our parents were not given opportunities to process their own emotional challenges. Without the ability to process their own fears, experiences, and vulnerable emotions, our parents struggle to hold the space necessary to mitigate the fears, challenges, and vulnerable emotions in their children. Emotions and sensations can quickly become overwhelming, like a piece of fruit or bite of dessert that is far too sweet.

I have spoken to many Asian Americans and children of Asian immigrants who woefully express how their parents respond to emotional distress by invalidating their experiences. Parents compare the unfamiliar challenges of their children to their own, sometimes unrelated experiences from childhood. Parents may say things like, "You think you have it bad? When I was your age, I had to work even harder at school and if I failed, I didn't get to eat dinner." Parents may also belittle their children's emotions by responding with statements such as, "That's a silly thing to be upset about." Others redirect their children's emotions by encouraging them to cultivate a stronger sense of faith. For example, many Filipino Americans with whom I spoke shared how frequently they hear parents assert, "Just pray about it and things will be okay" or "If only your faith was stronger, you would not feel as depressed." When our parents respond to emotional distress in these ways, we begin to internalize new cultural scripts:

Demonstrating vulnerability leads to conflict.
My feelings cannot be trusted.
I must keep my challenges, emotional burdens, and mental health distress to myself.
I cannot be fully accepted, loved, or valued for who I am.

Many of us carry these scripts around for so long that they practically become armor. Within our romantic adult relationships and friendships, we maintain a certain emotional distance and avoid expressing our true thoughts, feelings, and desires. We struggle to ask for help, feel resentment when partners can't read our minds, and believe that swallowing our emotions whole is the best way to avoid conflict. We engage in people-pleasing[6] behaviors rooted in fears that if we set boundaries, make our desires known, or deviate from what is expected from us, then we are unlovable and will be abandoned.

These scripts persist into the journey into parenthood. We experience emotional flashbacks when our children engage in behaviors for which we were indiscriminately punished. We struggle to apologize, validate the complex emotions of our little ones, and have difficulty holding space for big feelings. We face our own unresolved attachment wounds as we learn to re-parent ourselves while parenting our children. We struggle to ask for help, prefer to suffer in silence, and minimize our identities as perfectly imperfect people, partners, and parents.

Finally, the same internalized cultural scripts impact us within workplace settings. We develop unhelpful habits that link our inherent value to objective forms of productivity. We struggle to engage in flexible boundary setting, minimize the importance of self-nourishment, and believe that we should be grateful for any opportunities that come our way. We keep our heads down, work hard, and bite our tongues to avoid rocking the boat and upsetting our supervisors. We become fragmented pieces of ourselves who are experts at flaunting the performances reinforced throughout our lifetime.

Speaking Up About Mental Health

The pressure exerted by familial and cultural values is not the only obstacle that discourages our Asian American communities from discussing topics related to emotional well-being, psychological health, and the importance of unlearning toxic cultural scripts. Historically, our community simply has not had access to resources that enable us to overcome cultural barriers and enhance mental health literacy. Without the presence of these resources, our unhelpful cultural scripts remain unacknowledged, unaddressed, and unchallenged.

Though many cultural barriers to mental health access exist, language barriers, lack of awareness of and accessibility to available resources and services, the presence of stigma surrounding mental health issues, and general attitudes about professional mental health services are among the largest. According to Mental Health America,[6] between 7.4 and 9.4 percent of Pacific Islanders lack health insurance and approximately 32.6 percent of Asian Americans do not speak English fluently. Compared to other communities of color, Asian Americans are the least likely racial or ethnic group to seek professional mental health services and are three times less likely to seek counseling compared to our white counterparts. These barriers to mental health access and literacy contribute to high rates of mental health and substance use disorders among Asian Americans and Pacific Islanders (AAPIs). According to the Substance Abuse and Mental Health Services Administration (SAMHSA), a total of 2.7 million AAPIs meet the criteria for a mental health and/or substance use disorder each year.

Barriers to accessing mental health also intersect with tendencies for mental health professionals to view psychological concerns from an ethnocentric, Western, and individualistic perspective. These theoretical frameworks were largely developed to support middle-class white individuals and may therefore have limited applicability and cultural relevance for communities of color, such as Asian Americans. Adhering to such worldviews when conceptualizing the experiences of Asian Americans and other marginalized communities increases the likelihood of misdiagnosis, early termination, and other treatment-related concerns. Indeed, many Asian Americans and children of Asian immigrants feel wary about pursuing professional mental health services because they worry about being judged, misunderstood, or pathologized. Though the movement to decolonize current mental health frameworks by incorporating counseling strategies that address and dismantle colonialism[7] while detaching cultural ways of knowing from Western imperialism are gaining traction,[8] cultural competence represents an aspirational goal, and we still have a long way to go.

Dr. Valli describes the fears that many Asian Americans face when considering whether to pursue professional mental health services:

There was no way I could talk about my cultural and family concerns to a white counselor who would recklessly label it as enmeshment. I still struggle to talk to a counselor about my family. I know exactly what kind of diagnoses are out there in the DSM-5-TR, and how they can be twisted by an incompetent and insensitive therapist. So I focus on more surface level concerns, hoping desperately that they will notice I am Brown, that I am a first-generation immigrant, and that I have my own stories to tell.

As a member of the Filipino American diaspora, I am keenly aware of how our families face distinct challenges. Compared to other Asian American subgroups, Filipino Americans are the least likely ethnic subgroup to seek professional mental health services. Based on a 2003 study of over 2,000 Filipino Americans,[9] approximately 73 percent of those surveyed had never pursued any type of mental health service and only 17 percent had sought help from friends, community members, peers, and religious leaders. Compared to other Asian American ethnic subgroups, Filipino Americans also experience distinct forms of microaggressions,[10] face greater trauma symptoms following instances of discrimination,[11] and engage in specific stress responses that are uniquely grounded in Indigenous, religious, and cultural values.[12] Indeed, the stigma and taboo surrounding mental health usage within the Filipino American community are strong.[13] Within many Filipino American households, it is not uncommon to hear the statement "Only crazy people go to therapy."

In this first chapter, we identified how conspiracies of silence may perpetuate the development of unhelpful cultural scripts. We dispelled myths related to the Asian American community and outlined the harmful effects of the model minority myth. We reviewed traditional Asian American values and validated the struggles and sacrifices of our immigrant parents. We explored the challenges of expressing vulnerability and emotional distress and identified how our parents' responses can perpetuate overt and covert messages about who we are and who we are expected to become. Finally, we established the importance of breaking the silence around mental health distress, destigmatizing emotional vulnerability, and overcoming cultural barriers to mental health access and literacy. My hope is that as you read, some of the words resonate and the experiences feel familiar. Though it may seem as though you are alone in your journey toward healing, I assure you that you are in good company.

The Asian American population is growing at an exponential rate. According to the Pew Research Center, Asian Americans are projected to become the largest immigrant group by 2055.[14] Reports from the 2020 Census additionally noted that 24 million people residing in the United States identified as Asian and 1.6 million individuals identified as Native Hawaiian and Other Pacific Islander.[15] The growing rate of AAPI immigration to the United States illuminates the pressing need to engage in discourse that centers mental health literacy and the development of new culturally congruent pathways that prioritize emotional well-being and healthy relationship patterns among partners and parents.

Seemingly overnight, I have begun to see more and more Asian American content creators on social media platforms, on the news, and in media. The conversations I am witnessing are powerful. These conversations are educational, personal, and incredibly vulnerable. They are exploring topics related to internalized racism, the detrimental effects of the model minority stereotype, the historical sexualization of Asian bodies, and the process of overcoming intergenerational trauma. To create a rich tapestry that connects the diverse and nuanced experiences, challenges, and stories of Asian Americans and Asian children of immigrants, I interviewed many of these thought leaders for this book.

Inviting Storytellers and Collecting Stories

Prospective storytellers were recruited in two ways. First, I extended personal invitations to Asian American community members, mental health professionals, nonprofit organizers, educators, community leaders, social justice activists, and media reporters whom I believed could offer powerful stories that captured the multifaceted realities of being Asian American. Individuals were invited to respond to prompts about relationships, mental health, Asian American identity, sexuality, and cultural scripts through a popular social media platform. Asian American storytellers represented the Southern, Southeastern, Northeastern, Mid-Atlantic, Midwestern, West Coast, Pacific Northwest, and Hawaiian geographical regions, with ages ranging from 24 to 47. By the time this project finished, I had connected with a total of 30 Asian American individuals who held diverse ethnic, generational, sexual, and gender identities.

Storytellers were provided with information about the purpose of this book and had the option to meet virtually or respond to the book prompts on their own. Storytellers provided their name or pseudonym, generational status, age group, ethnic/racial identity, sexual identity, and any other salient identifiers. An asterisk is used throughout this book to indicate the use of pseudonyms. Virtual discussions were recorded (with storyteller consent), transcribed, and broken down into themes. Two objective assessors independently reviewed the transcribed sections and categorical themes to promote trustworthiness and accuracy. As the project came to a close, I reached out to storytellers to confirm that their interview excerpts were accurate and that the themes included in this book resonated with and reflected their lived experiences.

Although conversations naturally evolved, several semistructured interview questions guided the discussions. These included prompts such as the following:

> *How have historical trauma and intergenerational patterns impacted your emotional, psychological, and physical well-being?*
>
> *How would you describe your attachment style in current and past relationships?*
>
> *What are some examples of cultural scripts that have impacted important areas of your life?*
>
> *How can Asian Americans bridge the gap between our parents and ourselves to access greater mental health, abundance, and joy?*
>
> *How have sexual stereotypes toward Asian Americans impacted our community as well as your experiences?*

As new themes and categories of meaning emerged, additional prompts evolved until no new information was gathered. A participant table can be found in Appendix 2.

I believe when our stories and experiences are centered, it paves the way for future generations to thrive by providing the language and concepts necessary to cultivate mental health literacy in ways that my generation, and generations before me, simply did not have access to.

So many of our families have been silent about their stories. And yet, understanding our stories, and the histories they carry, is essential to unlocking the power we hold within ourselves. I hope this book will serve as a helpful resource for you as you begin journeying in this new and exciting way. Simply picking up this book represents an important step and a commitment to your own process of self-reflection and healing. When you're ready, take a deep breath. It's time to get started.

Too Long, Didn't Read (TLDR): Though Asian Americans are a heterogenous group, many of us share collectivist values that include respecting and honoring our parents as well as avoiding conflict and shame. These cultural values compound with overt and covert messages from our families of origin about what it means to be emotionally vulnerable. Because our immigrant parents often lacked the resources and space to resolve their own historical trauma, our experiences of emotional vulnerability and challenges are often met with invalidation, discomfort, and minimization. As a result, we tend to internalize the following cultural scripts: Demonstrating vulnerability leads to conflict; My feelings cannot be trusted; I must keep my challenges, emotional burdens, and mental health distress to myself; I cannot be fully accepted, loved, or valued for who I am. Carrying these cultural scripts without question has impacts on us as people, partners, and parents.

Questions to Ponder

1. To what extent have I felt invalidated or unseen when expressing vulnerable emotions?
2. What are some examples of covert and overt messages in my family of origin?
3. What is my family's migration story?
4. What were my parents' and ancestors' experiences of migration in America?
5. Upon migration to the United States, what did my parents or ancestors hope to accomplish or experience?

Questions to Bridge the Gap with Parents

1. What are some of your proudest moments and greatest challenges?
2. When thinking about your life, what have been some of the most exciting, challenging, or rewarding moments?
3. Upon migration to the United States, what did you hope to accomplish or experience?

2

Understanding Historical Trauma and Scarcity Mindsets

❧

I am sitting at the breakfast table with my brothers on Saturday morning. At nine years old, I am nearly as tall as my *kuya* (older brother) and still much taller than my two younger brothers. I swing my feet under the chair and they play loudly as the smells of *longanisa* (a sweet Filipino breakfast sausage made with ground pork, garlic, salt, pepper, vinegar, and brown sugar), rice, and eggs fill the air.

Mom walks across the kitchen to carry plates of food to the table. She proudly places the dishes in front of us, then turns to begin cleaning the kitchen. She always waits to eat until everyone else has already filled their bellies.

Kain na! (Let's eat!) My dad walks over from the other room and joins us. His place setting is already prepared and waiting for him at his usual seat.

If I don't act fast, there will be nothing left.

I quickly lean across the table and use my spoon to nudge three pieces of *longanisa* and two fried eggs onto my plate. I add a heaping scoop of steaming rice and begin to eat.

Our kitchen is filled with the sounds of running water and pans clanging around in the sink. As we all take those first few bites, the table falls silent. My mom's cooking has magical qualities. She tells me that cooking with love is what makes her dishes so delicious. Her meals have an uncanny way of bringing joy to your belly and your heart.

As the meal comes to an end, I look down at my plate with dismay. One and a half lonely sausages remain, along with some scrappy parts of crunchy egg white and a small lump of rice. I feel guilty wasting food, but I also can't bear to eat another bite.

I look across the table at my brothers, silently imploring them for help with my eyes. My *kuya* shoves the last spoonful of rice into his mouth before offering me a sweet chipmunk-cheeked smile and excusing himself from the table. My younger brother's plate is already cleared and the *bunso* (youngest in Tagalog) has had no trouble at all eating the food he was served.

I keep my head down, hoping my mom will be too busy with the dishes to notice.

She walks over to clear my *kuya's* plate and glances over to see if I am finished. By now, my brothers have all returned to the living room, where their Lego pirate ship battle continues. They know nothing of the battle happening back in the kitchen. My cheeks flush as waves of shame, embarrassment, and guilt crash over me.

My mom looks at my plate, disappointed to see a few pieces of *longanisa*, egg, and rice.

Sayang, anak! (What a waste, my child!) It's not good to waste. There are people back home in the Philippines who would love to eat this.

She reaches over me and swiftly packs the rest of my breakfast, sliding the contents of my plate into a resealable plastic bag.

For later. In case you get hungry.

As she opens the fridge to put away my leftovers, I can't help but watch. My fingers are grasping the sides of my chair. I squeeze so tightly my knuckles turn white. I wish the ground would swallow me up whole and I could just disappear into the floor. *There is nothing worse than disappointing my mother.*

The resealable plastic bag joins a community of containers that hold Filipino dishes from many nights before. Country Crock buckets filled with *sinigang* (a sour Filipino soup made of meat, tomatoes, onions, fish sauce, and tamarind), Cool Whip containers holding chicken *adobo (chicken or pork simmered in vinegar, soy sauce, garlic, bay leaves, and black pepper)*, and endless levels of Tupperware for every bit of leftover imaginable pack rows and rows of shelves.

I wonder if my American friends keep this much food around. In our home, nothing ever goes to waste. I walk away from the table carrying two heavy realizations:

My parents are committed to ensuring that my brothers and I never go hungry. and

Putting food on my plate without finishing it is an unforgivable sin.

Origin of Historical Trauma and Scarcity Mindsets

According to the latest Pew Research Center statistics,[1] approximately 71 percent of Asian Americans living in the United States are immigrants. Though our challenges cannot be collapsed into one monolithic experience, many of us carry the cultural beliefs and ripples of our immigrant parents' historical trauma in ways that result in scarcity mindsets.

Before we can dive into *what* a scarcity mindset entails and how it impacts the lives, careers, and relationships of Asian Americans and children of Asian immigrants, we must first understand *from where* the scarcity mindset originates.

The first big wave of Asian immigrants occurred between 1848 and 1855. During this time, approximately 15,000 to 20,000 Chinese immigrants arrived in the United States to complete construction of the Transcontinental Railroad. Although Chinese laborers worked sunrise to sunset six days per week, their monthly pay was between $24 and $35, which represented two-thirds of the amount paid to their white counterparts.[2] Chinese laborers were also forced to use their wages to pay for lodging, food, and tools, even though these supplies were provided to other workers at no cost.[3] Anti-Chinese sentiments among railroad companies were further evidenced as Chinese laborers were assigned to work in dangerous conditions and relegated to reside in segregated camps that had less access to fresh water.[4] Though many railroad companies did not keep records of worker casualties,[5] newspaper headlines reported that Chinese workers died from landslides, explosions, falls, avalanches, heatstroke, hypothermia, and other accidents. Researchers estimate as many as 1,200 Chinese workers died during the completion of the Transcontinental Railroad, resulting in a death rate of about 1 in 10 workers.[6]

This era in American history was characterized by anti-Asian sentiments and resentment toward Chinese workers and ultimately culminated in several exclusionary immigration laws that prohibited immigration to the United States from Asian countries.[7] First, the Chinese Exclusion Act of 1882 banned new immigrants for a period of 10 years and excluded Chinese immigrants and existing residents from becoming U.S. citizens. It was the first law to specifically discriminate against a group based solely on country of origin and ethnic identity.[8] Fueled by fears about national security during World War I, the 1917 Act continued to limit U.S. immigration by adding taxes to be paid upon arrival and requiring literacy tests for hopeful migrants over 16 years old. The 1917 Act also excluded entry to anyone born in the geographically defined "Asiatic Barred Zone," except for individuals from Japan and the Philippines, which was a U.S. colony. Seven years later, President Calvin Coolidge signed into law the Immigration Act of 1924, which completely prohibited all immigration from Asian countries and implemented a restrictive quota on the number of immigrants allowed to enter the United States.[9] These quotas remained in place until 1965.

The second big wave of Asian immigrants occurred following the 1965 Immigration and Nationality Act (commonly known as the Hart-Cellar Act).[10] This act prioritized highly educated immigrants, predominantly from Asian countries, who had professional skills within the fields of business, science, engineering, and medicine, and privileged individuals with family ties in the United States for reunification.[11] Following the Hart-Cellar Act, nearly half a million people immigrated to the United States each year, with only 20 percent of migrants from European countries. Individuals from China, India, and Japan flocked to the United States in the years immediately following the Hart-Cellar Act, nearly doubling the Chinese American population by 1975. By 1980, the vast majority of Asian Americans residing in the United States were formally educated professional-class members who were highly concentrated in a handful of professional fields.[12]

The stressful and occasionally traumatic experiences that contributed to our parents' and ancestors' migration from their countries of origin to the United States, as well as their financial hardships, experiences of discrimination, and unfamiliar socioeconomic landscapes upon arrival, may have contributed to instances of historical trauma. *Historical trauma* encompasses distressing or life-threatening events that have cross-generational effects and are collectively experienced by group members with shared identities.[13] These life-threatening events and "shocks" have the potential to "alter a person's biological, psychological, and social equilibrium to such a degree that the memory of one particular event comes to taint, and dominate, all other experiences, spoiling an appreciation of the present moment."[14] With this explanation in mind, it doesn't take much to consider how the traumatic "shocks" associated with immigration, as well as the contributing factors that led to the migration from our Asian countries to the United States, may continue to impact the perspectives, thoughts, and behaviors of our parents and ancestors.

An example of one of these "traumatic shocks" was captured beautifully by Monica Sok, a Cambodian American poet, in her essay "On Fear, Fearlessness, and Intergenerational Trauma":

> *My mother doesn't dwell in the past, so she smiles and shakes her head when I ask about her life during the Khmer Rouge regime. Mom, what did you do? Did you have to work? She shrugs. Her eyes are soft, then perplexed by my eagerness to bear witness to her story. What story? What do you want to know? In order to live her life and support me and my brother, she explains, it is necessary to move on. Forget the past. Don't think about it. But I am not like her. I can't forget the past and I always think about it. Yet, my mother seems to evade my questions on every rare visit home. Sometimes I give up asking. Her silence around her personal history often leaves me with doubts on how to begin telling my own.*

Sharon K., a second-generation Korean American woman in her early 40s, shares another example of how historical trauma is passed down across generations:

> *The long-term effects of the Korean War and continued militarization of Korea are something that my entire family shares, regardless of to which generation we belong. My father just turned 80 and he is the youngest of 6 siblings, two of whom*

are still living. My dad belongs to the generation who was directly impacted by the Korean War. He and his family escaped from North Korea to the South right before the war began. He was only a few years old, but he has so many memories from that time.

Dr. Ramya Avadhanam, a 1.5-generation Indian (Telugu) American woman in her late 30s from Andhra Pradesh, a state from the Southern Coastal region of India, shares another example of how historical patterns are passed through her family of origin:

My grandparents were part of the freedom fighter movement when India sought independence from the Colonial British. India gained independence in 1947, 10 years prior to the birth of my father and 11 years prior to the birth of my mother. Though my grandparents shared with my parents—and therefore my parents with me—some of the more glorified pieces of freedom fighting, their hardships are not explored at a personal level let alone shared with others.

Quan D., a second-generation multiracial man of Vietnamese, Chinese, and Malaysian descent in his early 40s, describes how his parents maintain the conspiracy of silence to provide a better life for their children:

My parents rarely talked about their hardships coming over to America. They never discussed how they escaped war, traveled by sea to another country on a flimsy boat with other refugees, and dealt with weird looks and instances of racism once they arrived in the states. Their main goal was for my brothers and I to focus on our education so that we could live a better life in America.

Jai Yang* (asterisk used to indicate a pseudonym), a second-generation queer Chinese American woman and social rights organizer in her early 30s, explains:

Both my parents are Chinese immigrants with different trauma experiences from growing up in China and surviving the Cultural Revolution. I didn't learn about the Cultural Revolution until I was in my early to mid-twenties. Needless to say, there was a culture of avoiding painful subjects while I was growing up.

Olivia,* a first-generation Vietnamese American woman and mental health professional in her early 30s, shares:

I've often wondered what it would be like to have a family where there were more transparent conversations about the traumatic experiences my parents and grandparents endured. The most I experienced was hearing my parents detail certain stories of their childhood and their struggles coming to the United States from Vietnam. In many ways, I internalized the idea that my life isn't as terrible as it could have been—how it truly was for my parents. At the same time, I was burdened to know that my parents struggled through food and housing insecurity, overt racism and discrimination, and threats to their own lives.

The extant body of research has explored how trauma can be transmitted across generations in a variety of populations, including Holocaust survivors, Indigenous communities, Cambodian genocide survivors, and Japanese Americans who were incarcerated during World War II.[15] Historical trauma, the cumulative and multigenerational experience of emotional and psychological injury that is passed down among communities and families, has profound impacts on the adaptation, adjustment, mental and physical health, and relationship quality of Asian American families.[16] Historical trauma can also be inherited through epigenetics, in which genes that promote survival and contribute to resilience become activated to prepare their children for stressful events.[17] Because these adaptive patterns promote short-term survival by helping us navigate traumatic instances, chronic exposure to fearful states, and acute scarcity, they are difficult to unlearn and are passed on to future generations. When families get stuck in survival states that perpetuate unhelpful cultural scripts like scarcity mindsets, the patterns that remain inhibit our abilities to thrive. Ultimately, the survival-based adaptations that are grounded in historical trauma and intergenerational patterns can result in the presence of a scarcity mentality or mindset (both terms are used interchangeably throughout this book).

Scarcity mentality refers to internalized beliefs that everyone exists within a spectrum of competition.[18] This attitude may have originated from employment competition during the construction of the Transcontinental Railroad as well as following the 1965 Hart-Cellar Act, which privileged highly educated and successful Asian immigrants in medical, engineering, business, and STEM fields. The additional impacts of war, political upheaval, intercommunity competition, and chronic resource scarcity among Asian countries have been prevalent through the 20th century and beyond, which may have further contributed to high rates of migration from Asian countries to the United States.[19]

Stacey, that's a lot of history, dates, and statistics, and I'm not sure I'm following (or interested). Can you just go over the high points and why this history is relevant?

Let's recap. In short, scarcity-driven competition among Asians in the United States may have begun as early as 1848 during the construction of the Transcontinental Railroad. This competition for (perceived) finite resources became exacerbated by the Hart-Cellar Act of 1965, where highly educated and skilled Asians who were trained in business, science, and medical fields were privileged to migrate to America. Those who did not meet these expectations were significantly less likely to be offered a "golden ticket" to America.

Because a scarcity mentality assumes that resources are finite and that one person's success comes at the expense of another, Asians may internalize beliefs that resources must be kept or reserved for ourselves and our families. We see this in the ways that our Asian parents conscientiously hoard and reuse every resource imaginable, such as tinfoil, clothing, and containers. The same mindset also appears to drive the deep sense of competition and status obsession that often exists within Asian American ethnic communities when it comes to educational, occupational, and milestone achievements: "*Your son was accepted into Cornell? My daughter was accepted into Stanford and the university offered her a full-ride scholarship.*"

Calypso,* a first-generation biracial Asian American woman and physician of white and Taiwanese descent in her mid-30s, shares another example:

> My brother, sister, and I are an extension of our family and represent our family status. I wanted to go to cosmetology school but instead I was encouraged to focus on academics. In my family, professions that require higher education are more respected; doctors, lawyers, pharmacists, and engineers who at the minimum need college degrees are prioritized. I am now a physician and love it, but I believe I could have married a male physician and still received the same or more recognition. The amount of money I make matters less than the status.

Though the scarcity mindset may have originally developed to contextualize forms of resource hoarding and within-group competition, dominant groups in positions of power have also historically limited the ability for marginalized individuals to thrive within the existing U.S. social structures. As a result, the scarcity mindset has evolved in ways that extend beyond simple survival to encompass an omnipresent awareness and socialized belief that marginalized individuals (e.g., Asian Americans) are "not enough" and, as a group, cannot acquire enough to access the full spectrum of opportunities available to the dominant (i.e., white) group.

Have you ever felt that intense desire to prove your value, intelligence, or worth through academic, career, and milestone achievements? When opportunities in academic or workplace settings arise, do you feel the need to take them on, even when your plate is full, because you fear that another opportunity may not present itself? If either of these instances resonates, that pesky scarcity mindset may be to blame.

With this short history lesson in mind, I offer the following possible takeaways:

First, when Asian parents meet to compare the accomplishments of their children, this is not an attempt to be malicious. Our parents are simply engaging in a time-honored practice that has become socialized and reinforced through a scarcity mindset. Comparing family achievements and experiences may therefore represent a critical form of social capital.

Second, since many of our parents and ancestors were only given access to immigration in America as a direct result of the 1965 Hart-Cellar Act, it is no wonder why they pushed us to become doctors, lawyers, and engineers. These career paths are deeply embedded components of our diasporic experiences and may represent the specific pathways that contributed to our parents' historical success. Our parents' career interests were emblematic of critical choices that became paramount to their survival and their ability to support and feed their families. Asian parents' beliefs about desirable labor markets continue to influence career decisions among Asian Americans today.[20]

When our Asian American parents say, "You have to work harder to be successful," "That career choice is not good enough; you should become a doctor instead," or "You earned an A? Why not an A+?" here is the meta-message our parents seek to communicate:

I struggled for a long time, and I don't want that life for you. As a result, I encourage you to work hard and achieve career success so that you can be happy, healthy, safe, and successful.

Yet, the message we tend to internalize is:

My parents cannot accept me for who I am, so therefore I am not good enough.
or
My accomplishments always seem to fall short, so therefore I am unworthy of love.
or even
If I do not succeed academically or occupationally or reach the milestones my parents have set for me, then I will be a disappointment.

Bottom line, our parents did the best they could with what they had. Many of them did not unpack their stories because they didn't feel the need to, were uncomfortable with the content, or wanted to avoid burdening us. Although open communication and role modeling emotional vulnerability could have saved us from the pain of fixed beliefs (e.g., "I'm not good enough unless I am a doctor, lawyer, or engineer"), strengthened our relationships, and improved our mental health as children, it is never too late to begin the healing and repair process.

TLDR: Though our immigrant parents and ancestors may have faced challenging immigration experiences, contended with historical trauma, and adhered to scarcity mindsets, these topics are rarely discussed among the Asian American diaspora. This lack of communication creates gaps in immigrant children's knowledge about who we are, what our families have overcome, and the ways in which we have demonstrated great resilience. Without access to our family's history, we are not able to develop a coherent and positive sense of identity. Rather than facilitating open, vulnerable, and honest discussions about their experiences, immigrant parents too often suffer the consequences of their trauma without recognizing it and children are left to fill in the blanks about why our parents behave in the ways that they do. Consequently, children of Asian immigrants may incorrectly attribute blame to their parents as the sole reason for their inherited patterns, scarcity mindsets, and internalized cultural scripts. In reality, the ways in which we internalize these concepts are far more nuanced, multifaceted, and complex.

Questions to Ponder

1. What might be some examples of patterns that you have inherited from your family of origin?
2. When reflecting on your parents' and ancestors' experiences, how may their struggles and/or successes have influenced their attitudes, thoughts, and behaviors today?
3. What are some of the internalized cultural scripts you carry?
4. To what extent might these internalized cultural scripts impact your ability to achieve happiness and well-being?
5. How has adhering to a scarcity mindset impacted the way you see the world?

Questions to Bridge the Gap with Parents

1. What are some hopes and dreams you had for me when I was a child? How have those changed as I became an adult?
2. Which values, attitudes, or beliefs helped you survive and adapt while raising a family in America? From where did those originate?
3. As you reflect on our family and on your life so far, what makes you most proud?

3

Patterns That Remain Among Asian Americans

స

It is Sunday morning, and my father is driving our family to church. I am 11 years old and desperately hoping that we will arrive late so we can stand in the back. Catholic Masses always seem to take forever, and it's much easier to make jokes with my brothers when we aren't under the watchful gaze of the other churchgoers sitting in the pews.

As we approach the main intersection and roll to a stop, I am surprised to see that my father has reached across to the console to turn down his favorite NPR show. He clears his throat and says: *"Education is the one thing they cannot take away from you. You are Asians living in America, which means you have to work twice as hard to get half as far. Do you understand?"*

I search his eyes in the rearview mirror for some semblance of emotion, but he is staring straight ahead, waiting for an opportunity to turn into the main road. My brothers and I nod in silence as the turn signal sends monotonous clicks into the background. I see my father quickly steal a peek at us through his reflection as he nods his head in apparent satisfaction.

Asian Americans and children of Asian immigrants are raised in environments with caring, hardworking, and dedicated parents who may focus so heavily on firmly establishing themselves into Western society that they overlook the importance of emotional and psychological well-being. Balance and moderation seem just out of reach when productivity, survival, and assimilation are foci that have historically served us well. As a result, we grow up internalizing cultural scripts and intergenerational patterns that prioritize hard work, gratitude, minimization of feelings, obedience, assimilation, and ethnic allegiance. Though these cultural scripts have undoubtedly contributed to the success of Asian immigrants who have migrated to the land now known as the United States since time immemorial, the meta-messages associated with these cultural scripts are toxic and unforgiving:

> *Work hard (at the expense of your own well-being).*
> *Be grateful (while silently enduring challenges, injustice, and unpleasant circumstances).*

Minimize feelings (because they do not serve you and elicit discomfort in others).
Be obedient and avoid standing out (to avoid discrimination).
Fit in (but don't forget where you come from).

Growing up, I held on tightly to these cultural scripts. They were ever-present in my relationships, in the ways I approached school and work, and how I interacted with the world and others around me. I stayed for too long in dead-end relationships with partners deemed "good enough," bit my tongue in moments of rage, and remained silent when I should have spoken up. I embodied these cultural scripts as best I could, believing these patterns would magically grant the white proximity needed to come out unscathed in a world filled with racial discrimination. By the time I reached my early 20s, these patterns had become so deeply intertwined into my sense of self that they were nearly indistinguishable facets of my personality. I had fallen victim to the model minority myth and espoused a scarcity mindset that pitted me in competition with other Asian Americans. As I grew older, I stopped seeing others as threats and began cultivating community.

I realize now that I wasn't alone. Countless Asian Americans and children of Asian immigrants internalize the same cultural scripts and patterns that remain from parents and ancestors. Let's take a look at some examples.

"Work Twice as Hard to Get Half as Far"

Asian parents and our ancestors focus on status and financial security because they endured aspects of resource, employment, and other forms of scarcity throughout their lifetimes. Consequently, they desperately seek to protect their children from experiencing those same struggles by funneling us toward career paths and lifestyle choices they hope will shield us from pain and suffering. Sometimes these messages are explicit. For instance, my father once shared how he was instructed to pursue a career in medicine despite his own desire to become an engineer. Dr. Avadhanam shares another example of how cultural messages about hard work can be explicitly communicated across generations:

My grandparents taught my parents that learning English was the only way to succeed in a post-British colonized India. My parents continued to teach me and my sister that speaking English, as well as pursuing educational opportunities, were imperative for survival. My father also explicitly shared that as a cisgender heterosexual woman of color, I would need to work even harder to prove myself.

Kareena,* a first-generation Indian American woman in her early 30s, similarly shares how her immigrant parents emphasized internalized cultural scripts while inadvertently invalidating her inner child:

> When I was growing up, I felt like many of my needs, desires, ideas, and interests were dismissed—they were replaced with what I "should" be doing (playing piano, getting straight A's, not speaking unless spoken to). That kind of childhood led to me live someone else's life. I wasn't able to explore who I am, what I want, and where I want to be until I became an adult and removed myself from that household.

Sacrificing our desires for more lucrative career options represents a tried-and-true strategy for many Asian Americans. Placing emphasis on hard work can also represent an important strategy for enhancing motivation, promoting success, and practicing filial piety. Quan D. shares how his immigrant parents' stories contributed to his own successful outcomes:

> Every time we complained about something my parents would say, "Well, when we were your age, we faced many challenges," and that made us work harder. We internalized their struggles as motivation and inspiration to better ourselves. My brothers and I have all graduated from college, received good-paying jobs, got married, and have started families. My parents can rest easy now because we do not let them pay for anything. It is like their hard work has paid off.

Gabriel K., a second-generation biracial Filipino American man and news reporter in his early 30s, shares another example of how our parents' struggles contribute positively to the internalized desires for success:

> When I think about my career path, I think about how both my parents wanted the best for me. My mother moved from the Philippines to the United States for the sake of opportunity. She wanted to be certain that her kids had an even better life, and I certainly feel the pressure to take advantage of that. I feel the pressure to do good in this world, and I feel the pressure to be a success story.

When our parents share their own experiences, it is as though they are allowing us fleeting glimpses of their fears, desires, and goals. The stories and messages our parents choose to pass down are important because they shed light on their values, belief systems, and internalized cultural scripts. Among ethnic and racial groups, storytelling represents an important part of how parents socialize their children and pass down meaningful messages.[1] More often than not, the messages our parents communicate are the ones that served them in some way. For instance, parents who experienced economic hardship may emphasize the importance of working hard.[2] Our parents may also communicate messages about the value of education, the risks of trusting outsiders, and the importance of maintaining interpersonal harmony by avoiding conflict and minimizing emotional expression. Ultimately, the stories passed down from our parents reflect their own socialized goals and are deeply rooted in their own experiences. Fortified by what they have learned, they are preparing us for success in the best way they know how.

"Just Be Grateful for the Opportunity"

When our parents and ancestors share their origin stories and historical trauma narratives, messages about the gratitude we should feel for their great sacrifices represent common themes. Asian parents and ancestors may allude to trauma experiences and challenges, both from their countries of origin and upon migrating to the United States, in ways that emphasize how fortunate their children are to grow up stateside.[3]

I.B.,* a pansexual Igorot Filipina Chinese American and first-generation woman in her early 30s, explains:

> My parents never exactly said, "Why are you complaining when you have it better than we did?" but they have shared similar things or would tell stories of their childhood like having to walk miles to go to school or waking up early to feed the pigs. Stories like that would invoke a sense of guilt because I never had to do that, which I am grateful for. I don't think my parents wanted us to experience that kind of hardship but the way they understand problems is, "Since you did not have to do it like I did then everything else should be easy."

In many ways, Asians in the United States are made to feel that their claim to an American identity is predicated on continued contributions.[4] The conditional nature of an American identity communicates an inherent lack of belonging in the United States and creates pressure on Asian Americans to continue "proving" ourselves as worthy in every aspect of our lives, including within educational, occupational, and even relationship settings. This pressure may perpetuate a scarcity mentality and can be evidenced in the ways in which we have learned to excel within occupational and education settings and give freely of ourselves within relationships.

Chamari De Silva, a Sri Lankan woman in her 30s who moved to the United States with her parents at 19 months of age, shares sentiments surrounding gratitude, scarcity, and competition:

I definitely had a scarcity mindset, especially when it came to my career. There were times when I would remain in situations because I was just grateful to have a job. I never negotiated my salary the way other American colleagues did. I would find out in retrospect, "Oh, my gosh, they're making so much more money than I am." Then I would get a new job and simply accept the compensation offer as is, because I was just so grateful for the new opportunity. I subconsciously must have felt that I needed validation from my social circles to affirm I was capable, intelligent, and that I had secured an opportunity that is reflective of my talents.

When our parents are unclear about how their previous experiences impact their current behaviors and expectations of us, we internalize cultural scripts about how we are *less than, unworthy of love,* or *not good enough* when we fail to meet high-achieving milestones. Children may struggle with feelings of guilt and fear about disappointing their parents and ethnic communities by falling short of academic, social, and professional expectations. The fear of disappointing our parents and community can subsequently drive future life decisions, such as school- and career-based choices.[5]

Chamari De Silva explains:

I think a lot of Asian kids put a ton of pressure on themselves right from grade school. They believe they need to go into prestigious baccalaureate programs, advanced programs, take all AP classes, and get straight A's. They aim to attend Harvard, Stanford, Cornell, or Carnegie Mellon—the best of the best. Their whole life is centered around that goal because they need that social recognition in their circles. The need for parents to brag about their children also exists and is so deeply rooted in Asian culture. We often validate each other based on academic accomplishments or career accolades instead of emotional accomplishments. I have so many friends who went to amazing schools and checked the right societal boxes and many of them seem deeply unhappy.

Though gratitude can be a powerful antidote to mitigate feelings of helplessness, shame, anxiety, and sadness, psychological well-being tends to pair well with moderation. Experiencing a sense of gratitude is great, but do you know what's even better? *Recognizing what a privilege it is to be able to leverage our parents' sacrifices by identifying and working through the patterns that remain.*

"We Don't Talk About Our Feelings in This Family"

Early messages associated with emotional restraint tend to be among the most common cultural scripts that are passed down through generations. Indeed, many Asian Americans and children of Asian immigrants struggle to express feelings of vulnerability and emotion in favor of avoidance, isolation, and withdrawal. We are experts at conflict avoidance and mere amateurs when it comes to expressing our feelings.

Because elements of historical trauma, intergenerational patterns, and cultural scripts are often passed from generation to generation, many individuals lack models for secure attachments, psychological safety, and deep, vulnerable connections. There is simply no time to reflect on mental health distress when survival is top of mind. Because many Asian American parents did not have access to coping strategies and language to contextualize their feelings, needs, and experiences, they were not always equipped to help us when we faced our own struggles growing up. As a result, covert messages, such as *we don't talk about our problems, I am not good enough, I cannot ask for help, I should not be emotionally expressive or vulnerable,* and *I must be grateful for what I have* are easily inherited.[6]

Christopher Vo, a first-generation Vietnamese American man, licensed marriage and family therapist, and founder of the Asian Mental Health Collective, describes how emotions are avoided in his family of origin:

> *I was driving to meet my parents to work on a commercial property when I received a phone call from my father. He said, "We were just in a head-on collision, the car is totaled, go handle business." And then he hung up. He hadn't even given me any time to form a proper response. I pulled over for a minute to collect my thoughts, arms shaking, eyes watery. Reeling from the confusion, I knew my father would scold me for being late, regardless of the circumstances. So, I put the car in drive and continued on. Later that evening I would learn the cop who arrived on scene had told them he was surprised they survived. We were home now, eating dinner across from each other in silence. I wanted to tell them how scared I was and how much they meant to me, but nothing came out. I smirk now at the irony of the situation; I had spent years teaching others how to be vulnerable for a living but when it came to family it felt foreign.*

Dr. Chris Cheung, a Chinese-Surinamese man, educator, and mental health professional in his late 30s, arrived in the United States at age 19. He describes another example of how vulnerability-focused cultural scripts were passed down in his family of origin:

> *For as long as I can remember, my parents and grandparents hinted at how awful it was to survive through poverty and a gambling addiction. They never shared openly about the past and would allude to how grateful they were to escape that*

life. As a child, the underlying messages I received were that we don't talk about painful experiences, and we avoid painful emotions as much as possible.

Dr. Monica P. Band, a third-generation biracial Chinese American woman, mental health professional, and thought leader in her early 30s, explains:

When it comes to intergenerational trauma, much is implied and little is communicated. I remember visiting my immigrant grandparents, and listening to everyone around me speak Cantonese while I did my best to pick up on facial expressions and nonverbal cues to keep up with the conversation. In hindsight, there was a lot of translating covert messaging to feel a part of my family. As a young adult, it didn't feel like there was a lot of safe space to have difficult or heavy emotionally driven conversations. Some of this may have been because my mother most likely never had these experiences with her mother/my grandmother. It's even harder to learn something when you don't have a model or secure base for support.

Tarm, a second-generation Chinese-Vietnamese diaspora woman in her late 20s, is Director of Partnerships for the Asian Mental Health Project. She shares:

After encountering trauma as immigrants who experienced the Vietnam war, my parents prioritized providing for the family to ensure there was food on the table and a home for us to live in. They worked really hard and sacrificed a lot to provide for our basic needs. At the same time, I didn't get very much emotional or psychological support. If I was sad or upset, there were not many conversations to discuss why I was sad or upset. I would be met with confusion or annoyance from belief systems that I had no reason to be upset. There were no efforts to engage in conflict resolution, so I had to learn how to let sadness or anger pass in silence. I would be forced to re-engage with my family during mealtimes and have everything return "back to normal."

Many of these stories share similar themes that convey the *conspiracy of silence* among Asian Americans about historical trauma.[7] Once they had immigrated to the United States, our parents were forced to focus on survival and assimilation, which may have kept them from processing their stressful experiences and de-emphasizing the importance of emotional expression and vulnerability. Of course, the extent to which our immigrant parents feel comfortable demonstrating these values exists on a spectrum; no two immigrant parents are alike.

In my work as a mental health professional and educator, and in conversations with Asian American community members, I have heard countless anecdotes about Asian American parents who would unexpectedly "blow their tops," have big reactions to seemingly small stressors, and then walk away, only to act as though the incident had never occurred. Issues are not addressed, and deeper problems are left unresolved. Apologies are not exchanged and attempts to revisit these emotional events are met with great resistance. We are met with pointed fingers and even sharper criticism one moment and are asked to pass the kimchi at the dinner table hours later. These reactions maintain family cycles of silence and perpetuate unhelpful cultural scripts about the minimization of feelings and emotional avoidance. We learn to adapt to these childhood patterns of silence by avoiding conflict and experiencing feelings of discomfort when we are faced with emotional distress. We grow up and become adults who struggle to identify our feelings, are quick to anger, shut down emotionally, and engage in distancing tactics that seem psychologically safer than addressing issues directly.

When our childhoods are not populated with parents who role-model healthy ways to resolve conflict, we experience deep confusion and internalize a misplaced sense of responsibility. We believe we are responsible for the feelings of others and become hypersensitive to the emotional needs and reactions of others. We find ourselves engaging in people-pleasing behaviors to avoid conflict and overanalyze the behaviors, words, and intentions of others. When we have parents and caregivers who are chronically stressed or who struggle with mental health issues, we learn to minimize our emotions to meet our needs for love and belonging. We continue downplaying our emotions and needs in adult relationships out of fear that we will overwhelm partners, friends, and other important people in our lives, ultimately maintaining conspiracies of silence.

"Don't Rock the Boat or Stand Out"

Deeply ingrained messages to avoid rocking the boat or standing out represent a longstanding acculturative strategy to avoid discrimination among Asian Americans. Our elders believed that fitting in, going with the flow, and not making waves represented valuable behaviors that enhanced our ability to assimilate into the melting pot of American society. As a result, many of us have learned not to speak up; not to advocate for our wants, needs, or desires; or not to challenge the status quo. Though there is something to be said for thinking before one speaks, the desire to fit in by avoiding conflict by all means necessary can perpetuate forms of injustice and social inequity and minimize our ability to achieve optimal happiness. The same cultural message that we believe shields us from discrimination also inadvertently perpetuates the model minority myth, impacts our ability to unlock deeper relationships, and maintains unhelpful patterns in educational and workplace settings.

Chamari de Silva explains how adhering to a scarcity mindset keeps our Asian American community from rocking the boat:

> *The scarcity mindset conditions Asian Americans to believe that we can't succeed if we don't achieve our parents' aspirational desires. Either we settle in certain areas of our life, or we feel unaccomplished and unfulfilled, and that can be emotionally crippling. When things happen at work, we feel afraid. We don't speak up when there's injustice. We don't want to mess with the status quo; we just want to maintain and survive. We believe we can't rock the boat.*

Christopher Vo describes how cultural messages and a lack of role modeling result in miscommunication among Asian American families:

> *In a society centered around the concepts of avoiding shame and saving face, you are expected to remain pleasant and not rock the boat, regardless of the circumstances. Unfortunately, Asian Americans are rarely shown what healthy and honest communication looks like. We don't have many models for compassionate, empathetic, and vulnerable discussions. As a result, biting criticism is seen as honesty.*

Cultural messages and internalized values can also contribute to unhelpful patterns within Asian and Asian American communities and families. Shoua Lee, a Hmong American woman and first-generation student in her mid-30s, explains:

> *I knew since childhood that my life as a female was not as valuable as a male. This message was sent overtly through cultural practices and covertly through family engagements. For instance, men always ate before women at traditional Hmong events. I can remember how my parents and the parents of my friends always hoped to have sons. This unbalanced valuing of the male sex was harmful in many ways. First, it paved the way for the growth [of] and ongoing domestic violence in the Hmong community. Second, it created a system that silenced women. Last but not least, this dichotomous view of humanity left no room for the queer community to exist.*

We can no longer afford to remain silent when injustice occurs. Our feelings, desires, and thoughts are real, valid, and matter. Rocking the boat creates ripples that lead the way for future generations to take meaningful action.

"Nako! You Have Become Too American!"

Looking back, I can't help but feel moments of shame for the deep internalized oppression I carried for so long. I beat others to the Asian punchline, worked at Abercrombie & Fitch because my white friends thought it was cool, and nearly fried my hair to a crisp with a straightening iron.

To avoid instances of ethnic and racial discrimination, many Asian American parents believed that assimilation was the most effective coping strategy to shield themselves and their children from pain. I have heard countless stories of Asian Americans and children of Asian immigrants who were denied access to their own language, aspects of their culture, and trips back to their home countries all because of their parents' desires to prevent them from standing out in ways that would further differentiate them from their white peers and lead to future instances of discrimination. In a personal anecdote, when my husband and I were deciding on names for our second child, I wanted to name him Lapu-Lapu. Lapu-Lapu vanquished Portuguese explorer Ferdinand Magellan in the Battle of Mactan on April 27, 1521, and is widely considered a national Filipino hero. Despite my best efforts to establish a healthy sense of ethnic identity in my child, we ultimately decided against it because my parents asserted the name was "too aggressive" and worried that our son would be teased for being too different.

Though well intentioned, gatekeeping Asian American children from these important aspects of our ethnic identities can have deleterious effects. Students, clients, and colleagues for whom this has happened often describe a crippling sense of disconnect from their ethnic communities, a sense of mourning for the whole person they could have become, and an internalized belief of not being "Asian enough." The latter belief becomes further reinforced through *intragroup othering*, a phenomenon that occurs when ethnic subgroups discriminate against in-group others who behave in ways considered less desirable. Asian Americans who struggle with internalized oppression engage in intragroup othering by deeming Asian immigrants "fresh off the boat" while referring to more assimilated community members as "twinkies" or "bananas" (yellow on the outside, white on the inside). Intragroup othering results in a Goldilocks-type mentality wherein Asian Americans may struggle to achieve bicultural identities—not *too* Asian, not *too* Western, just right.

Dr. Noelle,* a first-generation Filipina American woman and educator in her early 40s, describes an example of intragroup othering:

> I've talked to a lot of people who are children of immigrants and all of us agree, "Yep, there was a time when my parents told me I was becoming too American." It was like, Wait a minute. What do you mean, you brought me here. I am American.

And so are you, you became an American citizen! But I understand what they're saying. Culturally, they don't want you to be as American as white individuals.

Dr. Noelle's experience parallels research that illuminates how acculturation differences between Asian American parents and their children contribute to significant feelings of distress among parents. One common theme among Asian American parents in mental health spaces is the fear that their children will forget where they came from or abandon their family values. Indeed, many of us are still learning to walk a sensitive cultural tightrope where we honor and celebrate from where we came while fitting into the majority culture in which we live.

Dr. Valli shares:

I remember when my mum came to America for my doctoral graduation and we were getting into an argument. In my frustration, I spoke to her in English as opposed to Tamil (my native tongue). Although she is capable of speaking and understanding English, there is an unspoken rule in my family that Tamil is the more respectful language, especially when we are arguing. She retorted back by saying she didn't realize how American I had become! There have been several moments of such schism, and I look back at them with so much grief.

Dr. Avadhanam also captures how she learned that fitting in would result in greater perceived opportunities for acceptance and social capital:

Though it was not told to me, I very quickly understood that ridding myself of an Indian accent and taking on an American accent would grant me more privilege, and therefore, greater access to resources and possible success.

Dr. Daniela Pila, a 1.5-generation Filipina American woman and scholar-activist in her early 30s, shares:

There was a huge cultural disconnect with my parents. On one occasion, I asked my mom for $80 to take an AP test. I explained that I could earn college credit for it, but she said, "You're going to use the money to buy drugs. Why are you paying money to take a paper test?" Every time I needed something—money for a field trip, a book for college, school supplies—I felt guilty for asking my parents who did not understand.

The common theme across each of these stories is the sense of disconnect that develops between Asian American parents and their children upon moving to America. Indeed, Asian American children tend to acculturate into American society more quickly than our parents do. As a result, our parents may feel as though they are left behind, forgotten, undervalued, and forced to make sense of the majority culture alone. From their viewpoint, becoming "too American" is analogous to "abandoning your roots."

Healing from Historical Patterns of Silence

Trauma is in most cases multigenerational. The chain of transmission goes from parent to child, stretching from the past into the future. We pass on to our offspring what we haven't resolved in ourselves.
Gabor Maté and Daniel Maté, *The Myth of Normal: Trauma, Illness, and Healing in a Toxic Culture* (p. 34)

Asian Americans and children of Asian immigrants can be adversely affected by conspiracies of silence in various ways. It can be all too easy to develop feelings of frustration, resentment, or sadness for how our parents have historically shown affection and emotional support (or lack thereof) upon witnessing the more demonstrative ways our white friends and their parents may interact. Many of us watched family-friendly movies and sitcoms throughout our childhood that centered emotionally expressive adolescents and physically affectionate parents and wondered, *"Why can't my life be like that?"* However, when we contextualize the ways in which historical trauma, intergenerational patterns, and scarcity mindsets have prevented our parents from cultivating higher levels of vulnerability, demonstrating an openness to alternative career choices, and engaging in emotional expression, then the possibility for our own healing can occur.

In the end, our parents' and ancestors' labor and sacrifice have afforded us two realities:

1. A reality where we have internalized unhelpful patterns born out of historical trauma, intergenerational patterns, scarcity mindsets, and limiting cultural scripts
2. A reality where we are now afforded the time, privilege, and resources to break those unhelpful patterns, cultivate a deeper understanding and greater empathy for our parents' experiences, and rewrite cultural scripts from abundance mindsets.

As Asian Americans and children of Asian immigrants, I believe we can break these intergenerational patterns and learn to thrive in new ways. Scarcity mindsets and historical cultural scripts have created a deep sense of collective pressure among Asian Americans and children of Asian immigrants. Somewhere along the way, we have internalized the following fixed beliefs:

I can only make my parents proud when I am successful in certain professions.
Talking about emotions and being vulnerable is inappropriate.
I should work hard and accept every opportunity that arises because I may not
   get another one again.

However, we are not doomed to pass down these limiting narratives in silence. We have the ability, knowledge, and awareness to begin uprooting our ancestral histories, healing diasporic wounds, and unlocking the power within. Doing so has the potential to strengthen our relationships—the ones with ourselves, the ones with our partners and children, and the ones with our parents.

Cynthia Siadat, a Filipina American women and therapist who works in private practice, describes how learning about her parents' stories led to a powerful realization:

The stories my mom shared about her life in the Philippines were minimal and mostly surrounded her focus on academics and her penchant for self-sufficiency. After hearing these stories, I felt inadequate and like I didn't measure up. I believed I was not good enough and that I was too needy. Looking back now as a woman and mother in my 30s, I know more about my family thanks to people who researched and interviewed my now-deceased relatives. My grandparents were key figures in the Hukbalahap, a guerrilla organization whose mission was to free the Philippines from Japanese occupation. My mom was one of two children of Filipino revolutionaries.

As I continued reading, learning, and syncing up timelines of events, a different picture of my family history emerged: one that involved the silence and protection of my mom and her younger sister during a dangerous political uprising. My mother never knew that her parents were Filipino revolutionaries who frequently left her side to aid other family or community members. My grandfather was ultimately betrayed and executed. My grandmother became separated from her daughters and made her way as a single mother. She kept much of this information from my mom, knowing always the pain that it caused her. I learned that my mom wasn't just independent by nature, she had to become independent by nurture as well. She had to be self-sufficient to survive.

Cynthia's story illuminates the importance of unlocking our parents' historical trauma narratives to develop a more comprehensive picture and deeper understanding of who our parents are and why they behave in the ways they do. Before unearthing her family history, Cynthia filled in the blanks on her own, ultimately believing she was inadequate after hearing her mother's emphasis on independence and self-sufficiency. She describes how obtaining a deeper understanding of her mother's story allowed her to challenge internalized beliefs about inadequacy.

Noah,* a first-generation Laotian and Thai American man in his early 40s, works in the medical field. He shares another story about the power of understanding our parents' stories:

> Our parents' historical trauma wasn't really spoken about. I just had these expectations of what we needed to do to further ourselves and our lives. My parents' expectations were never questioned. There were no conversations about why we're not wasting food or not doing this or doing that. I didn't know how they were brought up, I didn't know about the environment in which they were raised or the daily struggles they had until I got to visit Laos and saw it all firsthand. Laos is still a third world country and not highly developed. After witnessing where they came from, I appreciate more and more what they've done for me, and I understand why they instilled the values that make me who I am today.

Gabriel K. similarly shares how understanding our immigrant parents and their experiences can promote forgiveness, healing, and connection:

> It's easy to see how different your parents are from other parents. As we enter adulthood, if these differences caused any conflict for us as teenagers or as kids, it's imperative that we recognize the fact that we have a privilege our parents didn't have. It's easy to wonder, "How come my mom didn't teach me as much about Filipino history as I would have liked?", "How come we didn't have more from our parents?", or "How come our parents treated us this one way and not the other?" You know, our parents were just trying to survive. Our parents were just trying to get by, lay low, not cause a stir, put a roof over our heads, put food on our table, and give us a safe environment that we can thrive in. That was their priority. The things we yearn for now as adults are things we can make a priority today because our parents have awarded us this privilege through their great sacrifice. So, I don't really fault my parents for their shortcomings. They had kids to raise on a tight budget and now my generation has the opportunity to think about generational trauma and preserving Filipino history.

I.B.* also shares the importance of understanding and contextualizing our parents' experiences:

> It's like as a family we're going through Maslow's Hierarchy of Needs. My parents struggled through the bottom part and tried to ensure security for us so we can get to the top part faster and with less struggle than they went through. As I have gotten older, I understand my parents a whole lot more. I know they love my sisters and I and have good intentions. I know they want to be understood and that they did the best they could in raising us. I always keep that in mind and appreciate them for that.

Yub Kim, a gay Korean man and first-generation immigrant in his late 30s, shares:

> *The idea of happiness often gets muddled in immigrant families. Parents often want to provide a life that they never had for their children or live a successful life vicariously through their children. Children of immigrants comply with their parents' wishes without agency. Building individuality and self-efficacy while acknowledging the effort and sacrifice our parents had made encouraged me to validate my parents' lives and focus on my emotional needs. Through the process, I have demonstrated to my parents that I am happy with my decisions and the outcomes, regardless of the results.*

I believe it is important to emphasize the unique privilege we hold as Asian Americans and as children of Asian immigrants. Regardless of the patterns that remain, our parents' sacrifices have gifted us with the flexibility, resources, space, and freedom to deepen our understanding of how their experiences, as well as the experiences of our ancestors, continue to impact our lives today. Our parents have invested in our survival so we can enjoy the freedom to heal and thrive. Thriving can only occur when individuals can cultivate a subjective experience of safety and security.[8] I stand alongside researchers and mental health professionals who believe in the importance of understanding and contextualizing our parents' experiences to understand their pain and begin moving toward secure relationships and abundance mentalities.

TLDR: Historical trauma refers to collectively shared group experiences that may contribute to the internalization of scarcity mentalities. Scarcity mentalities may have originated as a result of the Hart-Cellar Act of 1965, which privileged Asian immigrants who were highly educated, skilled, and trained in professional fields such as business, medicine, and the sciences. These mindsets compound with cultural notions and silence about historical trauma in ways that push Asian Americans and children of Asian immigrants to internalize unhelpful cultural scripts related to hard work, gratitude, emotion avoidance, obedience, and ethnic allegiance. Contextualizing our parents' and ancestors' experiences can help us cultivate empathy, compassion, and greater understanding for the ways in which they raised us.

Questions to Ponder

1. Which of these cultural scripts resonated with me?
2. How has adhering to these cultural scripts and patterns helped me?

3. To what extent may these cultural scripts have limited my ability to access joy, happiness, and abundance?
4. How might I begin learning more about my family's origin story?
5. What do I wish I knew about my family history, and how might I sensitively access this information?

Questions to Bridge the Gap with Parents

1. What do you wish I knew about your experience in America? What do you wish I knew about your experience growing up?
2. If there was one thing you might share to help me understand you better, what might that be?
3. Was there ever a time when you felt as though I was abandoning my roots or forgetting from where we came? What was that like for you and what were you afraid might happen?

4

Childhood Attachment Wounds
in Adult Relationships

౭

Imagine you are an infant.

Take a few moments to close your eyes, enjoy a few deep breaths, and immerse yourself into the world where infants find themselves.

Your earliest experiences, in the womb, are characterized by warmth, soothing darkness, and a sense of physical snugness that elicits a deep comfort. Moment to moment, you are bathed in the reassuring sounds of normal daily rhythms.

The sound of your parent's heartbeat.

The sound of your parent's breathing.

The vague sound of familiar voices.

You are happy, comfortable, warm, and whole. Your needs are met, and you feel safe. The world is predictable.

Now imagine the shock you experience upon being born into this world.

Without warning, the familiar sounds and physical experiences to which you are accustomed have been taken away and are replaced with a world that is bright, loud, cold, and unfamiliar.

This new world is unpredictable.

You are scared.

Your tiny limbs, which used to be balled up, warm, and snug around your body, are now extending and reaching further than they ever have. You experience hunger, fear, and temperature for the first time. All the newness feels strange and scary so you find yourself using a voice you never knew you had, pleading for help. Your tiny fists are balled so tightly and all you want in this moment is comfort, soothing, and familiarity.

For some infants, this sense of soothing comes quickly. You are wrapped tightly in a swaddle, and the warmth and familiarity of being contained once more elicits an immediate sense of comfort. Your heart rate begins to regulate, and you notice yourself feeling calmer. Safer. Voices you were once vaguely aware of now seem louder than ever and yet they are familiar and soothing. Soon your belly is warm and full. Before you know it, you are drifting off to sleep. In this moment, you feel content, calm, and safe. Over time, you come to learn that someone will tend to your needs when discomfort arises and you cry for help.

You believe that the world is safe, your caregivers are safe, and you are safe. You develop strong, secure attachments with your caregivers.

For other infants, obtaining a sense of comfort and soothing happens only intermittently, if at all. You don't know if your caregivers will respond to your cries for help and so you do everything you can to try and command their attention. You cry at different pitches, rates, and frequencies. You cry louder, softer, and every volume in between. Over time, you come to believe that when discomfort arises, your requests for help, soothing, and comfort will not be satisfied. If your needs are rarely met, you may eventually stop crying altogether.

You come to believe that the world is not safe, your caregivers are not safe, and you are not safe. You develop insecure or disorganized attachment with your caregivers.

History of Attachment Theory

The history of attachment theory is an interesting, albeit cruel, one. It involves baby monkeys, and if you've taken a Psychology 101 course, these studies may sound familiar. In this next section, I'm going to outline several historical research studies and describe how the scientific findings contributed to the fascinating concept of adult attachment styles as we know them today. Bear with me throughout this next section, and if you find that your eyes glaze over faster than a jelly donut, then feel free to just skip ahead to the Adult Attachment Styles section. This portion is just for my fellow nerds!

In the 1950s and 1960s, an American psychologist named Harry Harlow sought to explore the nature and function of attachment. At the time, there were two dominating theories about the origin of parent and child attachment. The first hypothesis was grounded in behavioral theory. This hypothesis posited that attachment forms as a response to a child's physical needs. Individuals who aligned with this idea asserted that children develop a sense of attachment to their parents because their parents provide food. In other words, children develop attachments because a caregiver's face, body, scent, touch, and other physical characteristics become associated with the alleviation of hunger and thirst.[1]

The second hypothesis was grounded in evolutionary theory. Proponents of this theory believed that infants are born with an innate need to touch and cling to their caregivers because it provides a sense of emotional closeness, comfort, and security. Individuals who aligned with this line of thought believed that proximity and closeness to one's caregivers provided helpful adaptations for survival.

In other words, children develop attachments to their caregivers because acting in ways that facilitate closeness in proximity increases one's likelihood of survival by ensuring the provision of protection, security, warmth, and food.

To explore the origin of attachment, Harlow conducted a series of experiments with baby rhesus monkeys. Before we dive into these experiments, rest assured that these studies would not be considered ethical by today's research standards!

In 1958, Harlow separated baby rhesus monkeys from their mothers and created two surrogate "mothers." The first one (grounded in the behavioral theory) looked like something straight out of a horror movie. This surrogate "mother" was made of bare metal wire, had a wooden head with a crude face, and provided milk through an artificial nipple. The second surrogate "mother" (consistent with the evolutionary theory hypothesis) resembled a stuffed toy. This "mother" did not provide food but was made from soft, fluffy terrycloth. The baby rhesus monkeys were forced to make an impossible choice: pick the "mother" who offered food but no comfort or the mother who offered comfort but no sustenance.[2] What's an innocent little monkey to do?

Harlow's experiments led to some fascinating discoveries. Although the baby monkeys had access to both surrogate mothers, the wire mother was only visited when it came time to satisfy their primary need for hunger. In fact, the baby monkeys spent far more time climbing, clinging, snuggling, and playing with the terrycloth mother, even preferring her to the warmth of a heating pad.[3] When Harlow would purposely frighten the baby monkeys by placing (creepy) moving toy bears into their cages, something interesting would happen. After scurrying to the fluffy surrogate for comforting snuggles, within a minute or two, the babies began to visually explore the very thing that elicited so much fear moments before. Harlow observed how the bravest of babies would leave their mother's protection and approach the object that had elicited fear just moments before.[4] Behold, the power of a comforting, nurturing caregiver!

Future experiments further evidenced the critical importance of nurturing caregivers. Baby rhesus monkeys who were denied access to the fluffy surrogates had softer feces compared to those who were given snuggly milk-providing surrogates.[5] Harlow believed that baby monkeys without nurturing figures experienced greater psychological distress and higher emotionality, which manifested in digestive issues. Baby rhesus monkeys without access to any surrogates also demonstrated more fearful behaviors as well as fewer exploratory and curiosity behaviors when placed in unfamiliar environments. In fact, these poor creatures curled up into a ball and froze in fear when left in open field-test rooms.[6] The results from these experiments highlight the importance of satisfying internal drives for contact comfort, security, and closeness and indicated how an infant's innate needs for comfort and security outweigh the primary drive to satisfy hunger.[7]

The scientific community was captivated by these studies, which evidenced support for the contact comfort drive, a theory embedded within evolutionary theory. The contact comfort drive posited that access to comforting and nurturing caregivers provides a secure and comforting base from which infants can explore unfamiliar challenges and develop effective coping skills.[8]

Though undeniably cruel, Harlow's experiments illuminated the importance of the caregiver–child relationship. It is not sufficient for parents to be *good providers*; they must also provide *love, comfort, and security.*

But, Stacey, we are not monkeys. Are there any studies that validate the importance of caregiver–child attachments among humans? And more importantly, how does all of this relate to Asian Americans and Asian children of immigrants?

Great questions.

Harlow's experiments inspired a revolutionary new theory about attachment that was proposed by British psychologist John Bowlby. Bowlby's attachment theory provided a framework for how children's early relationships and caregiving experiences result in the development of an internal working model (IWM), which later informs their sense of self-worth and the extent to which they believe they can depend on others for attention and care.[9]

Bowlby believed that the behaviors infants developed to avoid caregiver separation, as well as their responses to caregivers upon return, served distinct evolutionary purposes. Specifically, Bowlby posited that these behaviors develop because they increase an infant's chance of survival. In other words, because infants who remain in close physical proximity to their caregivers are more likely to have survival advantages (i.e., caregivers provide protection, warmth, security, and food), the ways in which infants behave to prevent separation or act in response to being reunited serve important survival purposes.[10] Remember that time your friend, sibling, or family member passed you their baby to enjoy a blissful hands-free moment and their little one immediately protested with loud cries? If that sweet little babe could speak, they might say, *Listen, I've seen you around and you seem great, but I'm not sure you will be able to meet my needs should something arise. I need to go back to my caregiver immediately because they best know what I need!*

Bowlby's theory was empirically supported by pioneering studies conducted by Canadian American psychologist Mary Ainsworth.[11] Using a standardized procedure called the *strange situation*, Ainsworth conducted a series of studies where infants were separated from their caregivers and placed in unfamiliar situations. Based on their responses, three distinct infant attachment styles were identified: secure attachment, ambivalent attachment, and avoidant attachment.[12]

Infants who demonstrated a secure attachment style became distressed when initially separated from their caregivers but were easily comforted upon their return. They acted in ways that demonstrated a sense of confidence in their caregivers as sources of protection, warmth, and survival.[13] Though infants obviously lack the ability to formulate complex thoughts, desires, and coping strategies, one might imagine how the internal dialogue of securely attached infants might include thoughts such as *my parent stepped away for a moment but they will be back soon* or *I am safe, whole, and happy and I can trust my caregivers to return and remind me of this.*

Infants who demonstrated an ambivalent attachment style experienced great distress when separated from their caregivers. These infants vacillated between feeling a sense of comfort upon being reunited with their caregivers and simultaneously attempting to "punish" them with avoidance for leaving.[14] If these infants could talk, they may express the notions *when you left, I wasn't sure if you were coming back. I am glad you returned but you better not do it again!*

Infants who demonstrated avoidant attachment styles expressed little distress upon caregiver separation and either ignored, avoided, or only approached their caregiver indirectly upon return.[15] It's almost as though these infants exhibited an *I could care less* attitude. Their internal thoughts may have consisted of phrases such as *I was so hurt when you abandoned me, and I can't bear the thought of experiencing that pain again. I will ignore my fears and push them deep down so I won't be disappointed by abandonment in the future. I can't count on anyone but myself to satisfy my needs for comfort, care, and soothing.*

As the body of attachment research expanded, researchers proposed a fourth attachment style: disorganized attachment.[16] Children who demonstrated this form of attachment typically experienced chronic and intense forms of abuse and neglect and exhibited no predictable pattern of attachment behaviors. These infants may have aligned with thoughts such as *I don't deserve to feel love, closeness, or security* and *I am broken and shameful.*

Adult Attachment Styles

Whereas infant–caregiver attachment styles focus on the caregivers' response when infants' attachment systems become activated, adult attachment styles focus on how individuals respond to their partners when distress occurs.[17] Though infant–caregiver attachment styles are distinct from adult attachment styles, researchers have established how these early templates continue to influence enduring patterns of emotional, cognitive, and behavioral responses within the context of intimate or romantic relationships.[18] The development of adult attachment styles is multifaceted and includes the ways in which our parents cared for us, our genes, and even our life experiences.[19] Though it may be tempting, we must avoid placing blame on our parents and ancestors for the behaviors we embody today. Our parents are but one of many influences on the ways in which we navigate our lives.

The need to be close to our special person is linked to a biological mechanism in our brain that is responsible for creating and regulating the connections to our attachment figures (e.g., parents, children, and romantic partners). This mechanism is called the *attachment system*, and it consists of our emotional and behavioral responses designed to keep us safe, protected, and close to our loved ones.[20] The ways in which individuals view intimacy and togetherness, respond to conflict, approach sex, and communicate their wishes and needs are largely influenced by their attachment styles. Consequently, the expectations we hold for our partners and our relationship also differ based on adult attachment styles.[21]

Dr. Amir Levine and Dr. Rachel S. F. Heller, co-authors of the book *Attached*, identified three main adult attachment styles, or ways that people perceive and respond to intimacy in romantic relationships. As you will notice, adult attachment styles parallel the attachment styles found in children: secure, anxious, and avoidant. Similar to the caregiver–infant attachment style of *disorganized*, a small percentage of adults may exhibit an anxious-avoidant attachment style.

The relationship style we strive for, and the style we aspire for in our partners, is a *secure* attachment style. Secure individuals are comfortable with intimacy and vulnerability and exhibit warm and loving relationship tendencies. When children experience consistent positive moments in which their early caregivers are perceived as caring and approachable, a secure attachment style develops. Securely attached adults regard their romantic adult relationships positively and perceive their partners as trustworthy and dependable.[22] Because they regard others as safe, securely attached adults tend to be lower in emotional avoidance and anxiety.[23] When distress and conflict occur, securely attached adults are able to address those challenges proactively and can lean into intimacy, connection, and communication as tools to help solve problems. Adults who develop secure attachments are also more likely to thrive emotionally compared to those who develop insecure (i.e., anxious or avoidant) attachment styles.[24] They have come to believe that they are safe, others are safe, and the world is safe.

Individuals with an *anxious* attachment style have extremely sensitive attachment systems and are consumed by their desires for closeness, connection, and intimacy. They are preoccupied with their relationships and frequently worry about their partner's ability to love them back. Though anxious adults desperately desire emotional closeness and intimacy, their deep fears of abandonment and rejection tend to get in the way. Because their parents were perceived as emotionally unavailable, adults with anxious attachment styles have developed activation strategies, such as protest behaviors, to reestablish physical or emotional closeness with partners.[25] *Protest behaviors* are hyperactive, emotion-focused coping responses that attempt to reestablish contact, connection, and security with loved ones.[26]

Have you ever found yourself in that stressful cycle of sending those quintessential *Are we okay? Are you sure nothing is wrong? Are you mad at me? Are you sure?* series of text messages? This is a classic protest behavior example. In addition to sending nonstop texts despite being left "on read," additional examples of protest behaviors include withdrawing, keeping score (*"You didn't text me back for 35 minutes, so I'm going to make you wait just as long before responding"*), acting hostile, threatening to leave (saying *"I don't think I can do this anymore!"* while packing a bag and preparing to walk away, all the while desperately hoping your partner will stop you), exhibiting manipulations (saying you're too busy and have plans despite your calendar being empty, or acting busy or unapproachable), and instilling jealousy (*"You'll never guess who hit on me today!"*).[27] Hyperactive forms of coping can be understood as forms of testing behaviors where individuals push, push, push, to ensure their partners are *really* committed, trustworthy, and safe. Though hyperactive forms of coping are intended to enhance a sense of relationship security, they ultimately contribute to feelings of stress and overwhelm in their partners, create distance, and, sadly, result in relationship loss over time.[28]

If pushing partners away when things start to get a little *too serious* is more your speed, perhaps you may resonate more closely with an avoidant attachment style. *Avoidant* adults struggle with chronic intimacy avoidance and strive to maintain a strong sense of independence, control, and autonomy in their relationships.[29] The closer partners get, the more avoidant adults pull away. Avoidant individuals equate intimacy with a loss of independence and minimize closeness. When distress occurs between romantic partners, avoidant adults employ distancing and deactivation strategies to suppress the attachment system and push away intimacy.[30] Although distancing and deactivation strategies can look different based on the individual and situation, they serve important purposes. *Distancing* others when distress occurs can be understood as a protective strategy. By pushing others away, avoidant adults can protect themselves from the disappointment and sadness that may arise from maintaining close, intimate connections.[31] Similarly, *deactivation* strategies are a form of "mental gymnastics" wherein avoidant adults convince themselves that they are better off alone. Because avoidant adults respond to conflict and emotional distress with distancing and deactivation strategies, intimate relationships are difficult to maintain and become associated with frustration and disappointment.[32]

Remember that individual who only shows interest or pursues you when you're in a relationship? Have you ever been overwhelmed with intense messages of affection and commitment, only for that person to unexpectedly disappear when things started to get serious? You may have had an avoidant adult on the other end of that message chain. Additional examples of deactivation and distancing strategies include focusing on small partner imperfections as reasons why things aren't going to work (*"They chew too loudly"*), obsessing about the idea of reconciling with an ex-partner (*"I never really had closure"*), pulling away without an explanation when things are going well ("ghosting"), avoiding physical closeness (*"I don't really do sleepovers"*), and pursuing relationships with an impossible future, like individuals who are not emotionally available or who are already married.[33]

Attachment Wounds and Growing Up Asian American

The meaning of the wound "trauma," in its Greek origin, is "wound." Whether we realize it or not, it is our woundedness, or how we cope with it, that dictates much of our behavior, shapes our social habits, and informs our ways of thinking about the world. It can even determine whether or not we are capable of rational thought at all in matters of the greatest importance to our lives. For many of us, it rears its head in our closest partnerships, causing all kinds of relational mischief.

—Gabor Maté and Daniel Maté, *The Myth of Normal: Trauma, Illness, and Healing in a Toxic Culture*[34]

Infant–caregiver attachment styles, and the attachment wounds that follow, represent a specific type of trauma that impacts how we see the world, ourselves, and our relationships.[35]

As you may have already come to suspect, the ways in which many Asian American parents respond to our distress, both as children and adults, can lead to attachment wounds and the development of an insecure attachment style.[36]

But, Stacey, how does this exactly happen? How is it possible that growing up with traditional Asian American values and the possibility of historical trauma have contributed to my insecure attachment wounds in adulthood?

I spoke with Dr. Band to find out:

Intergenerational trauma is carried down and passed down. You don't have to directly experience the same kinds of hardships to inherit intergenerational trauma. You wouldn't be a child of immigrants if your parents didn't remind you of the sacrifices they made. I see that a lot with my clients; this tension between wanting to work on these things and making sense of them but also feeling a sense of guilt or a lack of permission in approaching these topics because it didn't directly affect them. But it has. It has in the way that you feel close to your parents, it has in the way that you are currently operating and approaching work. It directly affects what motivates you and all your experiences around feeling gratitude or feeling permission to rest.

Because many of our Asian American parents and ancestors focused on survival and assimilation upon migrating to America, they rarely had the luxury of reflecting on their past experiences, emotions, or challenges. Furthermore, our immigrant parents lacked role models who demonstrated emotional vulnerability and openness in ways that could aid their ability to process distressing emotions. Rather than reflecting on from where they came, our immigrant parents were so consumed with working hard, feeding their children, and keeping a roof over our heads that deep personal reflection, discussions characterized by vulnerability, and acknowledging emotionally distressing experiences represented monumental distractions for which they had no time.

Vulnerable emotions are often interpreted as forms of weakness, and weak parents who allow themselves to become consumed with feelings of sadness, fear, and overwhelm may become paralyzed by the weight of their stress and historical struggles. This immobility could inhibit their abilities to pursue the American Dream and satisfy the desire to provide their children with greater opportunities for a better life. When our parents have minimal emotional currency to spend at the Big Feelings Restaurant, the only affordable menu options are *dismiss, minimize,* or *ignore.*

Indeed, many of our Asian American parents and ancestors carry unresolved stressful experiences, steeling themselves for survival by focusing solely on meeting the biological and pragmatic needs of their children. They clothe us, they feed us, and they ensure our physical needs are met because it represents a psychologically safer strategy for demonstrating care than exhibiting vulnerability and emotional nurturing.

Perhaps our parents behave in this way because providing objective forms of caregiving is the form of love that they are most comfortable offering. Our Asian American parents and ancestors speak the universal language of physical caregiving:

They ask, *"Have you eaten yet? Are you hungry? Come eat!"* as soon as we walk through the door.

Their homes are stocked with all our favorite meals and snacks.

They inquire, *"What do you need from Costco?"*

As Michelle Zauner writes in *Crying in H Mart*:[37]

Food was how my mother expressed her love. No matter how critical or cruel she could seem—constantly pushing me to meet her intractable expectations—I could always feel her affection radiating from the lunches she packed and the meals she prepared for me just the way I like them.

Asian American parents feel like wire surrogates: They may be experts at providing food, but they are wholly unequipped with the softness that vulnerability requires. It is important to remember that our parents and ancestors are doing the best they can with what they have and with what they are able to perform emotionally and psychologically. For many of our parents, emotional vulnerability represents a far riskier task than buying crates of rambutan at full price.

TLDR: From rhesus monkeys to adult humans, each of us are hardwired to seek caregivers who demonstrate nurturing, consistent, and comforting behaviors from which can learn, grow, and develop new coping responses to distressing events. Because many of our Asian American parents were not afforded the luxury to reflect on the emotional challenges associated with their historical trauma and intergenerational patterns, they may have struggled to respond with the consistent forms of validation, acceptance, and emotional vulnerability needed for us to cultivate secure attachment styles. In truth, providing more pragmatic sources of care may have been the psychologically safest way for our parents to demonstrate care because they may lack the emotional literacy to respond when big emotions arise. Despite their best efforts, minimizing, invalidating, and withdrawing responses following vulnerable emotional disclosures may inadvertently communicate covert messages that discourage emotional vulnerability in relationships and contribute to insecure attachment styles. Consequently, Asian children of immigrants may internalize cultural scripts such as *demonstrating vulnerability leads to conflict; my feelings cannot be trusted; I must keep my challenges, emotional burdens, and mental health distress to myself;* and *I cannot be fully accepted, loved, or valued for who I am.* We can learn to let go of these unhelpful cultural scripts and break enduring patterns of emotional, cognitive, and physical responses.

Questions to Ponder

1. Which adult attachment style most closely resembles my experiences in romantic relationships?
2. Which adult attachment style most closely resembles my current or past partners?
3. How might my early childhood experiences have impacted the development of my adult attachment style?

4. Which types of caring behaviors do my parents engage in that elicit deep feelings of love and connection?
5. How can I better begin to appreciate my parents' sacrifices and cultivate a deep sense of compassion for their experiences?

Questions to Bridge the Gap with Parents

1. What does a close parent–child relationship look like for you? Which activities might we engage in to deepen our relationship?
2. What are your proudest moments as my parent?
3. If you knew then what you know now, is there anything you would change about how I was raised?

5

Insecure Attachment Styles Among Asian Americans

It comes as no surprise that the critically acclaimed and award-winning 2022 movie *Everything Everywhere All At Once* resonates with Asian American viewers. Underneath the well-choreographed fight scenes, captivating costume designs, and outstanding performances, the movie's plot had heart. For many viewers, it stirred up the deep, unhealed attachment wounds and intergenerational patterns that many Asian Americans and children of Asian immigrants have carried for a lifetime. While Michelle Yeoh's character, Evelyn, tries to navigate the relationships with her father and husband while being audited by the IRS, Stephanie Hsu's character, Joy, travels through endless versions of the multiverse just to find a reality where she is wholeheartedly accepted by her mother. Her feelings of pain, anguish, hope, and resentment are represented by the chaotic nature of each multiverse that she travels to and destroys.

One doesn't have to be a professional movie critic to recognize the thematic power that drives the film's success. How many of us have longed for a reality where we feel unconditionally loved, accepted, and celebrated by our parents for all that we are, rather than for all that we are expected to become? How many nights have we lain awake wishing, wondering, and praying that one day we might be good enough for our parents' wholehearted approval?

Inheriting Our Parents' Attachment Styles

Studies have documented how Asian Americans and children of Asian immigrants tend to struggle with insecure forms of attachment stemming from our parents' challenges to understand and make sense of their own distressing emotional experiences and intergenerational narratives.[1] Based on my interviews, research, and anecdotal evidence, I have also found this to be true. Many of us have not only developed but have also *inherited* the attachment styles of our parents. They offer a master class in insecure attachment styles, and we learn from our caregivers through an intense and immersive lifetime apprenticeship.

Traditional Asian cultural values and societal messages can also intersect with our parents' responses to emotional distress, passing down covert and overt messages that communicate the importance of doing what it takes to survive (ignoring and suppressing emotions), maintaining interpersonal harmony (not discussing conflict with children), and emphasizing the importance of collectivism and filial piety (telling children they are ungrateful if they do not behave in ways that parents believe are best). This can be evidenced when our parents invalidate our career goals, partner selections, and life choices or when they withdraw or demonstrate discomfort when we disclose our feelings and emotions. Though it is not their intention, these responses communicate underlying messages that the full spectrum of our emotions, desires, and behaviors is not appropriate and should therefore be dismissed, minimized, or ignored. As adults, we may therefore internalize fixed beliefs that vulnerability has no place in the relationships we hold with our parents, and eventually with our romantic partners. We may internalize cultural scripts such as *demonstrating vulnerability leads to conflict*; *my feelings cannot be trusted*; *I must keep my challenges, emotional burdens, and mental health distress to myself*; and *I cannot be fully accepted, loved, or valued for who I am.*

We must also consider how traumatic experiences from childhood (e.g., instances of neglect or physical, emotional, and/or sexual abuse) contribute to challenges with achieving a secure attachment style in our adult romantic relationships. Just as the ways in which we internalize unhelpful cultural scripts are often multifaceted, so too is the development of our adult attachment style.

Kareena* shares how childhood trauma experiences have impacted her adult relationships:

> *I grew up in a physically, sexually, mentally, and emotionally abusive household. As a result of my childhood, I was involved in abusive relationships in my early adulthood. I didn't realize there were other options. I also found it incredibly difficult to trust because I didn't know who could hurt me. When I finally met my husband, a well-rounded, down-to-earth, kind, compassionate, furthest-thing-from-abusive type of man, I was constantly waiting for the other shoe to drop. I was waiting for the moment he would deem me unworthy, choke me up against a wall, or worse. I was nervous to open myself up and be vulnerable and I found myself running in the other direction at any sign of friction. Throughout my marriage, I had to learn what it means to give and show love, and how to receive and accept love. This is something I still struggle with today. In my family of origin, love was always conditional and could be taken away at any moment.*

Sharon K. expresses another example of how insecure attachment styles in her romantic relationships are rooted in the childhood relationship with her mother:

> *I have historically struggled with distorted thinking and assumptions about whether my partner is to be trusted and whether they have my best interest in mind. In therapy, I have been able to slowly work closer and closer to the origin of that anxiety and insecurity, which is tied to the relationship with my mother and her inability to provide the kind of love that I need. Learning what forgiveness is and how to radically accept these really hard truths about my mom is something that I'm actively working on.*

Let's check out at other examples of how adult attachment styles can look among Asian Americans and children of Asian immigrants.

The Emotional Distancers

Avoidant adults may have had parents who were not emotionally available or who struggled to validate and respond with unconditional acceptance when moments of emotional intimacy arose with their children. Though individuals who develop avoidant attachment styles have deep desires for intimacy, closeness, and connection, the very idea of vulnerability elicits discomfort because the presence of deep connection increases the likelihood of rejection. Because of internalized cultural scripts that minimize the value of emotional vulnerability as well as our own fears that if we are vulnerable we will experience rejection, many of us have learned to suppress our emotions. Indeed, many Asian American children grow up in households that do not encourage emotional intimacy, vulnerability, and open discussions about psychological distress in nonjudgmental environments.[2] As a result, we internalize the fixed beliefs that *other people are not safe* and *the only one I can rely on to meet my needs is myself.*
Shoua Lee reflects:

> *Not feeling safe in my own body led me to believe that nothing in the world was safe. Although I wanted to have close and intimate relationships, I struggled with letting anyone in.*

Dr. Band graciously shares an example of how her childhood experiences contributed to the development of an avoidant attachment style:

Broadly, avoidant attachment impacts what I share and how safe I feel to be vulnerable. This impacts my relationships in how comfortable I feel in sharing my innermost thoughts and feelings. When I was younger, I wouldn't feel completely safe to have big emotions and would often go to my room and cry into my pillow or listen to music. I learned that the only way to find safety and soothe myself was to be alone in isolation; not turning toward someone, rather turning away in a self-protective mode. When I got married and my partner and I began living together, of course that habit followed through with me. In the early stages and phases of living together, I would immediately do the same thing when big emotions would arise. I would isolate, go to our room, and be upset. I think to my partner at first, because he is securely attached, that was really hard to experience because on the outside my responses can be misinterpreted as stonewalling. Actually, it was really my inability to tolerate intense emotions around other people because that almost felt too vulnerable. In my present-day romantic relationship, I sometimes fall into old patterns of insecure attachment, especially when I am tired and my energy is low. I can avoid difficult or heavy conversations because I don't feel safe in spite of logically knowing I am. It can feel easier to self soothe by myself then ask for help.

Dr. Cheung's narrative echoes similar sentiments:

Even within the relationships I have with family and loved ones, I experience fear of judgment or worry that I will cause discomfort to others if I share my struggles.

As an adult, I understand now that I feel uncertain whether my attachment figures would still accept me if I were not good enough.

I.B.* shares:

A past partner once expressed that sometimes talking to me is like talking to a wall. I was shocked. It hurt a lot because although I have a lot to say and have constant thoughts and feelings, I was taught and shown to not always express them.

So many of us develop coping strategies that lead us to interpret our emotions as shameful or burdensome. We believe that distressing experiences must be dismissed, suppressed, and handled alone. And, we echo these patterns unconsciously with our partners, children, friends, and loved ones by engaging in isolation and emotional withdrawal when intense feelings arise.

The experiences of Kareena, Sharon, Dr. Band, Dr. Cheung, and I.B. are all consistent with attachment theories and research findings about the important role of emotionally available and nurturing caregivers. Without the presence of a secure and comforting base, it is difficult to develop new coping strategies in times of great emotional distress.[3] These behavioral, emotional, and cognitive patterns are carried with us into our adult relationships.[4]

The Security Seekers

Anxious adults may have perceived their caregivers as individuals who required great emotional care. As children, our parents may have come to us with adult problems such as expressing the challenging financial state of the household, the endless bills to be paid, or the grievances from their own marital struggle. Those with anxious adult attachments have developed people-pleasing abilities early on to cater to their parents' emotional distress. When we feel responsible for ensuring the happiness, stability, and well-being of our parents, we often cultivate caregiver identities. We form relationships with others whom we believe need us and attribute our value based on our perceived ability to give to others, often denying the same care for ourselves. In our romantic relationships, Asian Americans and children of Asian immigrants who develop an anxious adult attachment style internalize the fixed belief *I have to please my partner to avoid abandonment.*

Cynthia Siadat shares how anxious attachments have impacted her adult relationship:

> *When my husband and I were first dating and I realized I was entertaining the idea of being with him for the rest of my life, it terrified me. I was constantly afraid he would leave me; either alone or for another woman. I would seek to "win him over" and then felt devastated and abandoned when he couldn't respond (due to being at work, for instance). I had a number of desperate behaviors for getting his attention when my people-pleasing ones seemed to fall short. I would text relentlessly, pick fights, and on one occasion, I left our bed in the middle of the night. I have since learned that the behaviors I exhibited didn't foster long-term relationships and close connections. It did the opposite. It would push people away in a sort of self-fulling prophecy.*

Olivia* shares another example of how childhood attachment wounds can impact our adult relationships:

> *I'm deeply affected by my partners' and parents' sense of love or withdrawal from me. As the anxious one, I constantly feel the need to pursue my partner to feel validated and wanted. I find myself unconsciously trying to mitigate situations and control dynamics within my romantic relationship to avoid feeling unwanted and unloved. My anxious attachment style directly connects to my attachment wounds. My upbringing taught me to "do more" to feel more secure. This belief is a product of my parents' need to find safety and actual security (food, financial opportunity, etc.) and is now expressed in adulthood as a constant urge to "do more" in my relationships to prove I am worthy and to continuously receive love. I suspect that this stems from a lifetime of "accomplishment-reward" behavior from my mother, which was her sole way of showing love and support.*

Jennifer Alexander,* a transracial, transnational, adopted Chinese woman in her late 20s, describes how her adoption history may have impacted her anxious attachment style:

> *My adoptive mother describes the scene in China in 1994 as a sea of cribs and not enough nurses. I was a little over one year old when I was adopted. I couldn't walk and I could barely crawl. I clung to my parents, and I couldn't get enough physical attention. As an adult, I think this trauma shows up as feelings of distrust and uncertainty in my romantic relationships. I struggle with a deep fear of abandonment at times, and that's been challenging.*

As portrayed by each of these narratives, adults with anxious attachment styles seek to re-establish feelings of security and connection by implementing protest behaviors when relationship stress occurs. Anxiously attached adults are hardwired with hypersensitive attachment systems that, in some ways, are both a blessing and a curse. Though anxiously attached adults are more likely to notice subtle details and changes in their partners' behaviors (e.g., tone of voice, changes in body language) compared to individuals with other attachment styles, they are also more likely to falsely sound the alarm when problems do not actually exist.

The In-Betweeners

Individuals who embody a disorganized attachment style, also referred to as a fearful avoidant attachment style, struggle with elements of both anxious and avoidant adult attachment styles to higher degrees.[5] A disorganized adult attachment style can best be understood as having difficulty in responding appropriately when threats are perceived,[6] which leads to challenges with social cognition and identity development.[7] As a result, disorganized adults have an extreme need for closeness with their partners, struggle with an intense fear of rejection, and experience conflicting mental states and behaviors.[8]

Sophia, a biracial Asian American woman of East Asian and Middle Eastern descent in her early 30s, describes how anxious-avoidant attachment patterns have historically impacted her relationships:

> *As a child and even into my adulthood, if she was upset, my mom would explode and then she would withdraw and withhold. That created the most unhealthy attachment style: disorganized. It basically occurs when you're attached to that which you fear the most.*

The disorganized style is one that many children of immigrants experience and it's something that I definitely experience. I think unhealthy attachment styles play out in our adulthood a lot because we are afraid of being abandoned. We're afraid of not being accepted. It's very binary for a lot of immigrant parents and as children you carry that into your adulthood.

Calypso* shares how a disorganized attachment style has also impacted her:

Being an immigrant's daughter is a special kind of unstable footing. I witnessed as a child how much my mother praised my father for his hard work. It seemed like hard work made one lovable. Because of this message, I've become hyper independent and guard my autonomy to a fault. This exaggeration made it difficult to find well-balanced and healthy romantic relationships. Each failed relationship felt like a failure in self-worth. I would also become very insecurely attached; if I became hurt or felt small and worthless, I'd revert back to, "I can do good all by myself" and quickly run from the conflict. I had multiple relationships in which I felt I was not enough. I tried really hard to make past partners love me. Love in exchange for service was natural to me. I would show surges of emotion out of desperation when I felt unloved. I feared I'd be alone because of my behavior.

Kimmy Wu, a first-generation Taiwanese American woman and mental health professional in her late 20s, shares:

Surviving as a disorganized-attached individual feels like a constant cycle of emotional dysregulation, projection, and unresolved ruptures. I found intimate and close relationships to be confusing and unsettling. It showed up in dichotomous and all-or-nothing patterns of thinking and behaviors due to an extreme fear of rejection and abandonment, coupled with difficulty connecting to and trusting others. This impacted my relationships with friends, family, and partners because disorganized attachment behaviors can often seem unpredictable and ambivalent. My inner child finds its source of safety to also be a source of fear—which showed up as beliefs that I was undeserving of love and closeness in relationships.

We circle back to Shoua, Dr. Band, Dr. Cheung, Calypso*, Cynthia, Olivia*, Sophia, Jennifer, and Kimmy in a future chapter. Spoiler alert: Each of them have managed to break those old patterns and cultivate secure attachments with loving partners—and so can you!

TLDR: Though distinct, our adult attachment styles are informed by our infant–caregiver relationships. When our emotional, psychological, and physiological needs are met from an early age, adults may develop secure attachment styles. Adults who cultivate secure attachment styles are flexible, comfortable with intimacy, and creative when conflict occurs. Conversely, individuals whose needs were not consistently met as children may develop insecure (i.e., anxious, avoidant, or disorganized) attachment styles. Adults with anxious attachment styles are consumed by intense desires for intimacy and their sensitive attachment systems often result in problematic coping behaviors, called protest behaviors. Adults who have avoidant attachment styles prioritize independence in their relationships and engage in distancing and/or deactivation responses to minimize the psychological distress associated with intimacy and disappointment.

Questions to Ponder

1. When I experience relationship stress with my partner, how do I respond?
2. When reflecting on past relationships, how have my patterns changed? How might they have remained the same?
3. To what extent do I feel able to be vulnerable, trusting, and authentic with my current and/or past partners?
4. When I expressed vulnerability and emotional challenges to my parents/caregivers, how did they respond?
5. When I express vulnerability and emotional challenges with my partner, how do they respond?

Questions to Bridge the Gap with Parents

1. What was it like for you growing up?
2. How have your childhood experiences impacted the way you understand yourself, your relationships, and the world today?
3. With whom do you feel you can be your most authentic self?

6

Identifying and Challenging Sexual Scripts

❦

I am 11 years old and standing at the end of the driveway, waiting for the bus that will take me to my new school. It is a warm morning in late August, and I feel excited and nervous about what the first day will bring. I wonder whether I will make new friends, enjoy my teachers, and fit in with my classmates.

My father received an incredible offer to join a private practice in Cleveland, Ohio, so our family relocated from Texas to a suburb just 10 minutes west of the city. As I hear the familiar groan of a school bus engine, I look down at my shoes. Small chunks of dried mud have caked around the edges of my white sneakers from catching grasshoppers a few days before. I hope nobody notices.

The school bus halts to a loud stop in front of me and the smell of diesel fills my nose. I tightly clutch the straps of my backpack and climb the four steps into the school bus.

By the second step, I immediately miss my best friend back in Texas, a quiet Korean American girl named Jenny Kim. Though her house was only a few blocks away, our eyes would frantically search for one another the moment I entered the bus. We were the only Asian American kids in our class and shared a deep sense of cultural familiarity and understanding. Our bus seat was always the same: fourth one down on the right. She preferred to sit next to the window because there was a small cushion tear close to the aisle and she worried about bugs that may have crawled into the stuffing. I could always count on Jenny to save me a seat, and we would spend the entire school ride trading small toy animals from our Littlest Pet Shop collections.

Once inside the bus, I am met with a sea of unfamiliar white faces. As I try to force a brave smile, my mouth suddenly feels dry, and my lips can't seem to stretch across my face. Everyone avoids eye contact as I slowly start walking toward the back of the bus. I slide into an empty seat over the tire well as the vehicle jolts forward.

Behind me, I hear a voice call, "Hey, Asian!" and I am immediately filled with a complex mixture of emotions. Fueled by apprehension, curiosity, and hopefulness, my heart races as my muddy white sneakers push me toward the aisle.

I peek around the seat and see a blond-haired boy. He is snickering and sitting with a small group of friends. "Hey, Asian!" he repeats, this time preparing to pose a question: "Is your vagina slanted sideways, like your chinky eyes?"

My cheeks immediately flush and my face feels scorching hot. I whip around as fast as I can and stare out the window, doing my best to ignore the loud cackles of laughter that fill my ears. My eyes are stinging with tears that threaten to spill out at any moment, so I squeeze them tightly, resigned not to let them see me cry. I learned two things that day:

Don't turn around when someone calls you outside your name.
and
There is something sexual in nature about being an Asian girl.

The History of Asian American Sexual Stereotypes

I've lost track of how many Asian American women have shared similar childhood stories and experiences. How many of us have received messages from society, media, and potential partners that centered sexuality as a primary part of our identities?

The sexual stereotypes and misguided beliefs about the innately hypersexual and submissive nature of Asian American women followed me through young adulthood and into my college-aged years. When I started dating, men were often shocked to learn I was not the submissive, hypersexual, demure, and well-behaved Asian woman they were expecting. I had opinions (strong ones at that!) and made them known. I was confused when I would receive pet names that essentialized my identity, such as "China Doll" and "Fili-peanut." Couldn't these men see that I was more than my Filipina and Chinese heritage?

It turns out, these ill-suited lovers may have fallen prey to the same beliefs about Asian women that American men have carried since the 1875 Page Act, the Immigration Act of 1924, and the War Brides Act of 1945.

Stacey, what's the point of reviewing all this history, and what does this have to do with the sexual stereotypes that Asian American women face today?

Excellent question, dear reader.

As it turns out, the very same experiences that modern Asian American women face today echo centuries of oppressive sexual stereotypes and cultural scripts.

Asian women have been historically portrayed through the U.S. lens as sexually promiscuous, manipulative, and cunning prostitutes as early as the late 19th century. Fueled by decades of anti-Chinese sentiments and the yellow peril discourse, the 1875 Page Act banned the immigration of "Oriental" laborers who were brought against their will or who sought to immigrate for "lewd and immoral purposes" (i.e., prostitution). Although the 1875 Page Act was designed to combat forced labor exploitation, only the latter criterion was enforced, which effectively banned all East Asian women from migrating into the United States. Through the lens of the yellow peril discourse, which was deeply embedded into the minds of Americans at the time, Asian women were framed in propaganda as prostitutes, carriers of sexual disease, and immoral temptations to white men.

As World War II began, things only became more complicated and divisive for Asian women. Following the Rape of Nanking on December 13, 1937, a human rights violation in which between 20,000 and 80,000 Chinese women were raped by Japanese soldiers, the Japanese government developed a plan to ensure that such an atrocity would never occur again. The Japanese government attributed the Rape of Nanking to the unfulfilled sexual desires of the military and forcibly abducted and trafficked over 200,000 women from China, Korea, and the Philippines. These women, referred to as *comfort women*, were forced into sex work to satisfy the desires of American and Japanese allies. An estimated 80 percent of comfort women were of Korean descent.

The lives of comfort women were punctuated by moments of tragedy, shame, and psychological distress. Comfort women were forced to submit to the needs, wants, and desires of Japanese allies around military camps and were even deployed alongside soldiers who were stationed in different places. In times when the military was forced to withdraw, the comfort women would be abandoned, leaving them at the mercy of the enemy. Due to these harsh conditions, high rates of suicide, and lack of medical care, 90 percent of comfort women did not survive the end of WWII.

Human sex trafficking among Asian countries continued through both the Vietnam and Korean wars. Though gruesome, emotionally distressing, and potentially activating, the experiences and realities of comfort women play an important role in the enduring sexual stereotypes that Asian American women face today. In other words:

The first interaction that three generations of American men had with Asian women were ones that positioned us as submissive sex objects.

Surprise! Scarlett Johansson Didn't Invent Yellowface

The stories, experiences, and fantasies shared by American servicemen about Asian women during WWII became part of American Western consciousness and played itself out time and time again in media, books, and movies. Tropes portraying Asian American women as mere objects of sexual desire can be traced back to the 1920s when Wong Liu Tsong, known professionally as Anna May Wong, became the first Chinese American actress to grace the silver screen.

Though Anna May Wong achieved international acclaim as a film star in a time when Hollywood was fraught with racism, anti-miscegenation laws (which prevented on-screen kisses between individuals of different races), stereotyping, and yellowface (hiring white actors to portray Asian American characters), she was frequently typecast in roles that centered her sexuality. Wong earned her first leading role at age 17 in *The Toll of the Sea*, a film that was loosely based on Giacomo Puccini's three-act opera *Madame Butterfly*. The film tells the tragic story of an American soldier who travels to Japan to find a wife. The opera was inspired by John Luther Long's short story *Madame Butterfly*, which in turn was based on Pierre Loti's semi-autobiographical French novel *Madame Chrysanthème*.

Loti's novel takes the form of the journal of a white naval officer who marries a Japanese woman while stationed in Nagasaki, Japan, in the summer of 1885. The book begins with a conversation between the protagonist and his friend, who eagerly await their ship's arrival in Japan the following morning. As he imagines the traits for an ideal wife, Loti posits:

> Yes—I shall choose a little, creamy-skinned woman with black hair and cat's eyes. She must be pretty and not much bigger than a doll.

Scholars credit *Madame Chrysanthème* for shaping Western attitudes toward Japan at the turn of the 20th century. The novel became increasingly popular following the War Brides Act of 1945, which allowed U.S. servicemen to bring home women whom they married abroad on a non-quota basis and without regard to racial exclusion laws.

According to the National Origins Formula, part of the Immigration Act of 1924, immigration visas were only given to 2 percent of the total number of people of each nationality in the United States as of the 1890 national census.[1] The Immigration Act of 1924 also included the Asian Exclusion Act, which prohibited all Asian immigration to the United States with the exception of Filipinos, who were considered U.S. nationals due to the Philippines' status as a U.S. colony.[2] Though between 60,000 and 70,000 women married American servicemen during and immediately after WWII, many of them were unable to reunite with their husbands in the United States because of restrictive immigration laws. The War Brides Act therefore became a loophole wherein white soldiers could marry and bring home Asian women who were specifically excluded from immigration to the United States as part of the Immigration Act of 1924.[3]

An Oriental Fetish to Be Consumed

Orientalism is the notion that portrays Eastern cultures, societies, histories, and people as wild, disordered, and needing to be civilized.[4] The drive to "civilize" Indigenous Asian natives through the forcible insertion of Western law, religion, language, and cultural norms was deemed "the white man's burden" in a poem by Rudyard Kipling.[5]

These dangerous Western desires intersect with race, ethnicity, gender, and sexuality in complex and nuanced ways. First, "orientalizing" Asian women as "the exotic other" strips us of our humanity and minimizes the amount of empathy afforded to us. It also places Asian women outside of white feminism,[6] resulting in tension among women and adding to the fetishization of Asian women. Indeed, those deemed less than human may also be considered less deserving of respect, care, and justice. Positioning Asian women as overtly hypersexual, demure, and submissive "others" who only exist to please the white male gaze has justified behaviors designed to conquer, discipline, and police the racialized bodies of Asian women for centuries.[7]

Through this lens, Asian American women have been historically perceived as a fetish to be consumed, an experience to be encountered, and an adventure to be had. The sexual stereotypes that portray Asian women as exotically attractive extend beyond the cultural commodification of sexuality to encompass even a literal commodification. For example, Asian women's sexuality is believed to attribute to us the powerful ability to provide a means of financial security. Case in point: I have yet to see an episode of *90-Day Fiancé* that does not feature an Asian woman dating an American in pursuit of a T-visa.

What About Asian Men?

Whereas the bodies of Asian American women have been historically positioned in ways that frame us as overtly sexual, the opposite holds true for Asian American men. In fact, the stereotype of Asian and Asian American men as effeminate, sexually undesirable, and less masculine compared to other ethnic and racial groups goes back all the way to—you guessed it—the late 18th century.

When Chinese immigrants were completing the Transcontinental Railroad, it was not a fun time to be Asian. As you may recall from our previous chapter, the early experiences of Asian immigrants in the United States were punctuated with anti-Asian sentiments. Remember the Chinese Exclusion Act? That dusty old document that prevented Chinese individuals from immigrating to the States for a period of 10 years? One of the significant consequences following this law was that Chinese migrants were unable to reconnect with their wives or start families. Anti-miscegenation laws in the 1920s also made it illegal for Asian men to marry white women in the United States. In fact, non-white women could lose their American citizenship if they married Asian men. Without the prospect of romantic partners or the ability to start families, white Westerners began creating false narratives about Asian men as less masculine, less desirable, and even queer.[8] Many of these persist today.

Asian men faced further discrimination through other forms of legislation that attacked their rights to own land and pursue livelihood. In 1913, the Alien Land Acts prohibited Asian immigrants from owning real estate, while other laws kept Asian men from working in heavy industry. These laws forced Asian men to begin working in industries traditionally portrayed as feminine, such as within laundromats, housekeeping, and restaurants.[9]

The compounding impacts of these laws attacked Asian men's abilities to marry, start families, and work in diverse, traditionally "masculine" settings. The result?

Asian men were deemed effeminate and were emasculated, symbolically castrated, and portrayed as less desirable as potential husbands or sexual partners.

False tropes about Asian men perpetuate stereotypes that position Asian masculinity as deficient,[10] deviant, and queer.[11] Researchers have even proposed a term for this, *Asianized attribution*, which refers to the ways in which masculinity, race, and sexuality intersect among Asian men in ways that frame them as adhering to traditional patriarchal values while also being less emotionally receptive and physically unattractive. This notion results in racial isolation and the symbolic castration of Asian men.[12] Asian men are therefore forced to contend with harmful sexual stereotypes about their masculinity, genital size, and physical appearance, which can result in high rates of psychological distress, internalized racism, and feelings of shame.

As I dove deeper into the literature about this topic, I discovered that researchers had quantified what many of us had already known. In one study that explored the presence of stereotypes aimed at Asian Americans at the intersection of gender and ethnicity, Asian women were perceived to be exotic, passive, and overtly sexualized while Asian men were perceived to be weak and asexual.[13]

Another study conducted with a group of 158 college-aged Asian American men explored their perceptions of people's stereotypes about them. Stereotypes included beliefs that Asian American men embodied unflattering physical attributes and were deficient as sexual and romantic partners.[14] Many Asian men have described pressures to adhere to Western portrayals of traditional masculinity in order to be deemed attractive by white women. As you can see, contextualizing the stereotypes and cultural scripts faced by Asian Americans must be situated within the sociohistorical context in which they occur.

Queer Asians Face Unique Challenges

Communities outside the majority culture are viewed through androcentric, ethnocentric, and heteronormative perspectives. Thus, individuals outside the majority culture (i.e., cisgender, heterosexual, white men) are positioned against this backdrop in ways that frame us as different and "less than." Gay men, for example, may experience overt rejection in sexual encounters on the basis of sexuality, race, or ethnicity.[15] They may face homonegativity from the largely straight Asian American community while also experiencing racism from the predominantly white gay community. These experiences are even more heightened among Asian Americans who identify as transgender, non-binary, gender expansive, and gender non-conforming.[16] Because of how queer Asian American men's identities intersect with one another, they are commonly viewed as meta-minorities.

Impact of Sexuality-Based Stereotypes

I began to wonder how these sexuality-based stereotypes impacted the well-being and sexual development of our Asian American community members and children of Asian immigrants. Here is what I found.

Assumptions of Hypersexuality Among Asian Women

Many individuals with whom I spoke expressed how messages about sexuality began early in their lives and continued to impact them into adulthood.
Calypso* recalls:

Even to this very day, the space where I feel most discomfort is around white heterosexual men. These feelings began in middle school when my fifth-grade ex-boyfriend kept saying, "Sucky sucky for a dollar." I was confused because I wasn't raised watching TV, but I knew that it meant something sexual. The Asian accent in his voice was distinct and painful. The layers of embarrassment settled in. Throughout my adolescence, I was not asked on dates, but I received a lot of sexual attention from older white men in public. In college, a boyfriend accused me of having a sexually transmitted infection and called me a "rotten egg roll." As an adult, I struggle with an internal battle between being a feminist who celebrates sexuality and also an Asian woman who wants to be seen as separate from her sexuality. Even when I am the most powerful person in the room, I feel outside of myself and uncomfortable as more straight men enter my space.

It feels as though the more hetero male the room becomes, the more vulnerable I become.

Jeanine*, a third-generation multiracial Asian American woman, shares:

Asian women and femmes are generally seen as submissive, quiet, passive, child-like, or babydoll-like. In this way, they are objectified, tokenized to be dominated, and dehumanized. Asian women and femmes are seen as validators of masculine superiority. They are hypersexualized due to their exotic nature and are influenced by white supremacy and imperialism.

Sharon K. describes how the presence of these harmful sexual stereotypes has empowered her to advocate for herself and others:

General racist archetypes about what an East Asian Femme is (hypersexual vs. docile, Dragon Lady vs. submissive decorative object) have been really disturbing to see play out in real-life experiences and exchanges. I believe this is in part why I am so direct and outspoken.

The thread carried through each of these narratives is the pain and internalized shame among each of the women with whom I spoke. Unfortunately, it seems that childhood and adolescent stories shared by Asian American women who grew up in the United States collectively share moments where they have felt sexually objectified, essentialized, or shamed.

Sexual Stereotypes Among Asian American Men

Feelings of pain, disconnect, and sexual shame also impact Asian American men. Though the media have begun to expand their purview of Asian masculine roles to include handsome protagonists rather than bumbling nerds, society at large continues to perpetuate harmful sexual tropes toward Asian American men.
YanYan* shares:

The stereotype I see most often that affects Asian American men is that they are not sexual or romantic. This sexual stereotype has caused a great deal of confusion and false expectations for me. For example, I mostly maintain a passive role in dating and when looking for potential dating partners. This led to feelings of self-doubt, self-criticism, and feelings of rejection. When I started dating my wife, there was a lot of uncertainty on how to lead and that frustrated her. Through the grace of God and honest communication, we have been able to overcome many of these challenges.

Jeanine* expresses:

Heterosexual Asian men have been stereotyped as overly feminine, passive, nerdy, and emasculated in ways that presume they have small penises. I think this has recently changed as we are seeing more representation in pop culture of Asian men taking on many forms, roles, and sexualities.

Asian American men have a long history of being emasculated, castrated, and feminized. These stereotypes also seem to extend into the lesbian, gay, bisexual, transgender, and queer communities in ways that position gay Asian men as submissive.

Drake M., a first-generation cisgender gay man in his early 30s of white and Filipino heritage, states:

I have seen or personally heard stereotypes about Asian and Asian American men regarding body size, height, and penis size. I have personally felt inadequate or believed that if I were "whiter" I would receive more attention on dating and hookup apps. These are self-esteem issues for sure, but I think that they stem from real-life experiences and ideals that are pushed upon us by the media.

Bayani* similarly shares how his identity as a gay Asian American man affects expectations of him within sexuality and kink spaces:

Sexuality stereotypes about gay Asian men make me hyper aware of how people interact with me—especially when romance or dating is in play, and in social situations. I might play into them for the sake of smoothing over perceived social strain or scripts. I sometimes am hesitant to reveal my race in dominant/ submissive relationships for fear that my sub may perceive that my dominant power is weakened because of my race. I generally think Asian men are typically less sought after without an air of submissiveness being assumed (e.g., someone wants/expects to dominate me) so I perceive that our masculinity is lowest on the tier of racial ranking. Examples of this are typically seen in porn. The only thing that shakes up the racial hierarchy of who dominates whom in porn tends to be from muscle definition.

Yub Kim explains how sexual stereotypes toward Asian men are prevalent in media and describes how they have impacted his sexual experiences:

Although some American men have expressed their sexual interest in and sexual fantasies of me, I believe the more common expectation is that Asian men are desexualized or automatically submissive. You can easily see examples of the stereotype: Iago from the Broadway show Aladdin *or Waymond Wang from the Academy Award–winning movie* Everything Everywhere All at Once. *Before entering the kink scenes, I could brush off rejection as merely a difference in attraction. However, when I was rejected in the kink community, I could not help but feel that American men sometimes do not know how to feel attracted to me. I am a cis-gender gay Asian male who is a dominant and assertive bottom. Being an Asian bottom already sets up an expectation that I am submissive. So, when I approach somebody I am interested in with straightforward interest and flirtation, I feel they do not know how to feel attracted to me. The experiences have made me doubt that I will ever be good enough to be as attractive as other white males. Sometimes I would put up a façade and act more submissive. Back then, fake sex was better than no sex. It pushed me to participate in performative sex and not put my pleasure at the center.*

Breaking the Stigma and Liberating our Sexual Selves

Looking back, I can't remember a time where my parents explicitly sat me down to discuss topics related to sex and sexuality. I don't think these challenges are limited to Asian American parents or even immigrant parents, either. Instead, I suspect many parents struggle to broach these difficult and vulnerable conversations because of their own internalized feelings of shame and discomfort about sexuality and our identities as sexual beings. Beyond our racial and ethnic identities, I suspect that this challenge is simply emblematic of the Western culture in which we live.

For many individuals, the ways that parents broach sex and sexuality are largely influenced by gender. I'll never forget how my mother casually gifted my *kuya* a box of condoms when he left for college. Purchased dutifully from Costco, she slid the box under the bed and assured him, *Just in case, anak* (*my child*). I can't help but feel entertained at the thought of a college-aged man pulling out a wholesale-size box of condoms before initiating sex with his partner.

When my mom addressed sexuality with me, there were no overtures about protection or discussions about the importance of safer sex practices. Compared to the proactive approach she took with my *kuya*, my mom's approach held a distinctly threatening tone: *You better not get pregnant out of wedlock.*

My experiences echo those shared by Asian American thought leaders and community advocates. Themes around silence, discomfort, and internalized shame appear to be consistent with the individuals with whom I spoke.

YanYan,* a multiracial Asian American man in his 30s, expresses:

For Asian American men, there aren't a lot of overt discussions about sexuality within our community. This often leads to confusion or repression; Asian American men do not have a space to talk and become educated about sex. As a result, we are often embarrassed to seek advice or talk to anyone about sex. There is little to no discussion about sex and dating in my family. I learned that this is common in first-generation Asian American families. In my family, the closest thing to modeling or teaching is through media or hoping that teachers would provide the education. It seems that my family does not have the understanding or knowledge on how to discuss topics related to sex with younger generations.

Jeanine* echoes:

The assumptions and biases about people's sexuality, gender identity, and gender expressions all come from the sociopolitical messaging that attempts to control these aspects. On a micro level, messaging about sexuality and gender expression comes from our families, their values, and our communities. Our families are often informed by tradition, religion, and spirituality. In this way, we can internalize these messages. In collectivistic cultures, our bodies are not often seen as our own and may be both protected, loved, nurtured, and commented on in regards to size and expression. It's very common for Asian American caregivers to comment on their children's bodies, particularly their size and what they look like when it comes to food, finding a romantic partner, or even how attractive they are.

Sexual stigma among Asian American communities may also be embedded within cultural narratives, cultures, and practices. Shoua Lee recalls:

Although it occurs less frequently now, Hmong men practiced polygamy. Hmong men were allowed to take many wives and were praised for their ability to have many children. Meanwhile, Hmong women were prohibited to express their desire. Having children out of wedlock led to ostracization and shame. I believe that prohibiting Hmong women from acknowledging and accepting their desires keeps a part [of] them deeply hidden and plays a key role in inhibiting their ability to truly access their authenticity.

Breaking the stigma around sexuality as Asian Americans can be a powerful strategy to reclaim our identities as whole beings. Whether we have internalized sexuality-based scripts from parents, partners, the media, or society as a whole, many of us have not received opportunities to reflect on our sexual scripts, liberate our sexual selves, and incorporate the fragmented parts of our sexual identities.

In my work as a sexuality counselor and educator, empowering others to reclaim their sexual identities and liberate their sexual selves is some of my very favorite work. Though everyone's journey is different, it seems as though many individuals struggle with similar internalized scripts related to their sexuality. These often include notions such as:

> *I cannot trust my body.*
> *I am not deserving of sexual pleasure.*
> *I must meet my partner's sexual expectations to avoid being abandoned.*
> *Sexual pleasure, and who I am as a sexual being, is linked to sexual shame.*

One way to overcome these sexuality-based stereotypes is to give ourselves permission to tap into and explore different parts of our sexual selves and identities. A few questions to guide this exploration may include:

> *What qualities of my sexual self would I like to cultivate?*
> *Which types of behaviors might I engage in that would indicate my progress toward sexual liberation?*
> *How might exploring new sides of my sexual self increase my ability to connect with my partner(s), satisfy desires, and access pleasure?*

Bayani* shares an example of how he has begun working toward sexual liberation, within the context of an ethically non-monogamous partnership:

> *Exploring my interests in the kinkspace regarding Dominance/submission (i.e., D/s) has been useful because while I do primarily take a naturally submissive role with my partner in real life, D/s dynamics allow me to exercise the mental/emotional aspect of my dominance with people online without engaging them physically.*

Yub Kim also shares how the kink community has been impactful in liberating his sexual self:

> *One of the many reasons I love the kink community is that people are accepted for who they are. Unfortunately, we grow up with restricted sexual scripts and are given narrow ideas of what sexual appropriateness looks like. My partner, who also introduced me to the community, allowed me to expand how I understand sex and my sexuality. I didn't have to feel bound by all the rules I carried with*

me. Instead, I could develop my rules and did not have to apologize for sticking to them. The community, for the most part, understood this idea and allowed me to develop my individuality. Being loved for who I am helped me realize I do not have to feel othered and I am not broken in any way.

What Happens When We Challenge Sexual Stereotypes?

Challenging sexual stereotypes as Asian Americans can be a tricky business. Because many of us may experience discomfort at the thought of asserting our wants, needs, and desires, the tendency to exhibit go-with-the-flow attitudes when it comes to topics related to sex and sexuality is at an all-time high within our community.

However, this does not mean we cannot familiarize ourselves with the language and processes needed to challenge sexual stereotypes. If you are ready and willing to speak up when sexual stereotypes arise, I have a few helpful considerations to keep in mind. Each of these suggestions is informed by research and anecdotal evidence and through my lens as a clinical sexologist and sex-positive mental health professional.

Research on Asian American stereotypes has established the presence of two kinds of racial stereotypes: *descriptive*, which reflect beliefs about how racial groups are different, and *prescriptive*, which reflect beliefs about how racial groups should be.[17]

A descriptive stereotype about Asian Americans is that we embody collectivistic mentalities that place high value on our families and communities. In this way, Asian Americans may differ from the more individualistic values of white Westerners. Descriptive stereotypes also intersect with the model minority myth by positioning Asian Americans as universally successful. Other descriptive stereotypes about Asian Americans portray us as more competent, less warm, and less dominant compared to our white counterparts.[18] When individuals challenge descriptive stereotypes, the outcome ranges from pleasant surprise to curiosity. Within academic or workplace settings, peers and colleagues may laud our friendly demeanor or be genuinely shocked when assignments do not come easily.

Prescriptive stereotypes about Asian Americans are that we are submissive and soft-spoken. When Asian Americans speak up and engage in assertive behaviors within occupational, educational, societal, or relationship settings, individuals may experience shock, surprise, or even anger. Our assertive behaviors are labeled inappropriate, out of place, unprofessional, and disrespectful. When prescriptive stereotypes are violated, individuals may be more likely to respond with social disapproval and even backlash.[19]

Interestingly, the stereotype that Asian Americans are less dominant compared to whites is also a prescriptive one. In other words, Asian Americans who are perceived to be more expressive, assertive, and outspoken are also more likely to be disliked, believed to lack social skills, and experience racial harassment. [20]

I'll never forget the time a student described me as "loud" in a course evaluation. Was I actually loud or had I simply violated a prescriptive stereotype about how society deems I *should* be? I have also had past partners label me as "difficult." Was I truly difficult, or did I simply challenge internalized expectations that I was supposed to be submissive and easygoing?

When it comes to racial stereotypes in relationships, violating social scripts about how we are supposed to behave can have serious consequences. Up to 55 percent of Asian women in the United States reported experiencing physical and/or sexual violence[21] compared to 9 percent of Asian and Pacific Islander men who reported experiencing contact sexual violence and 9 percent of Asian and Pacific Islander men who reported non-contact unwanted sexual experiences across their lifetimes. [22] A 2012 report from the National Domestic Violence Hotline indicated that 6 percent of Asian and 6 percent of Native Hawaiian and Pacific Islander callers reported sexual violence experiences compared to 5 percent of Hispanic, 5 percent of African American, 6 percent of Caucasian, and 7 percent of Native American and Alaskan Native callers. [23] Rates of intimate partner violence may be especially high among specific Asian American communities. According to a national study of 143 domestic violence survivors, 56 percent of Filipinas and 64 percent of Indian and Pakistani women reported experiencing sexual violence by an intimate partner. [24] Another study consisting of 385 South Asian Americans living in New York underscored how members of the South Asian queer community were far more likely to face sexual violence compared to their heterosexual counterparts.[25]

Though these rates of sexual violence among Asian American communities are alarming, it is important to keep a few things in mind. First, these statistics reflect *reported* experiences rather than *actual* experiences. Unfortunately, the true prevalence of intimate partner violence that exists in our community is much more difficult to extrapolate. Next, we must remember that our disaggregated Asian American community is extremely unique and rates of intimate partner violence among specific groups will differ based on a variety of influences including, perhaps, family history of generational violence, substance abuse, presence of mental health issues, poverty, level of education, undocumented status, and access to resources, to name a few.

Prescriptive gender stereotypes and prescriptive racial stereotypes are grounded in the sociohistorical roles and inequalities that have maintained the status quo by evoking instances of discrimination. Though I spent the better part of an hour scouring the deepest corners of the internet, I couldn't find any studies that explored whether Asian American sexual stereotypes were descriptive or prescriptive. However, based on the interviews I conducted with Asian American thought leaders and storytellers, Asian American sexual stereotypes appear to be prescriptive.

Thalia,* a first-generation Indian American woman in her early 30s, states:

> I was involved in a toxic and abusive relationship where my ex expected me to be silent. He trumpeted traditional patriarchal views and looking back, it's clear that he expected me to be a subservient and submissive "doll." It took years to rebuild my confidence and learn how to speak up for myself. Even to this day, it can be hard to advocate for myself—a little voice in my head struggles with beliefs that perhaps I would be better liked if I didn't rock the boat so much. I am grateful to have married someone who loves to hear my thoughts, wants me to speak up more, and makes space for me to be who I am. For years, my husband has been asking, "What do you like to do in the bedroom? What's most pleasurable for you? What do you like?" I have no idea, because it's hard for me to believe I'm worth that kind of sexual enjoyment.

Prescriptive stereotypes maintain status and power differences between groups in ways that evoke social retribution when conformity does not occur. We see examples of this among women who violate prescriptive gender stereotypes about how they are "supposed" to act; these women are more likely to face sexual harassment compared to women who adhere to gender stereotypes.[26]

The prescriptive and descriptive sexual stereotypes attributed to Asian Americans compound with aspects of fetishization and become even more nuanced when they intersect with other identities, such as sexual and gender identities.

Jackson,* a gay biracial Asian American man of Filipino and white descent, shares:

> When I used to date white men, there were situations where I was assumed to be the submissive or subordinate partner. Other times, racial stereotypes came to the fore. A white Grindr hookup once looked over at my bookshelf and made a fetishizing comment about how smart Asians are, as if the revelation of intelligence somehow heightened his arousal. Another time, a white man disappointedly commented that I had too much body hair—contrary to the tendency among East and Southeast Asian men.

Challenging Potential Partners and Avoiding Fetishization

I could write an entire book on how to spot someone who claims to have "yellow fever." Though each individual (and each scenario) must be considered on a case-by-case basis, there are a few things I encourage my clients, students, friends, and community members to be curious about when entertaining the thought of a potential partner.

How Do I Know If Someone Is Sexually Objectifying Me?

It can be difficult to know for sure if someone may be sexually objectifying you as an Asian American person (or as a person with any marginalized identity). Some things to look for may include the following:

- Does the person center one or more of your identities in a way that elicits feelings of discomfort?
- Does the person honor who you are as a whole, complex person or do they focus on one specific identity (e.g., your race, ethnicity, disability status, queer identity, etc.)?
- If you identify as an Asian American woman, does the person overtly or covertly communicate expectations for you to be submissive, docile, and hypersexual?
- Does the person have tattoos that are representative of Asian culture or our histories without context (e.g., geishas, tribal patterns grounded in Pacific Islander and Native Hawaiian cultures, koi fish, yin and yang symbols, and samurais)?

These are all helpful questions that may be considered.

What Do You Tell People Who Claim, "Asians Are Just My Type"?

To answer this question, we must take a step back and consider the development of romantic and sexual attraction. Ultimately, we know that romantic and sexual attractions are socially constructed and largely influenced by our culture. [27] In the United States, our culture continues to be driven by notions that center whiteness, heterosexual monogamous relationships, able-bodied status, and more. So, people who have a "type" often have not done the work to identify and challenge the internalization of harmful narratives that bind them to their "type." If someone claims to "just have a preference for Asian women," I would be curious about *why*. Listen for reductionistic responses that essentialize Asian American women in stereotypical ways. Examples of red flag responses might be, "*They are just better behaved and take excellent care of their partners*" (i.e., internalized racist belief that Asian American women are submissive, docile lotus flowers) and "*Their sex drive is just more congruent with my own*" (i.e., internalized racist belief that hypersexualizes Asian women).

How Might Sexual Trauma Survivors Regain a Sense of Power by Centering Pleasure?

If someone has experienced sexual trauma and would like to regain their sense of power by centering their pleasure, I would begin by validating their challenges, fears, and desires. A great first step toward healing is *permission giving*. This includes permission to stay the same; permission to explore their ideas, thoughts, and desires; or permission to make a change. Connecting with a trauma-informed and culturally responsive healer who can support you in learning the grounding and resourcing skills needed to calm your body and mind when physiological activation occurs is also recommended. Regaining a sense of power after your body may not feel like it belongs to you can take time, but the work is worth it. Ultimately, the work may involve learning to identify and let go of self-talk and narratives characterized by shame, doubt, and unworthiness. Finding a partner or partners with whom you feel safe to explore aspects of intimacy, touch, and pleasure is also critically important. Finally, learning to re-acquaint yourself with your body and learning the touch, pressure, and speeds that feel good and bring pleasure can additionally be helpful. Giving yourself the power, space, and time to explore what feels pleasurable, safe, and satisfying is a great first step to centering your pleasure. You can also bring up this topic with a culturally responsive and sex-affirming mental health professional.

TLDR: Dating is hard enough without having to worry whether potential partners are sexually objectifying, fetishizing, or placing sexual stereotypes onto you. Though these experiences can certainly feel daunting, they echo centuries of oppressive anti-Asian sentiments that go all the way back to the late 18th century. Sexual stereotypes can be *descriptive*, which reflect beliefs about how racial groups are different, or *prescriptive*, which reflect beliefs about how racial groups should be. Violating descriptive stereotypes elicits feelings ranging from curiosity to pleasant surprise, whereas challenging prescriptive stereotypes evokes social disapproval and backlash. The jury is still out and waiting for evidence-based studies that properly quantify the extent to which Asian American sexual stereotypes are descriptive or prescriptive (anyone looking for a fun dissertation topic?). This chapter wraps up with a few helpful tips on how to liberate our sexual selves and determine to what extent someone may be pursuing you for the absolute gem that you are, or whether they are merely trying to satisfy a sexual fantasy.

Questions to Ponder

1. How might the presence of sexual stereotypes have impacted the ways in which I show up in my romantic relationships?
2. To what extent do I feel comfortable setting boundaries and challenging the presence of sexual stereotypes, when they arise?
3. What are some ways that sexual stereotypes have personally impacted who I am and who I am expected to be in relationships?
4. How might liberating my sexual self allow me to strengthen my relationships, satisfy my desires, and access pleasure?
5. Who do I want to grow into, as a sexual being?

Questions to Bridge the Gap with Parents

1. What are some stereotypes about Asian men and women you have noticed in media? How do you feel about those stereotypes?
2. What are some early messages you learned about sex, intimacy, and relationships from your parents?
3. What are the most important lessons about sex, intimacy, and relationships that you think I should know?

7

Becoming Balanced People

How Patterns Impact Our Well-Being

I am one-and-a-half years old and living in Cubao, Quezon City, with my *kuya,* mama, and *yaya* Shirley. I love eating the coconuts that grow in our front yard and laughing loudly as my *yaya* chases me around the house with spoonfuls of *arroz caldo* (Filipino chicken and rice porridge).

The Philippines is a wonderful place to grow up. The air is always warm, there is plenty of room to run, and I love the feeling of my bare feet as they plod along the marble floors of our home. Though I am not allowed to run outside without shoes, the feeling of my skin on the sun-warmed earth is what I love the most.

My days are filled with joy and my nights are filled with stories about a stranger. There is a photograph next to my crib, the only photo I can see in my room. Though we share the same eyes and a similar nose, I have never met this man before. Every night, as my mom takes me into her arms and rocks me to sleep, she holds my finger and gently places it on his face. She says:

Stacey, this is your father. Your papa. He is in America working hard so we can have a better life. When the time is right, we will go there and meet him.

I am a baby with no sense of time. Though my father left for America two years prior, to me he has been gone a lifetime.

I don't have an adult brain filled with logic, knowledge, and understanding to contextualize the sacrifices my parents are making. I can't possibly understand that over 8,000 miles away, my father works 80 hours a week to make ends meet. I have no sense of appreciation for how he is forced to complete his oncology residency and fellowship again in the States even though he has already completed the same training in our home country.

I know nothing of my mother's sacrifices. How she misses my father every day but wholeheartedly dedicates herself to succeeding as a pharmacist and raising two young children. She simply does not have the luxury to think of herself or reflect on her emotions. How she spends her daily lunch breaks journeying back home so she can breastfeed before returning to work. How she wishes she could hear my father's voice and share stories about his children but understands the little money he earns must be spent toward food instead of a phone card. How she takes endless rolls of photographs for my baby albums and painstakingly labels each one, filling them with heartfelt captions to bridge an ocean:

Look papa, I can walk now!
I can roll over and see myself in my mirror. Peek-a-boo!
Playing with my kuya. Papa, I miss you!

As a baby, I know none of this. All I know is that the man whom my mother calls my papa is not here with me. *I feel abandoned.*

On an unconscious level, these feelings lead me to internalize fixed beliefs from an early age:

I am not good enough.
I am not needed.
I am not wanted.

Cultural Scripts of Shame That Drive Productivity

In his book *The Myth of Normal*, Hungarian-Canadian physician Gabor Maté describes how early traumatic childhood experiences have deleterious impacts on our worldviews, sense of balance, and emotional well-being. At 14 months old, Maté recounts how his mother, a Jewish Hungarian woman living in Nazi-occupied territories in post–World War II Budapest, entrusted her baby to a stranger for protection and survival. Although his adult brain now understands the logic of his mother's decision, his infant brain internalized a deep sense of abandonment and unworthiness. Maté contextualizes this early experience as a driving reason for why he pursued a career in medicine and uses his early childhood experience to explain how he developed "workaholic tendencies":

> *My own workaholism as a physician earned me much respect, gratitude, remuneration, and status in the world, even as it undermined my mental health and my family's emotional balance. And why was I a workaholic? Because, stemming from my early experiences, I needed to be needed, wanted, and admired as a substitute for love. I never consciously decided to be driven that way, and yet it "worked" all too well for me in the social and professional realms.*
> Gabor Maté and Daniel Maté, *The Myth of Normal: Trauma, Illness, and Healing in a Toxic Culture* (2022)[1]

How many of us can see ourselves in that narrative? How many of us have adapted to the internalized scripts of *I am not enough, I am not needed, I am not wanted*, and *I must prove my worth*? How many of us have considered that these internalized cultural scripts lead us to bury ourselves in our work and overvalue productivity?

When considering the compounding influence of internalized shame scripts and insecure attachment styles among Asian Americans and children of Asian immigrants, it is pretty clear how these worldviews can have deleterious impacts on our ability to achieve a healthy work–life balance. We develop a community of voices who whisper (or scream) cacophonies of fixed culturally bound beliefs that originate from generations of unhealed historical trauma, intergenerational patterns, toxic cultural scripts, unchecked scarcity mindsets, and painful insecure attachments.

The intergenerational patterns and toxic cultural scripts assert: *I have to work twice as hard to get half as far. I must keep my head down and can never stop to reflect on my emotions or talk about my problems.*

The scarcity mindset voice whispers: *I have to succeed in school and career settings; otherwise, I will fail and disappoint my parents. I must take every opportunity that arises because I never know if another one will present itself. I have to prove to others that I am good enough.*

The insecure attachment voice coerces: *I have to overcome challenges on my own because it is too painful to ask for help, be vulnerable, and experience disappointment. I cannot trust other people to meet my needs for comfort, affection, or care. I will be abandoned if I ask for support because something about me is needy, "less than," or unworthy of love, connection, acceptance, and belonging.*

Our inner child, the wounded, needy, injured part of us, has no sense of time and is not housed in our logical adult brain. The disconnect between *logically knowing and understanding* (our adult brain) and *emotionally sensing and feeling* (our infancy and childhood experiences) creates gaps between what we need to heal our attachment wounds and the strategies we use to adapt. In fact, the extant body of research has established how avoidant adults tend to resist and avoid help-seeking behaviors, preferring instead to protect themselves from disappointment by demonstrating independence.[2]

Though these coping skills may have kept us safe, helped avoid conflict, instilled the value of hard work, and promoted success, they do not allow us to inhabit our fully integrated and whole selves. Nor do they allow us to achieve optimal well-being. Compared to our white counterparts, Asian Americans may be more likely to somaticize psychological distress rather than describe Western-based concepts associated with emotions.[3] For example, we don't say "I feel depressed" or "I feel anxious" when we allow ourselves to become buried in work. Instead, we are far more likely to report feelings of dizziness, sleep difficulties, challenges with concentration and breathing, and physical complaints such as headaches, stomach problems, and chronic pain.[4] Specific somaticized symptoms may also exist among the Filipino American diaspora. Filipino Americans who face feelings of overwhelm, stress, and emotional/psychological distress report bodily-based responses such as shallow breathing, hyperventilation, pacing, aches and pains, as well as chest pressure.[5]

The intention of this chapter is not to minimize the importance and value of a strong work ethic. Instead, the goal is to explore the extent to which we may have developed unhelpful tendencies that lead us to overvalue aspects of hard work, productivity, and external forms of achievement as mechanisms to prove our worth and to honor the sense of indebtedness we hold to our parents in exchange for their sacrifices. We may find ourselves working exceptionally hard, often at the expense of caring for ourselves, our partners, and others, as a form of gratitude to our families of origin for the privileged lives they have gifted us.

Shoua Lee describes how her sense of worth has been historically tied to notions of productivity:

> *Although others view me as someone who is capable, I lived with a deep sense of unworthiness for all my adolescent years and through most of my young adult years. Seeking external validation was my full-time job at home, school, and social relationships. My expectations for myself were extremely high. There were times when this toughness served me; however, it always left me feeling isolated and deeper in shame. My insecurities bled into my dating life. This would leave me to try too hard, which often resulted in my own heart breaking. The shame that came along with this further deepened the grooves of unworthiness in my mind.*

Bayani,* a second-generation gay Filipino American man in his early 30s, described a similar instance:

> *Something I've keyed in on specifically came from my father. He explained that the smartest and most resourceful Filipinos were stateside because it takes resources (typically financial or professional skills) to make it in the U.S. From this, the necessity to prove my worth through achievement was planted deeply. My parents never directly expressed their expectations about what we should do in our career lives; it was more indirect or phrased as suggestions.*

Calypso* similarly shares how our need for parental approval can impact the ways in which we navigate the world:

> *Not having my mother's approval is an ongoing sore spot for me. I grew up seeking my mother's approval, which translated into this need to prove myself. The good thing about this trait is that my parents supported my accomplishments and I became a very confident and successful individual in the world. The downside is*

that even in my most important relationships, I feel the need to perform in order to be loved.

Our inner child, who continues to crave the emotional and comforting words of our parents, has learned to navigate the world in ways that align with our community of voices. The community of voices consists of all the internalized messages we have carried with us since childhood. They may be words of advice about who we are, who we are meant to become, and how we are supposed to think, feel, and act as well as what we can anticipate about ourselves, others, and the world. These voices can represent various forms of internal dialogue, from supportive and encouraging (*I am worthy of love and belonging*) to disparaging (*Why do I even bother?*). Though the specific messages, intensity, and impact of our community of voices are unique, they often consist of the messages we have heard and swallowed whole from our ancestors, parents, ethnic communities, religious communities, friends, and even past partners. And, if we don't learn how to challenge them, these communities of voices can become driving narratives that shape maladaptive coping behaviors into adulthood.

As a Filipina child of immigrants, I am not immune to the narratives espoused by my own community of voices.

In 2009 I was a young adult searching for viable career options. In the process of earning my bachelor's degree in psychology, I attended the University of Cincinnati and John Carroll University. I did not know what I wanted to be when I grew up, but I was convinced I was not smart enough to succeed in medicine.

Perhaps this belief came from my proud mother's good-natured assertion. Each time I expressed fears about not being successful in my career or not having what it takes to thrive in medicine, she brushed my concerns aside:

Stacey, you can do anything you put your mind to. You've always been smart; you were the class valedictorian!

Dearest reader, there are three things you should know about that statement.

First, she is right. Yours truly was, in fact, honored with an esteemed valedictorian title.

Second, it was in *the fourth grade.*

Third, and this is the biggie, there is one detail I never had the heart to admit to my (very Catholic and very Filipina) mother, even to this day: *I cheated.* Throughout the academic year, each time my teacher would ask us to go around the room and report our grade on math tests, spelling quizzes, or phonics exams, I always added one point to my score. Funny how I could never admit that to my own mother and yet here I am, writing it out for the world to read.

Though my mother's unwavering belief that I could accomplish anything should have been encouraging, it had the opposite effect. Through the lens of my wounded inner child, it felt like my accomplishments were being minimized, dismissed, or invalidated. Each award, scholarship, and accomplishment was met with comments like:

Stacey, you've always been smart, success comes easy for you!
Of course you did well, I prayed for you!

And, of course, the kicker:

You are the valedictorian!

I internalized these moments as pieces of evidence that my successes and accomplishments were a farce: fake, insignificant, no good. I began to believe I could only convince my parents of my worth with the *next* award; I would finally prove my value with the *next* accomplishment. The vicious cycle continued all the way into adulthood.

As one can imagine, the validation I so badly desired never came. Time and time again, I was met with the same responses. *Of course, no surprise there, job well done!* followed by *Pass the vegetables, anak* (child in Tagalog).

Armed with the fixed cultural scripts of *I am not good enough, I am not worthy,* and *I am not needed,* I pursued graduate programs. I enrolled in a clinical mental health counseling program and began working as a mental health professional. I cultivated a unique specialization that allowed me to support high-need client populations such as human sex trafficking survivors, individuals with co-occurring substance use and mental health concerns, and other underserved, marginalized client populations who faced complex trauma.

Somewhere in the back of my mind, the community of voices praised:

I was not needed or wanted when I was younger, but look at me now! My clients always need me. People constantly tell me what a good person I am, and what valuable work I am doing.

It was not enough. I applied to a counselor education and supervision doctoral program and earned my PhD in three years by keeping my head down and working hard. I published peer-reviewed research, spoke at countless national conferences, and engaged in professional service at the national and international levels. I drove myself into the ground, all the while hoping to be seen, celebrated, and lauded as good enough. I grasped every opportunity that presented itself as the community of voices in my head screamed:

If I don't take this opportunity, someone else will, and then they will get ahead of me. They will succeed and I will fail.

I accepted a position as an assistant professor in a counselor education graduate program. I published over 30 peer-reviewed academic papers and studies in three years. I checked my email constantly and even responded to student questions on the weekend. Email became my lifeline, and I found myself obsessively refreshing my browser, careful not to let a single correspondence fall through the cracks. I checked my email in the middle of dates, during meals with family, and when I randomly woke up at four in the morning. I made myself available for all questions, all events, all needs but my own. Who had time to rest? On an unconscious level, the community of voices asserted:

I was not needed or wanted when I was young, but look at me now. My colleagues and students always need me. I cannot let myself rest because if I do, someone else will get ahead of me. They will succeed and I will fail.

Focusing on Output Until We Burn Out

The prioritization and value of hard work above all else may be reminiscent of our parents' and ancestors' fears that we will never have enough or that we will never be enough. It also seems to be a collective experience shared by our Asian American community. Because many of us operate from scarcity mindsets, we continue to blindly embody these values. We attribute our own sense of internal value to our productivity, rather than to more vulnerable, authentic, and emotional forms of accomplishments. Our lack of balance can contribute to burnout and emotional fatigue in our workplaces, negatively impact our relationships, and wreak havoc on our inner peace.

Though our parents, ancestors, and Asian American community members never explicitly sat us down and told us to work hard and focus on output at the expense of our own well-being and relationships, it seems as though we have not escaped covert messages about prioritizing academic and workplace success from our families of origin and communities. As a result, Asian Americans and children of Asian immigrants tend to measure our internal sense of self-worth by our external achievements. We overlook the value of relationships and the quality of connection and equate our success with tangible milestones. We struggle to set flexible boundaries, say "no," and achieve a healthy balance between our personal and professional roles. We accomplish a great many things in our careers without allowing ourselves the gifts of rest and restoration.

Many of the individuals with whom I spoke share similar challenges. Jennifer Alexander* shares:

Historically, setting boundaries has been really hard for me. Even in the last few years, I have attributed my value and worth to career performance. Working more than my 40-hour-a-week schedule made me miserable. I was trying to meet unrealistic expectations and always feeling like I was falling short.

Calypso* describes internal messages about productivity:

Nobody specifically told me that accolades measure my worth. I just remember being a child and seeing how much my mother praised my father for his hard work. It seemed to me like hard work made one lovable. To this day, I strive to be the best and do my best. I rarely rest. I graduated medical school top of my class. I skipped vacations and quality time with friends. As a physician, I've grown in my practice exponentially because of my dedication, willingness, and accessibility. I'm only in my 8th year and I'm already so tired. I can't stop because success is so tied to my self-worth. This message . . . it's deep in my bones.

Dr. Band shares a similar narrative:

When I am feeling low or anxious, work has always been a constant source of validation. I can overwork myself and place a higher value on my productivity rather than on my health. I watched both my parents elevate in social class and status through their work ethic, so outside of my personal vices, the messaging around work has always been part of a larger sacrifice to obtain success for yourself and everyone. I want to make myself proud as much as I want to make my parents proud as a tribute to them.

I.B.* shares:

I think at a young age I learned to attach my value to my productivity. I believed that if I was successful it would reflect well on me and show that I am valuable. When I was in college and I wasn't getting a good GPA I figured I could compensate by participating in a lot of leadership activities and by doing a lot of work with other organizations. I overcompensated because I believed I was only as good as the work that I did. I have the urge and tendency to constantly work and push my emotional and mental health to the side.

Finally, Bayani* describes:

I crave individualized acknowledgement as an extrinsic motivator and I have a high need for recognition, both formally and informally. Professional awards and competitions are always high on my achievement list and are major sources of pride.

Perhaps the workplace is where we feel seen, valued, heard, and worthy. After all, there are clear expectations, roles, and responsibilities associated with educational and workplace settings that may feel congruent with our own internalized cultural scripts of "work hard," "keep your head down," and "don't rock the boat." Over time, we can begin to attribute our sense of value and worth to our job titles, salary bands, and other career-based achievements. Education and workplace settings provide clear objectives about what we are supposed to do, how we are supposed to do it, and when. Furthermore, professional behavior expectations within school and workplace settings minimize the value of emotional expression and encourage the prioritization of others over one's own self-interest, especially within the medical field.[6] Expectations to act professionally create a natural sense of separation and psychological comfort that allow us to operate on autopilot without accessing the vulnerable emotions we have not historically been modeled to value.

Or maybe we have come to believe that our workplace accomplishments will finally make our parents proud. Perhaps we believe our hard work, accomplishments, and areas of success will finally make our parents see us in the ways that we have so badly wanted them to. Maybe we feel like we are one achievement away from finally making them proud.

For others, focusing on work may create a natural barrier that protects us from the intimacy and vulnerability of forming and maintaining relationships. Work is a constant; it will always need something from us. It is reliable, predictable, and therefore safe. Our assignments, projects, and workplace tasks ask very little of us when it comes to demonstrating vulnerability or addressing attachment injuries. They are emotionally and psychologically easier to navigate compared to the unpredictability of people, who can activate uncomfortable emotions grounded in our deep-seated fears of abandonment, disappointment, invalidation, and loss of independence. Unlike our relationship with work, relationships with people can be unpredictable. They require emotional, psychological, and other forms of investment. Though they have the potential to bring joy, they can also lead to feelings of disappointment, anger, rejection, and abandonment. When we perceive work to be a "safer" investment of our time than our relationships, it's understandable why so many of us prefer to chase productivity over cultivating close relationships with parents, partners, children, and friends.

Ultimately, the reasons why we overvalue productivity at the expense of our well-being and relationships are multifaceted and undoubtedly influenced by our community of voices, internalized fixed beliefs, intergenerational patterns, early experiences, and cultural scripts. The question is not *Is this mentality working for you?*—because we know that it is. It must be working on some level for us to continue engaging in the behavior.

Instead, the question is *How might focusing so much on work serve our emotional, psychological, and physical well-being? To what extent is our focus on work impacting the relationships we have with ourselves and with our loved ones?*

Engaging in Self-Nourishment, Abundance, and Balance

As a recovering workaholic, I am intimately acquainted with the all-too-familiar dopamine hit that is linked to meeting deadlines, crushing goals, and establishing objective accomplishments. Hard work, conscientiousness, and commitment to productivity all represent critical values that promote our success and undoubtedly serve us well. Similar values have also worked well for our parents and ancestors. So, what gives? How can we begin to find workplace balance, let go of scarcity mindsets, cultivate abundance mentalities, and practice intentional acts of self-nourishment in an increasingly capitalistic, disconnected, and outcome-oriented society?

First, it is important to note that what works for one will not work for everyone. As much as I wish I had the answers, challenging these specific narratives will require a bit of individualized self-reflection, and compassion. As a starting point to your healing journey, I offer what works for me, as well as what has worked for the storytellers with whom I have spoken.

Honoring and Uncovering Your Windows of Productivity

When I think about productivity, I reflect on the times when I *feel* most productive. For me, this window of productivity is between 6 a.m. and 11 a.m. After that block of time, I find myself scrolling on social media, texting friends and family, and struggling to maintain focus. I have learned to unapologetically protect this window of productivity with ferocity. Prioritizing my work during this window of productivity has been invaluable in creating opportunities for rest, self-nourishment, and abundance mentalities.

Curious about how to locate your own window of productivity? Here are a few reflection questions to consider:

During which part of the day do I perform the best?
When does my mind operate most clearly?
When do I feel most motivated to accomplish my goals?
At what time of day does my concentration hold longer and my thoughts align most easily?

For some, it's not about *when* productivity naturally flows but *what must align* for productivity to *begin*. My window of productivity changed substantially when I became a mother. Enjoying those protected hours of productive silence evaporated the moment tiny mouths needed nourishment and small hands wanted to be held. Even when I scheduled childcare that lined up within my window, I struggled to make the most out of that space. I found myself distracted with never-ending worries about my sons: *Are they hungry? Are they safe? Do they need me?* It took a while to realize what needed to happen to regain my focus. It wasn't just finding childcare; it was finding *the right kind of childcare*. I needed to wholeheartedly trust that the person watching my boys would be patient and caring and would love them without question. So, I stopped hiring nannies and interviewing au pairs and asked my parents and in-laws to help care for our sons. (I realize what a privilege it is to have family whom I can trust for this task!) I also needed to know that their meals, snacks, and drinks were prepared. So, I portioned lunches, made bottles, and ensured they were ready to start the day before family arrived and I began my workday. Once I uncovered *what needed to align* before productivity could flow, I was able to unlock my new window of productivity. I also learned to be much more efficient with my time.

Remember that what you need and what works for you will undoubtedly evolve and grow throughout your lifetime. As a starting point, here are a few prompts to explore what must align for you:

What needs to happen before I can focus?
Which needs must be met so that I can achieve peace of mind and optimal focus?
Whom can I trust to help meet these needs?
How can I protect my window of productivity by ensuring these needs are met?

Establishing windows of time around dopamine-seeking behavior has been helpful to begin breaking my own unhelpful patterns. For example, I limit blue-light exposure and work-related checking behaviors one hour from waking and two hours before bed. Limiting blue-light exposure a couple hours before bedtime can also help regulate our circadian rhythm and promote greater sleep quality and duration.[7] I resist the urge to look at screens until after I have intentionally settled into my morning and have finished my coffee (or at least until

I have enjoyed the first sip!). For me, this represents a world of difference from earlier moments in life when I would groggily roll over, reach for my phone, and refresh my inbox first thing in the morning. Once we establish and honor our windows of productivity, we can be more flexible in how we spend the rest of our time. We can set boundaries around moments where we are most productive while mitigating workplace burnout and overwhelm by sprinkling in intentional moments of joy, abundance, and connection.

Practice makes progress, and there will be times when we fall back on old un-helpful habits. Case in point: I emailed my editor a question about this very book only a few days after giving birth to my second child! When these slipups occur, I invite you to recognize these moments of growth, without judgment, and prac-tice a little self-compassion. Each new moment is an opportunity to reinvest in balance, boundaries, and restoration.

When it comes to finding workplace balance, there is no such thing as "one size fits all." Here are a few examples of what some of the storytellers have shared. Jennifer Alexander* describes:

I have learned that boundaries are about me and not about other people. When I prioritize myself and my well-being over deadlines, my boss, or a report, I am much happier.

I.B.* shares how engaging in self-awareness has helped her achieve a healthier work–life balance:

When I moved to Hawaii, I told myself that I was going to focus on what makes me live a happy life and that I wasn't going to overwork anymore. I started set-ting boundaries at work and made sure to leave at a certain time. I committed to focusing on activities I truly enjoyed, like acting and family time. I also realized that as much as I love certain parts of my job, if there is not enough institutional support and people bank on my goodwill and good attitude, then I need to leave. I do so much for my job, my students, and for others, and I realized that I need to focus on doing something for me. I began to wonder, "At what point will I have nothing to give?"

Finally, Kimmy Wu explains:

To get to this point of my healing, I had to learn to draw and maintain better boundaries and improve my verbal and nonverbal communication skills to better understand and be understood by others.

Giving to Others at the Expense of Ourselves

Beyond the voices that drive us to measure our worth based on external accomplishments, we also carry cultural scripts that espouse the importance of engaging in self-sacrifice for our families, friends, and communities, often at the expense of our own well-being.

As Dr. Jenny T. Wang explains, Asian Americans may struggle to set boundaries:

> *Many members of Asian diasporas have shared with me that they struggle intensely with boundaries. I believe one of the reasons for this struggle is because we are living between cultural worlds that hold different perspectives on boundaries, so setting boundaries as an act of preserving the self may feel like a betrayal of our cultural upbringing or even those we love.*
>
> Jenny Wang, *Permission to Come Home: Reclaiming Mental.*
> *Health as Asian Americans* (2022)[8]

From an early age, we have learned to give freely of ourselves. As children, we learned to anticipate our parents' or siblings' emotional needs and triggers to cultivate a sense of peace and safety in the home. This tendency evolved into people-pleasing behaviors that underlie deep needs for connection and relationships. Consistent with this challenge, Kareena* expresses:

> *I came from a family that didn't know how to apologize, express love, or repair from fights. Issues were swept under the carpet, adults were always right, and as a child, I had to find a way to move on without any reconciliation. Growing up, the temperament of my household was like an unpredictable rollercoaster. I never knew when something would trigger someone else to hit their peak. Rather than gradually coming down from conflict with communication and active listening, it was a straight shot down, usually accompanied by the silent treatment until the next ride up. As an adult, I became a people pleaser who constantly worried about losing relationships.*

Bayani* similarly shares:

> *I grew up anticipating others' needs as a way to fulfill them and build on our relationship. This became a skill I am often complimented on. However, having such deeply developed emotional intelligence comes at the cost of never turning it off. It always runs in the background of my mind, taking up cognitive and emotional space that could be dedicated toward other, more conscious tasks.*

Noelle* describes the internalized belief to sacrifice for her parents:

There's this whole idea that we have to take care of our parents. Of course we want to, but at the same time, that's a pressure a lot of Filipino and Asian cultures instill in you. We [children of immigrants] will sit there saying, "I'm not doing enough, I'm a bad kid," because we have heard it so much. We start to believe it. I just bought my parents a new water heater and a new washer and dryer because neither of them works anymore. I take care of my parents and pay for their phones. I also give them a monthly stipend and all I ask in exchange is that they watch my little one a few days a week. It's validating when you hear your partner say, "You do a lot, you are a good kid, you show them your love, you treat your parents better than anyone else." Sometimes I still don't believe it, because it is a deep emotional wound. I know I'm not alone in this.

Many of us have learned to give freely to others at the expense of ourselves as a result of limiting cultural scripts. Our Asian American parents often had no choice but to role model self-sacrifice to better the lives of their children. The impact of intergenerational patterns and how they intersect with self-sacrifice was described by Dr. Avadhanam:

Another pattern that is generationally apparent from my grandparents and parents is self-sacrifice for the benefit of others. My grandparents taught my parents about the importance of equal justice for all people and the importance of taking on more socialistic attitudes. My parents learned this and taught my younger sister and I that we must do our duty (dharma), regardless of circumstance. I often saw my parents sacrificing their time, resources, and love even when it was not reciprocated at the most minimal level.

Self-sacrifice is a funny thing. On one hand, it represents an important cultural value that is shared among many Asian American communities. On the other hand, it may come at dire costs to our emotional, psychological, and interpersonal well-being. Learning to set flexible boundaries therefore represents an important skill to achieving a greater sense of balance. If we pour from our cup until we are empty, what can possibly be left to offer our loved ones?

A Crash Course on Flexible Boundary Setting

Not sure how to start setting flexible boundaries? Here are a few tips to get started.

First, get curious about *why the boundary needs to be set.* Once we are clear about our desires and how what we want aligns with one or more of our core values, the likelihood that we will maintain the flexible boundaries we create increases. A few examples of possible core values include altruism, authenticity, balance, compassion, courage, curiosity, creativity, family, innovation, integrity, kindness, loyalty, rest, respect, and self-nourishment.

Next, identify the *goal.* What are we hoping this flexible boundary will achieve? Will it protect our emotional well-being, time, energy, or relationship? Might it enable us to better focus on important aspects of our lives? Remember, too, that goals associated with boundaries can change over time as relationships evolve.

When you are ready to begin setting flexible boundaries with your partner, friends, or family of origin, practice using "I" statements. Doing so promotes accountability while keeping the listener from responding in a defensive way. For example, communicating emotional consequences after conflict may be expressed with statements such as, *"I feel [emotion] when [circumstance]."* Another good example statement is, *"I am not interested in engaging in this conversation when spoken to in that tone."* As a side note in emotion identification, be sure that "I feel" is followed by an actual emotion rather than a phrase such as "like you" or "that." Saying "I feel like" or "I feel that" is a way to express a *thought* rather than an emotion. For example:

> *I feel disappointed when you offer advice and I need you to listen* (sharing an emotion and circumstance).
> *I feel like you don't listen to me when you offer advice* (sharing a thought).

Challenge yourself to express the emotion you *feel* and let the thoughts follow later.

Setting flexible boundaries within educational and workplace settings can look a little different. In this case, speaking from a place of gratitude while honoring your current commitments represents an effective way to politely decline additional projects. Here are a few of my favorites:

> *Thank you for thinking of me for this opportunity, but I am not able to commit to any new projects/commitments/roles at this time.*
> *I can't commit to this project/opportunity/role at this time.*
> *Let me think more about whether this project/opportunity/role is a good fit. Can I get back to you at a later date?*

Remember, you are worthy of cultivating space for self-nourishment, restoration, and self-compassion. You do not need to earn the right to rest. Rest is a radical act of resistance and is something that you inherently deserve.

Silencing Our Voices to Avoid Conflict

Though many Asian American communities prioritize collectivist values associated with maintaining interpersonal harmony, avoiding conflict, and minimizing emotional expression, these belief systems don't always align when we carry them into a Western individualistic society. As Asian Americans and children of Asian immigrants, we often feel forced to keep one foot in each world, carrying the collectivist-based internalized cultural scripts from our parents and ancestors while trying to navigate the individualistic expectations embedded in the United States.

This internal struggle is evidenced when we choose to remain silent when faced with conflict, struggle, or discomfort. Because we have not had practice in cultivating vulnerable and authentic selves that set boundaries and ask for help, we fall back on minimization, avoidance, and silence that are rooted in our desires to avoid abandonment, save face, and evade conflict.

Dr. Avadhanam shares how her community of voices has historically taught her that silence can help avoid conflict:

I have seen that when my parents struggle, they are unlikely to seek help or consult others. Similarly, in the deepest moments of struggle, I have historically chosen to take on the consequences of my actions alone while pushing out those I love in fear of burdening them. This leaves me to feel even more isolated. When I make choices, I feel a sense of responsibility to respect my parents' values and rise to the expectations of others. Often, what feels most appropriate is just to silence my own voice. I stopped sharing what I think, feel, and believe, and started conforming. In most cases, the fear of not receiving acceptance was what drove a lot of my behavior.

Dr. Cheung shares a similar story about how internalized messages about silencing discomfort may impact our workplace mentalities:

Avoiding pain and discomfort was certainly easy for me. As I became an adult, this limited me in different areas of life. At first, I was unable to deal with life pressures and felt that I was not able to talk about them. Talking about pressures felt painful and unnatural. This also became a problem in my first job. Because I felt that I couldn't approach colleagues about my feelings of stress, my work suffered while I tried to push through the pain. Looking back, I had internalized the beliefs from my parents that silently enduring pain is better than letting others know about my negative experiences.

Kimmy Wu recalls:

Growing up Asian means growing up in a collectivistic culture where love is expressed through actions and a mutual understanding of the belief that social harmony, respectfulness, and group needs are more important than individualistic needs is ever present. The "unspoken rules" in such a society suggest that "socially-acceptable behaviors" such as compromise, indirect communication to avoid conflict, group loyalty, and personal interdependence are favored. There is also often a tendency for emotional downplay because intense emotions can be received as impolite gestures. Being shut down and invalidated for my emotions taught me to believe that my feelings did not matter—that I did not matter. Instead of explicitly explaining the societal norms and expectations, the "corrective" and disciplinary practices often involved the act of shaming, which was devastating to my ability to feel loved, adequate, and worthy and even caused me to harbor deeply rooted shame.

Le* shares how conflict avoidance has historically impacted her in school, the workplace, and relationships:

I come from a family culture where emotional and psychological well-being wasn't a norm. As a result, a big part of my identity has been becoming an independent woman who didn't need anyone and who can do everything on her own. When it came to my work life, it has been (and still is to this day) difficult to ask for help or accommodations because I don't want to seem stupid, lazy, or difficult. When I dated in college, I approached it from a place of partnership instead of seeking romance and intimacy. If conflict happened between past partners and I, I would just sweep it under the rug because I didn't want to cause "drama" or more conflict.

Carmel,* a second-generation Filipina American woman in her 20s, recalls:

I have a hard time sharing my feelings with others because my parents also grew up not being able to do so. They never had the outlet to be honest due to the belief that speaking your mind is equivalent to "not being thankful" for everything your family has done for you. Every time I do speak up, my parents always blame me for being ungrateful instead of acknowledging my feelings.

There is something deeply healing about seeing ourselves in the narratives and experiences of others. As Asian Americans and children of Asian immigrants, many of us have dealt with our fears, struggles, and feelings of shame in silence. Somewhere along the line, we may have come to believe that nobody could, or would, ever want to understand us. We may have worried that if they did, they would abandon us upon recognizing that we are broken, bad, or somehow unworthy.

All that aside, do you want to hear a secret?

That deep underlying fear that screams, "*If I truly allow myself to be authentic, ask for help, express my needs, or be vulnerable, then people will deem me unworthy, and I will be abandoned*" is shared by nearly everyone. This collective fear seems to be embedded among people across age, race, ethnicity, class, culture, and ability status. This shared fear is protective: It has historically kept us safe from painful rejections, attachment injuries, and disappointments. But when we let that fear grow unchecked, it steals our abilities to thrive and keeps us from operating from places of emotional well-being, joy, and great abundance. I give you permission to begin exploring a reality where this fear no longer keeps you from accessing the fullness of expression to which you are deserving.

Consider the following:

What might I be giving up by silencing my voice?

To what extent is this fear limiting my ability to access abundance, joy, and well-being?

What evidence is there that this fear is serving me?

How does minimizing emotional expression serve me? How might it keep me from accessing a life full of joy, abundance, and whole-heartedness?

When are times that expressing myself, engaging in vulnerability, and asking for help worked well?

Wearing Abercrombie & Fitch in High School Didn't Hide Your Asian Identity

As a young girl, I have vivid memories of my mother telling me not to play outside for too long because I would get too dark. Growing up, this message confused me: What would be so wrong about embracing my naturally dark skin?

I eventually learned that experiences of colorism and internalized oppression were shared by other Filipino Americans, as well as Asian Americans across various ethnic subgroups. Internalized oppression refers to the ways in which racial and ethnic individuals internalize the racist stereotypes, values, images, and ideologies perpetuated by white culture.[9] This phenomenon results in feelings of self-doubt, disgust, and disrespect for one's racial or ethnic community. For example, Asian Americans are forced to contend with messages from our parents, the media, and Western society that communicate American beauty standards as the norm. These messages celebrate traditionally European physical attributes, such as light skin, straight hair, slim bodies, and a tall nose.[10] As a child, my identities were not represented in movies, film, or music. Desperately trying to fit in, I begged my mom for blonde highlights and asked for clothes from Abercrombie & Fitch for birthdays and on Christmas. When I heard Lucy Liu was cast in the 2000 rendition of *Charlie's Angels*, I was thrilled. I had never seen an Asian American woman portrayed in a leading role, and I fantasized about a reality where boys would ask me on dates instead of mockingly tease, *Me love you long time*. Unfortunately, the film did little to quiet the internalized voices in my mind about idealized Western beauty standards. Lucy's tall nose, light skin, and straight hair didn't seem to match the button nose, golden skin, and wavy hair that was reflected back when I looked in the mirror.

The skin-whitening business in Asian countries represents a multi-billion-dollar industry. Asians and Asian Americans alike seem to have internalized the limiting cultural scripts that acting and appearing "more white" is inherently better than aligning with one's own ethnic identity. In reality, seeking white proximity (e.g., adjusting one's appearance, behaviors, and values in ways that more closely align you with the majority group) is a specific kind of oppressive experience that lies at the intersection of white supremacy and internalized racism. Because whiteness continues to be the norm in American society, non-white communities believe they can garner more social power and social capital by aligning with whiteness. These beliefs are the same ones that maintain the model minority myth. Looking back on my childhood, I vividly remember finding any excuse to speak English without the hint of a Filipina accent when my family and I would go for dim sum after church on Sundays. Before challenging (or even recognizing) my internalized oppression and ethnic shame scripts, I was convinced that white patrons would hear my impeccable English pronunciation and deem me *one of the good Asians*.

Filipino Americans can also experience colonial mentality. Colonial mentality refers to the preference for the values, beliefs, and cultural practices of the majority culture and the denigration of one's own indigenous Filipino identity.[11] Among Filipino Americans and Filipinos, this preference can be understood as developing after nearly 400 years of colonization by Spain and the United States and may be evidenced through practices that are perceived to align oneself closer to whiteness. Filipinos may press the bridges of children's noses in hopes of training a tall, more attractive nose, avoid sun exposure out of fears of becoming too *etim* (dark in Tagalog), and avoid bringing home-cooked Filipino cuisine in public (even though it's quickly becoming *en vogue!*).

Internalized oppression may also intersect with complex messages about assimilation. Asians and Asian Americans who deviate from messages about *fitting in* are often slapped with pejorative "FOB" (fresh off the boat) labels and teased, and they elicit feelings of judgment and shame from others who have yet to challenge their own internalized oppression and ethnic shame narratives.

Growing up in a predominantly white Ohio suburb, it took longer for me to recognize and overcome feelings of ethnic shame than I would like to admit. Although I had befriended two Asian American women in high school, a part of me always felt as though we were in competition. I never spoke candidly about my feelings and continued to carry an underlying distrust of other Asian women into young adulthood. In college, I joined an Asian American student organization that role modeled community values and acceptance. Through these friendships, I began coming to terms with the uncomfortable realization that my feelings toward other Asian Americans (especially women) stemmed from the internalization of harmful stereotypes about our community such as the lotus blossom myth, yellow peril, and perpetual foreigner. I recognized my own ethnic shame and misguided belief that achieving white proximity would protect me from racial discrimination. Once I began challenging my own internalized oppression scripts, I started seeing things differently for the first time. I stopped feeling embarrassed when Asian international students would eat pizza with chopsticks, thinking, "You're ruining this for the rest of us!" and I began feeling empathy and compassion for the discomfort they must be experiencing as they learned to adapt in an entirely new country. I realized that the nerdy Asian table and the cool Asian table portrayed in the *Mean Girls* film was actually representative of inter-group othering and was a joke layered with race-based stereotypes, misogyny, and the exoticization of Asian women.

When we take a step back and view each of these internalized cultural scripts more critically, we realize how these messages represent attempts to ingratiate ourselves into American society. I've often questioned, though, *What is the cost of abandoning who we are to fit in?* I spoke with Asian American thought leaders and storytellers to find out more.

Carmel* shares:

> Growing up, I never referred to myself as Filipino-American. Interestingly enough, a lot of the cultural values that impacted me were mostly part of what we call "toxic Filipino culture." In a physical sense, I admit I grew up having the colonial mentality that light skin is better. Although I do appreciate my tan skin color, I would always think I looked better with lighter skin for makeup and picture purposes. I stopped playing outside to stay out of the sun and I always looked for skincare products that had brightening ingredients to lighten my dark spots. I also quit marching band in high school because all the long hours under the strong summer sun gave me skin discoloration and a darker facial complexion than the rest of my body.

Anecdotally, it seems as though the struggle to find one's place as an Asian American in the majority culture is a challenging, individualized, and unique process. Many of us have received messages from an early age that communicated meta-messages about how to behave to promote belongingness. As a result, we grow up with narratives that convey a conditional sense of belonging and secure our identities as a perpetual foreigner. We are Asians first, before ever being considered American.

Learning to Embrace Asian American Identity

To feel distinctly different while embodying a visceral sense of ethnic shame is part of the Asian American experience. Dr. Jean Kim captured this process through an Asian American identity development model.[12]

The first stage, *ethnic awareness*, begins in early childhood and centers the family's ethnic expression as a significant contribution to one's identity and ethnic attitudes. Once children begin school and face racial discrimination, they may enter the *white identification stage*, wherein individuals realize they are different and seek to fit into white society while distancing themselves from their Asian heritage. The *awakening to social political consciousness stage* occurs when individuals' worldviews and perspectives expand in ways that recognize oppression and embody a political awareness that stops them from wanting to identify with white society. Individuals rediscover their sense of Asian pride and reconnect with their culture in the *redirection stage*. Because part of this stage encompasses the realization of white privilege and an awareness of how white supremacy is linked to Asian oppression, individuals may experience feelings of anger in this stage. Asian Americans achieve the highest form of identity development, *incorporation*, when they hold a positive and comfortable identity as an Asian American person and demonstrate respect for other groups.

The ways in which Asian Americans move through their identity development process is unique and influenced by a variety of factors including family of origin, lifetime experiences, presence of supportive peers, internalized overt and covert messages from families of origin, as well as by individual factors such as one's coping processes, meaning-making tendencies, and psychological readiness. Many of the storytellers and thought leaders with whom I spoke shared their own personal stories about growing up Asian American.

Carmel* shares:

As a second-generation American, I knew that I never completely fit in anywhere. I hated typical American lunches but forced myself to eat cold cut sandwiches so I could sit with other kids for lunch. I made myself believe I was always the odd one out. When I began college, I realized that was not true and learned I just needed to surround myself with people who understood me for who I am. It took years to find a crowd I can be myself in. Of course, I won't vibe with all Asian Americans, but at least I know I'm capable of finding a safe space that makes me feel comfortable.

Jennifer Alexander* recalls:

I've always felt a little lost and believed I had been missing a sense of belonging in terms of race and culture. My adoptive parents are white and though I have always told myself that they did the best they could, I don't know if that's true. My parents were not open about the fact that they adopted two children from Asian countries and then effectively erased our cultures. This has impacted my well-being because I never quite fit into any of the "boxes." Growing up in a very rural and conservative Michigan community, I was never white enough and never Asian enough. I can remember being told, "You're not really Asian, you're white." I grew up thinking that there was something wrong with me.

Dr. Valli also alludes to feelings of disconnect in America:

For most Americans, I will never be seen as one. I will always be the outsider who has a name with far too many syllables, who has familial experiences that are not relatable, who always has to plan around her long trips to India, and who has festivities when I wear "costumes."

Quan D.* describes how bullying was a part of his childhood experience:

I was fortunate enough to live in the same neighborhood and attend the same multicultural school with many children of immigrants. Our families went through similar life experiences and we all had the same goal: for everyone to become successful in life. In high school, things began to change. When many of my friends moved to the suburbs, their parents wanted them to become doctors and lawyers, get on the honor roll, and earn straight A's. Their classmates expected them to be super smart at everything and math wizards. As for me, I continued my educational path through the inner-city school system and had to deal with typical experiences of racism. I was called "Ching-Chong" and "Chun Li and Liu Kang" from video game characters. I also got bullied because everyone assumed all Asians were kung fu masters like Bruce Lee.

Each of these stories capture powerful experiences of what it was like growing up as an Asian American. These moments represent snapshots of time that many Asian Americans and children of Asian immigrants can appreciate, understand, and relate to regardless of our own histories, experiences, and worldviews.

I believe we can overcome the historical patterns and unhelpful internalized cultural scripts about productivity, silence, and internalized oppression. Though the path toward healing is challenging, small steps can pave the way for larger accomplishments. Give yourself permission to set flexible boundaries, speak up, embody a full range of emotions, and embrace your full identity as an Asian American person. When you are ready, take a deep breath. The next chapter is one of my favorites.

TLDR: Though our logical adult brains may objectively understand why our Asian American parents acted, thought, and behaved in certain ways, our emotional childhood brain is still trying to catch up. As a result, many of us struggle with internalized shame scripts driven by a community of voices that perpetuate unhelpful cultural scripts that lead us to focus on output until we burn out, give to others at the expense of ourselves, and silence our voices to avoid conflict. We can learn to challenge these shame scripts by recognizing the complex and nuanced ways that historical trauma, internalized shame scripts, scarcity mindsets, and insecure attachment styles compound in ways that impact on our ability to achieve a healthy work–life balance and a perspective of abundance.

Questions to Ponder

1. What are some messages expressed by my community of voices?
2. To what extent do the cultural scripts described in this chapter resonate with my experience?
3. With whom might I consider setting flexible boundaries?
4. What are some specific strategies I can begin today that would promote self-nourishment?
5. What are my experiences with Asian American identity development?

Questions to Bridge the Gap with Parents

1. How have values of hard work, sacrifice, and avoiding conflict served you well? What might be some drawbacks of these values?
2. What does your identity as an Asian or Asian American mean to you?
3. Under which kinds of circumstances might it benefit someone to speak up or remain silent?

8
Wholehearted Acceptance
Toward a Healing Orientation

It is a chilly Tuesday evening and I have just returned home from a 12-hour workday. By 8:30 p.m., I have little energy to cook and an even smaller desire for conversation. I am every man's trifecta of a universally pleasant partner: hungry, tired, and cranky.

Despite my appetite, fatigue, and irritability, I feel gratitude for the sense of peace and quiet that is visiting our home. By this point in the evening, my husband has already ensured that our son is fed, bathed, and asleep in his crib. Our dog is fed, content, and curled up like a furry brown loaf on the couch. The hard work of the day is done, and yet I am still left with an all-consuming question: *What do I eat for dinner?*

And, perhaps more importantly, *How quickly can I eat it?*

As I stand in the light of the fridge, I am distantly aware that my husband is watching television on the couch. Some sportsball team, no doubt. I know he has already had dinner and I'm just cooking for one.

I close the fridge and migrate to the pantry, desperate for a quick and easy answer. Boxes and canned goods stare back at me as I scour the shelves for something quick, easy, and satisfying. As I scan the shelves once more, willing the products to convince me that they're the right choice, I come across a package of ramen.

Not exactly healthy, but definitely quick and easy. Perfect.

I boil water for the ramen in one pot and plop a few eggs into a swirling bath of vinegar and water in another. A few minutes later, I am delighted with my dinner of prepackaged ramen and poached eggs.

As I make my way to the couch, bowl of ramen in hand, my husband picks up the remote, selects Netflix, and asks the most unexpected question:

Which cooking show would you like to watch? I know you like to watch cooking shows while you eat, and you've had a really long day.

At this moment, I am dumbfounded. Speechless. It's a small miracle that I don't drop my dinner.

I feel so deeply seen, valued, and *known*.

I think to myself, *To be fully and wholeheartedly accepted, without conditions ... is this the sixth love language? How did such a small question evoke such a deeply healing response?* And, *If this healing orientation exists, is it something that may be collectively shared by other Asian Americans and children of Asian immigrants?*

I had to find out.

Expanding on the Five Love Languages

The five love languages were proposed by Gary Chapman to capture the five ways people felt the most loved. As a marriage counselor, Chapman began noticing that couples often misunderstood each other's needs and struggled to communicate care and affection in ways that resonated. His book *The Five Love Languages: The Secrets to Love That Lasts*[1] is a *New York Times* bestseller and has sold over 5 million copies. It has been translated into 38 different languages and has established itself at the forefront of relationship tools.

According to Chapman's theory, there are five love languages that individuals use to speak and understand love or emotions. These are Words of Affirmation, Quality Time, Receiving Gifts, Acts of Service, and Physical Touch.

Whereas individuals who resonate with *Words of Affirmation* feel most loved when they receive praise or positive feedback from their loved ones, those in the *Quality Time* category feel loved when their partners give them their undivided attention. *Receiving Gifts* befits individuals who feel most loved when their partners give them presents or surprises. Those who primarily speak *Acts of Service* feel most loved and connected to partners who sincerely offer and provide help. Finally, those who speak *Physical Touch* fluently feel loved by receiving caresses and skin-to-skin contact. Though this last category is often misunderstood as sexual touch, Chapman is quick to differentiate this love language from more explicit sexual acts.

I never really felt as though any of the love languages resonated deeply with me. The closest one that remotely satisfied my innermost experience of connection was Words of Affirmation. Yet, nice compliments and gestures of verbal gratitude elicited nothing close to what my husband had just awoken inside me when he anticipated my desire to watch a cooking show. My husband's statement communicated the following meta-message:

I know who you are deep down; I know your preferences, desires, and shortcomings ...

and the clincher,

… and I love and accept you anyway, as you are, without conditions.

I still feel warm, fuzzy feelings when I think back to that moment.

As Asian Americans and children of Asian immigrants, we tend to struggle with the very idea of being wholeheartedly loved and accepted, for who we are, without conditions. Our insecure attachment styles keep us from accepting intimacy, emotional closeness, and vulnerability. Trusting that others can accept us without condition is a foreign concept when our parents encourage us to eat more at mealtimes and comment on our bodies in the next breath.

Many Asian Americans have learned from an early age that if we make our preferences known, we will be dismissed, invalidated, minimized, or ignored.[2] After some time, we may learn to stop expressing emotions altogether, preferring instead to prioritize the interpersonal harmony that comes from conflict avoidance. So, we finish the food that is served to us and bite our tongues when the critical auntie remarks on our weight.

And yet, conflict avoidance in relationships does not serve us. It can't serve us because it keeps us from honoring our identities as whole people and unlocking the power of communication, vulnerability, and the secure attachments of which we are truly deserving.

If we want to become better parents, partners, and people, we need to begin healing the attachment wounds of our inner child and cultivate secure attachments and worldviews characterized by abundance rather than scarcity. One way to do this is by leaning into what I believe is a healing orientation of unconditional acceptance and knowing.

How Does This Orientation Resonate?

Achieving an orientation with our romantic partner that is characterized by full and wholehearted acceptance, without conditions, represents a powerful way to heal our inner childhood wounds and move toward an identity of wholeness. From the secure base of this healing orientation, we can begin to give ourselves permission to feel, act, think, and behave in all the different ways we have learned to shut down, silence, or ignore from childhood.

For example, since our childhoods, many Asian Americans learn that explicit disclosure of vulnerable feelings is discouraged, minimized, or invalidated. When we share, "I had a bad day at school," our parents may remind us of their sacrifices and struggles or encourage us to simply move forward. Though our parents' intentions are likely meant to promote resilience and success, we learn to adapt by creating walls around these vulnerable parts of ourselves. We shield ourselves from access to these vulnerable emotions to avoid conflict with our parents, and later our romantic partners, and avoid activating parts of ourselves that we have deemed shameful, unworthy, or burdensome. When our partners gift us with full and wholehearted acceptance without conditions, we can begin occupying those unfamiliar spaces in ways that empower us to develop effective coping skills when vulnerable emotions arise, learn communication strategies to effectively navigate challenges, and even (gasp!) ask for help when needed.

Achieving this orientation with our partner can heal the wounded inner child within us who did not feel safe to be their full, authentic, emotional self.

Sophia describes:

I have grown into a head and heart space of learning that acceptance is essential to loving. I think a lot of our immigrant parents have relationships that are really fraught because they don't have acceptance as a part of how they love. Love isn't really even a verb for a lot of our parents and so practicing acceptance as part of this broader action of loving is so important. This orientation is something that I've seen in my own life. I realized I can't love myself if I don't accept myself and that has been something that I've intellectually known but haven't emotionally felt until very recently. I can't feel love by someone else unless I feel accepted.

Dr. Avadhanam shares:

There is tremendous pressure to be perfect as a child of immigrants. I always felt as though I could not afford to make mistakes because of the sacrifices that not only my parents made, but also my grandparents, great grandparents, and so on. For as long as I can remember, I wanted the freedom and ability to make my own choices without the pressures of living up to expectations and without the fear of letting my loved ones down. Due to that, especially in my friendships and partnerships, I have sought spaces of immense safety and comfort where I truly do feel unconditionally loved and accepted. I have an innate need to be loved without conditions, expectations, or even consequences.

Both of these interview excerpts evidence our deep desires for, as well as the fundamentally healing nature of, wholehearted acceptance as a necessary element in our adult romantic partnerships. As a researcher by nature, I couldn't ignore the powerful itch to identify the specific orienting elements that make up this healing orientation. What are the ingredients to this intoxicating recipe?

And more importantly, how can I empower others to achieve this healing orientation in meaningful ways?

The Healing Orientation Model Elements (HOME)

The healing relationship orientation that I believe resonates with Asian Americans and children of Asian immigrants is *to be deeply seen, known, understood, and yet wholeheartedly accepted by our partners, without condition.*

So, what are the possible elements associated with this exciting new way of being? What are the parts and pieces of this deeply freeing, undeniably healing, and viscerally connecting orientation? Here is what I've come up with and why I believe it is especially healing for many of us:

1. In this orientation, our partners *understand* us. They know who we are, our likes and dislikes, our beliefs and values, and our goals. They have a deep sense of knowing what will bring us joy, sadness, pain, and peace. They recognize what we need to feel connected, appreciated, and seen.
2. They *anticipate our needs.* Building upon their deep understanding of us, our partners can anticipate our needs. In many cases, our partners may even know what we want, desire, or feel before we do. There is a sense of acknowledgment followed by action.
3. They are *intentional.* The deeply healing actions that our partners engage in aren't just limited to the high-stakes moments of crises and big emotions. Instead, they are mostly embedded within the everyday mundanity of being in one another's presence and sharing time and space.
4. They are not *transactional.* For many of us, the act of simply giving of oneself without expecting something in return is a wholly unfamiliar concept. Our partners are role modeling what it means to simply *be loved with no expectation for anything in return.* In my case, I could continue eating my noodles on the couch without feeling pressure to have a conversation or even to improve my grumpy demeanor. Our partners extend the freedom to *simply be.*
5. When these elements combine over time, we experience a greater *sense of freedom and healing.* We can love ourselves and others more deeply and grow into new parts of who we are. And, we become better positioned to tend to the attachment wounds we have carried since childhood in ways that heal our inner child and allow us to move toward wholeness.

When I think about the components of this new love language, it brings to mind a counseling orientation I've studied: person-centered counseling.

Applying Theory to Our Relationships

Developed by Carl Ransom Rogers, person-centered theory is based on the assumption that people have a natural tendency to move toward growth in a process called self-actualization.[3]

One of the tenets of person-centered theory is how children's self-concepts are shaped through their interactions with important people in their lives.[4] If the messages children internalize about themselves include conditions of worth, then their ability to grow may be negatively impacted. *Conditions of worth* encompass the judgmental and critical messages that communicate to children that they are only worthwhile and lovable if they think, feel, and act in ways that meet the needs of others. Because children desperately seek love, connection, belonging, and acceptance, they may learn to act in ways that are incongruent with who they truly are to receive love, acceptance, and positive regard from others.[5]

How many of us believe that we must act, think, or behave in ways that better position us to receive the affection and acceptance of our loved ones? How might these conditions of worth impact our well-being?

To explore the necessary and sufficient elements that allow people to overcome their conditions of worth, Rogers sought to identify the psychological elements that elicit what he refers to as *constructive personality change*. This concept includes change in the personality structure of individuals at surface and deeper levels, in a direction toward greater integration, less internal conflict, and more energy available for effective living.[6]

According to Rogers,[7] the necessary and sufficient conditions for positive personality change are two people in psychological contact, one of whom who is incongruent (e.g., vulnerable or anxious), the other of whom is congruent (e.g., securely attached and fully integrated). The congruent person experiences unconditional positive regard and empathy for the other and seeks to communicate this to the other person, who accepts this.

Empathy, according to Rogers,[8] was a core component of this healing orientation. He described empathy as one's ability to cultivate an awareness of how another person is experiencing an event as if you were occupying their private world.

The second necessary element for positive change is unconditional positive regard. Rogers[9] conceptualized this concept as the extent to which one feels a warm acceptance toward each aspect of another's experience as part of that person. It is prizing of a person—a valuing of another individual for their whole self, even the messy bits.

Stacey, this framework was developed for therapist–client dyads. Rogers's ideas have no bearing for the relationships I have with my loved ones.

On the contrary, my dear reader.

In the very same paper where Rogers outlined his conditions for positive personality change, he added some very specific caveats. He explained that the conditions for healing represent "a heightening of the constructive qualities which often exist in part in other relationships,"[10] such as within romantic relationships. He also reassured readers that one does not need to have specialized training or be a professional therapist to demonstrate these healing qualities. Instead, one can simply be in a meaningful relationship with another person. Finally, one person does not need to have a formal diagnosis to experience fundamental healing. The storytellers with whom I spoke are full of examples of this.

Note: Person-centered theory and the five love languages are grounded in European, Western, and individualized notions of mental health and wellness, which may not be culturally congruent with Asian Americans or other racial and ethnic communities. Though I incorporate Western theories as helpful frameworks that guide this book, it is important to decolonize the standard mental health framework and expand our ways of understanding optimal psychological health and well-being through Indigenous, culturally grounded, and healing-centered frameworks.

A Deep Sense of Understanding and Wholehearted Acceptance

In this healing orientation, our partners demonstrate a deep sense of understanding and wholehearted acceptance. They know and understand our preferences, values, beliefs, desires, quirks, and even our shortcomings. They hold and honor the qualities that we may believe are bad, broken, and shameful until we are ready to own them for ourselves. Our partners know us, prize us, and celebrate us for who we are as whole, imperfect people, even though we may not have allowed ourselves to do the same. I have experienced this phenomenon throughout the relationship with my husband, and others seem to have captured these moments too.

Matthew*, a 1.5-generation queer man of Filipino and white descent in his early 30s, shares:

> My partner and I understand each other at a different level and accept all of the various differences that we bring to the table. We experience mutual oppression and have a shared sense of political values because of those things. Because of our commonalities in our backgrounds (class backgrounds, immigrant backgrounds, all that stuff), that is why I feel comfortable marrying this person. Where we live now is not the most forgiving place as a queer Filipino person. It's quite homogenous. Fortunately, we can be so much for each other in a space like this because

we come from similar families and similar backgrounds. It does feel healing. After dating my partner, it's just so hard to imagine dating anyone else because of the way that he knows how to love me and because of the depth and holisticness with which he's able to care about what I care about, accept who I am, and understand me.

Following a stressful moment with her partner, Olivia* shares:

I wanted so badly for my partner to say—"It's okay. I got you. I hear you." Perhaps on some level, I wanted to hear that I was enough. I wanted our relationship to be the superseding validation that no matter what was going on in my professional life, no matter what had happened—my partner would be there for me unconditionally. I wanted to know and believe that I was worthy of that type of love and attention.

Kareena* shares the importance of being deeply understood and wholeheartedly accepted:

For me, the feeling of being seen and heard is unmatched. The space to say my piece, to share my truth, to recount my own history—and for people to care about that—is life changing. At first, I was scared to bring up my past traumas with my husband, and he was rightfully shocked by much of it. To be at a place now where he completely understands my triggers, holds me when I'm feeling down, and knows what to do because he knows who I am, is such a validating and loving feeling.

It seems as though there are reasons why acceptance and understanding may be deeply healing. According to Dr. Band:

Acceptance is a form of validation. Validation is a recognition that your thoughts, feelings, and actions have value—and by extension, so do you. Acceptance is also a way of seeing someone for who they are, which is probably one of the most healing experiences someone can have and offer to another. Acceptance is a reciprocal process and an aspect of unconditional love. The only way to truly gain acceptance is to be vulnerable around someone. Vulnerability is often thought of as being authentically emotional.

As evidenced across each of these narratives, feeling deeply understood and accepted by our romantic partner can unlock a vulnerable need for connection. Many of us have adapted to our ancestral historical trauma narratives, intergenerational patterns, and internalized cultural scripts by over-emphasizing independence or keeping others at an arm's length. As a result, the very thought of vulnerability can elicit intense feelings of discomfort.

Taken all together, here is what I believe to be the underlying secret of this healing element:

> *When our partners deeply understand and accept us, they give us permission to do the same. Our partners therefore create the necessary condition to engage in the vulnerability required to deeply understand and fully accept ourselves— sometimes for the first time.*

Intentionally Anticipating Our Needs, Wants, and Desires Without Reciprocity

How many of us secretly side-eye our partners when they engage in intentional acts of kindness or anticipate our needs? Perhaps we feel inclined to "keep score" or immediately reciprocate with our own act of kindness to ensure our debt is repaid.

Accepting when partners anticipate our needs, wants, and desires without an expectation for reciprocity can be another orienting element that many of us may struggle to accept. This challenge may originate from the fact that Asian American households are characterized by a seemingly endless list of transactional behaviors and actions. For example, our parents made enormous sacrifices to keep a roof over our head, food on our plates, and clothes on our back so we could succeed academically. We may be constantly reminded of these sacrifices and expected to reciprocate by succeeding in academic and career settings, earning social capital that benefits our families of origin, serving as caregivers to our older adult parents, and sacrificing our own personal boundaries to placate their collective wishes.

Within Filipinx culture, the sense of eternal indebtedness to our parents and ancestors for their sacrifices is called *utang ng loob*. Though nuanced and largely dependent on context, this Tagalog phrase refers to the Filipino cultural belief that upon receiving acts of kindness from others, we become indebted to them. As a result, many Filipino Americans and Filipino individuals carry expectations to continue sending money back home to family, to care for parents and other family members, to remain silent when conflict arises, and to disregard personal boundary violations. Though the Filipino American diaspora prides ourselves on maintaining Indigenous notions of generosity, kindness, and hospitality, the concept of *utang ng loob* can extend beyond cultural values in ways that maintain unhelpful relationships and perpetuate toxic cultural scripts.

With these concepts and experiences in mind, it doesn't take much to see how receiving acts of care, thoughtfulness, and intentionality from our partners, without expectations for reciprocity, can feel like navigating uncharted territory. Over time, however, learning to simply accept these acts of kindness and allowing ourselves to feel connected and cared for can bring us one step closer to achieving a healing orientation with our partners.

Chamari De Silva shares:

I went through a reconstructive surgery in 2005 and the decision to make that was actually with the help of my ex. I had been in so much physical pain, and he was the first person with whom I really shared how deep that pain was. There were times where he would observe me in social settings and just come over and rub my shoulders. At first, that made me feel uncomfortable. I was like, okay, okay, don't bring attention to this. But what that act of kindness ultimately broke down for me was, "Oh, wow, he actually notices changes in the way that I'm carrying myself," or maybe I'm making some sort of gesture and it's indicating that I'm in pain. And he sees that. I became so appreciative of him for noticing my discomfort when no one else had. Giving me the comfort of knowing that he wasn't dating me for how I physically looked, but for the soul of the person that I am, was powerful. It allowed me the freedom to make life choices and decisions that benefitted my overall health and well-being.

Angelika Holleran, a second-generation biracial Filipina American and therapist in her early 30s, explains:

With my partner, it's all about the small everyday moments. When we are at a restaurant and the waiter places our meals in front of us, instead of immediately digging into his plate, my partner will patiently wait for me to take a photo of our food because he knows I enjoy posting it on social media. He has even taken up the role as an assistant by positioning the centerpiece candle or flower arrangement to help with the photo's aesthetics. That effort is just so beautiful. It's like, "Oh wow, he knows how weird I am, and he loves it anyway."

Matthew* similarly expresses:

My partner will just remember things. He will come home from work and bring me a bubble tea, or maybe he will have my favorite snack from the corner store. I don't ask for these things, he just remembers what I like and buys it. He just listens, receives, and he is always curious about my take on things. When I sing karaoke, the way that this man looks at me, it's just like I'm Beyoncé, you know?

My voice could be cracking, I could be flat, but he's still sitting right there with his phone out, filming, and just amazed. We live together now in a two-bedroom apartment in the Midwest with one of my elder Filipino family members, who has needs and is particular. I'm just amazed at how he's able to deal with that situation without a single complaint. He is so respectful, so generous, and just seeing the way he treats her is incredible. I feel like when people don't have immigrant parents, sometimes there's a learning curve in terms of how to communicate with them and engage with them. And for him, it was never like that. The way he's able to care for my people as a way of caring for me is so very healing.

Tarm shares how her partner anticipates her needs while they navigate a long-distance relationship:

I am pursuing my Psy.D. on the east coast and he is on the west coast. One of the wonderful things about my partner is his ability to think one step ahead and be supportive and helpful. My partner engages in these daily acts of thoughtfulness. One prime example is when he knows I have long clinical days, he'll order food delivery so that when I get home I don't need to cook and can eat right away. Even when I don't want to accept his offer (because I don't want to "take" his hard-earned money), he'll still send me food and it can be a meal for the next day. He knows I'm overwhelmed and wants to make sure that I eat and that I am taken care of. He does these things without expecting me to do anything in return. It means so much and makes me feel deeply seen, appreciated, and connected to him.

Michelle Zauner captures similar themes when she recalls her marriage vows in her book, *Crying in H Mart*:

I talked about how love was an action, an instinct, a response roused by un-planned moments and small gestures, an inconvenience in someone else's favor. How I felt it most when he drove up to New York after work at three in the morning just to hold me in a warehouse in Brooklyn after I'd discovered my mother was sick. The many times these months he'd flown three thousand miles whenever I needed him. While he listened patiently through the five calls a day I'd been making since June. And though I wished our marriage could begin under more ideal circumstances, it had been these very trials that had assured me he was everything I needed to brave the future that lay ahead.[11]

Learning to accept our partners' acts of thoughtfulness without immediately wanting to "even the playing field" can move us closer toward a healing orientation. When we learn to overcome the unhelpful cultural scripts that have positioned transactional relationships as the norm, the benefit is clear: *When our partners anticipate our needs, wants, and desires without an expectation for reciprocity, we learn that we are deserving of kindness, patience, and love. We can begin to challenge deeply held notions that contributed to conditions of worth. And, in doing so, we can recognize that we are worthy of love and belonging.*

The Freedom to Grow

Remember that earlier chapter about healing childhood attachment wounds and the importance of cultivating secure attachments? All of that comes into play right here.

Specifically, recall how achieving a secure attachment represents a safe place from which we can learn and grow. This same element also exists when a healing orientation with our partner occurs.

Bayani* states:

> *The greatest part about my partner is that he takes me as I am. I don't have to filter what I say around him because I'm not worried about being wrong or being put on the defensive. I'm more free to express what I want and how I feel even if it's problematic. There is no need to prove myself to him. We are walking the same path, ensuring we're guiding each other along. He allows me to work on myself, exist as myself, and grow into myself.*

Calypso* recounts how her partner's love empowers her with a deeper freedom to grow:

> *Atlas became my friend as I was exiting a dark chapter of my life. He gave me space without judgment. He treated me gently and required nothing from me. I've had many romantic relationships but never truly a partner. We are on the same side. In times of serious conflict, I can feel some of my previous insecure reactions resurge. I'll want to either avoid or declare my independence. However, because we are on the same team, we've repeatedly worked through it productively and lovingly. This is only possible because I feel free, and seen, and safe. He considers my emotional and physical well-being in a way which makes my life more peaceful and restful. He encourages me to be the best version of myself, without his own expectation or self-interest. This is pure acceptance. This means everything to me.*

Lisa Factora-Borchers, a first-generation American-born Filipinx woman, author, and activist in her early 40s, echoes similar sentiments in her relationship:

The practice of honoring someone the way Nick practices and honors our relationship—the constancy, the absolute devotion to showing up no matter how big or small—is the most extraordinary gift I've been given. His presence and ability to completely accept me is the foundation of my strength as an adult. He has a different way of expressing himself, but there has never been one moment where I have ever wondered if he honored me. That kind of love is very difficult to articulate because it's the highest form of freedom you can find with another human.

Recognizing how our partners act in ways that move us closer to a securely attached relationship characterized by unconditional love, safety, and acceptance has an incredible impact on our ability to develop into whole people. *From the theoretical lens of attachment theory, when our partners unconditionally love, accept, and celebrate who we are, we are gifted with the freedom to grow. More specifically, we are better able to grow into the people we aspire to become deep down, not simply the people whom we believe we were supposed to be in order to achieve acceptance.*

The Freedom to Heal

Achieving a secure attachment and a healing orientation with our partner is not only a springboard for growth, it is also a catalyst for healing. When our partners accept and love us without conditions, we can learn to accept and love ourselves without conditions. In doing so, we also unlock the freedom to heal our wounded inner child.

Lisa Factora-Borchers shares how her relationship elicits the freedom to heal:

There is so much reimagining of love when you have a partner who is loving you all the time, no matter what. And in the best way, you get to turn around and deal with your shit because you don't have someone throwing it back at you or using it to degrade you. It's not just that my partner accepts who I am; it's that he profoundly honors it. He honors me and honors every struggle I've ever had as if it were his own. It's the most incredible gift of healing when someone simply loves you as you contend with your own issues and says, "That's not my stuff, I've got my own stuff. That's your stuff and I'm going to love you every second through that." It's impossible to center my healing without recognizing our relationship building and the labor that went into my/our deepening. I wouldn't even know how to talk about my healing without him.

Dr. Daniela Pila shares:

I have been with my husband for over a decade, and he has never commented negatively about my body. He reminds me every day how much he loves me and how attractive I am to him. When we first started dating, he was confused why no one had told me that I was beautiful. In the Philippines, my classmates would literally call me "pig" and "fat" simply for not being a size 0. His unconditional love, no matter my weight, has helped me embrace my curves and define myself outside of the scale. This was so important especially after I had our daughter. I am currently the heaviest I have ever been, but I know this is a phase. I am grateful for my able-bodiedness and the things my body is able to do, like create life.

Shoua Lee expresses the healing effects of her husband's wholehearted love:

I prayed for someone exactly like my husband. The relationship with my husband was something I deeply needed yet was not prepared for. I experienced something I had never felt before with him, not even from my parents: wholehearted acceptance. Given my insecure attachment style, our relationship started off very rocky because I did not believe I could be loved in this way. I tried to push him away and he continued to stay present and soft with me. His patience and kindness were like water for my fiery heart. His love for me showed me that I was loveable and helped me learn how to love myself. When I would make mistakes, his nurturing of my spirit showed me I did not have to be so hard on myself. His holding of me lifted me up from my wallow. His sweet words replayed in my mind instead of my harsh inner critic. Over time, his words became my words. Being accepted wholeheartedly as the foundation to our relationship provided me with a sense of ease. As our relationship progressed, I found myself never having to worry about any infidelity. His full trust in me helped me trust him fully. Never having to worry has this way of allowing one to just flower. Not having to worry about why he was coming home late meant that I could be present for my dinners and baths in the evening. This also meant that I slept better. Although this may seem minuscule, these days add to years, and it makes all the difference.

A similar story was shared by Noelle*:

In our relationship, my husband followed and supported me every step of the way. When I got a job that required us to move we were engaged and he was like,

"That's fine, take the leap out of the state and I will do my best to find a job as soon as I can." And then I found a job at a large private midwestern university and he's like, "Take it, I'll figure it out." He followed me there. A lot of men can feel threatened when their wife is the breadwinner of the home and has a higher title, but he's never felt threatened or upset. He actually celebrates it. He's like, "Yeah, I'd be happy to have you become university president, that's great. I'll take care of the kids, I'll drive you wherever you want to go," because he knows I hate driving. That deep sense of understanding is such a gift. It's so good to have somebody who is your partner who doesn't make you feel any of the pressure or any of those expectations that my family places on us. When our partners see us, it fills the gaps we had as children because we didn't get the ability to freely be who we are and do what we wanted and be trusted for our passion. When our partner give us that freedom, I just imagine a scar or a wound and our partners are the salve.

The Salve for Our Wounds

I once worked with a fabulous counselor, Maria, who said, "*It sounds like your partner heals the wounds from your childhood.*" It was the first time I cried in therapy (instead of just dissociating) and it opened my eyes to a new possibility for my own healing.

Because many of us are unable to embrace our whole selves, in their entirety, as children, we enter into adulthood as fragmented pieces. Somewhere along the line, we have come to believe that if we enter relationships or navigate the world as one integrated being, with the full spectrum of human experiences and emotions, then we will be abandoned, face rejection, or elicit disappointment, shame, or discomfort in others.

We have carried these fragmented parts of ourselves for a lifetime. We have become experts in using these broken pieces as shields for battles with vulnerability, comfort, or expression.

When our partners *deeply see, know, understand, and yet wholeheartedly accept us, without conditions*, this experience is healing. It communicates the message *I see you, all of you, and I love you in spite of your flaws.*

A beautiful example of this was shared by Dr. Cheung:

In just these past five years, I have encountered some significant events that have repeatedly activated my attachment wounds. My wife demonstrated patience and a willingness to understand. It did involve a lot of tears, yelling, disagreements, and confrontation of my core beliefs, yet unconditional acceptance was present. I felt understood and supported because there was trust and openness in our conversations. In these difficult and vulnerable moments, I didn't have to make my partner proud and I didn't have to put on a mask and pretend I can handle it. All I needed was to be myself. Her acceptance was healing for me to make positive changes in my life. This process consisted of many dialogues to help me clarify my needs and be honest while helping my partner understand how she can help me. It was deeply healing to know that I am allowed to fail, to come up short, and to disappoint, but still be loved.

Perhaps the acceptance we feel from our partners gives us the freedom to finally heal from our childhood wounds and occupy new places within ourselves. Through this healing orientation, we can learn to grow into the parts of ourselves that have felt scary, unfamiliar, or too vulnerable. Allowing ourselves to be vulnerable gives others, as well as ourselves, opportunities to accept every aspect of who we are. Through vulnerability, we can learn to inhabit our bodies, our minds, and our emotions in ways that we haven't given ourselves permission to do before.

Dr. Band explains:

To receive acceptance, you must take the risk of being vulnerable and emotional in front of someone, which can be scary and feel risky—especially when you're healing from your own attachment wounds. If you are asking [for] and needing acceptance, you also want to be thinking about how often you give acceptance— not just to others, but yourself. For example, I had a lot of experiences not fitting in and feeling othered growing up. I didn't feel accepted by others and while wanting to feel a sense of belonging, there were critical parts of myself that didn't really accept me either. Working on these parts and coming together as one with self-compassion has made the difference in feeling loved.

There is something deeply healing and connecting about demonstrating vulnerability and receiving acceptance and praise in light of our imperfections. Perhaps this is why so many Asian Americans, especially Korean and Filipino communities, feel drawn to karaoke. Singing in front of others is a particularly vulnerable group activity. Though we may go with friends, we are also surrounded by strangers. Karaoke is interesting because enthusiasm is valued just as much as talent. Both the powerhouse family singer and the out-of-tune uncle who misses key parts of the chorus receive five-minute standing ovations. We are baring our souls and showing emotion in arguably one of the only culturally appropriate ways, and we are celebrated for it. The extent to which we are talented singers doesn't seem to matter. What matters instead is that we are willing to step into the light, lower the protective façades that we have built across a lifetime, and simply exist in a vulnerable, uninhibited way. Taking this same leap of faith with our partners can be a powerful first step to achieving a healing orientation with our romantic partners. Our relationships become more harmonious when we are in tune with one another.

TLDR: Using the theoretical lens of person-centered theory, Carl Rogers describes how children often internalize conditions of worth from caregivers, community members, and others in their lives in ways that impact their self-concept. I believe similar conditions are present in adult relationships that lead to a healing orientation among Asian Americans and children of Asian immigrants. The healing relationship orientation that I believe resonates with children of immigrants is characterized by being deeply seen, known, understood, and yet wholeheartedly accepted by our partners, without condition. It incorporates elements of secure adult attachment styles, supports the healing of our wounded inner child, and empowers us to recognize how acceptance, understanding, and a willingness to receive intentional acts of kindness from our partners can become a catalyst for personal growth and healing. Because many immigrant households are characterized by transactional relationships, it is challenging to learn how to accept kindness from our partners without immediately seeking to return the favor. However, learning to accept these loving gestures represents an important step to achieving a healing relationship orientation and letting go of unhelpful cultural scripts. When this healing orientation among partners is achieved, we are better positioned to become an integrated, whole person who recognizes they are worthy of love, belonging, and acceptance.

Questions to Ponder

1. What thoughts or emotions did this chapter evoke as I read through it?
2. What are some conditions of worth that I may have learned from childhood?
3. To what extent have my partner and I achieved this healing orientation?
4. Which of these healing elements do my partner and I share?
5. How can my partner and I begin practicing these orienting elements today?

Questions to Bridge the Gap with Parents

1. When do you feel most connected to your partner?
2. How have you and your partner grown together or changed since the beginning of your relationship? How did you manage to do that?
3. What do you believe are the most important qualities of a happy, healthy, successful relationship?

9

Pattern-Breaking Strategies for Self-Nourishment

൭

When we do not question the powerful frameworks that influence our lives, we lack awareness. Without awareness, we lose agency and freedom of choice over our lives. When we lack awareness, we react out of impulse or instinct to triggers and situations, instead of responding with intention. We replay old dynamics and maintain patterns of living that keep us stuck.

Jenny T. Wang, *Permission to Come Home*[1]

We have covered quite a bit of ground on this journey toward healing. Together, we have unearthed how historical trauma, intergenerational patterns, and anti-Asian oppression contribute to the internalization of overt and covert messages and result in limiting cultural scripts. We have explored how these cultural scripts, scarcity mindsets, and childhood attachment wounds limit our abilities to access joy, achieve secure attachments, and find balance within the workplace, in our lives, and within our relationships. Finally, we have outlined the elements to an important relationship orientation that promotes healing, unconditional acceptance, freedom, and growth.

So, what do we do with all this information? How can we integrate what we have learned into the next steps of our healing journey?

The following two chapters were developed to address the inevitable question: *What do I do now with the information I have?*

Healing Our Inner Child

Today is my son's second birthday.

As I look across the room and see his jubilant face, bright eyes, and messy hair, I am filled with a deep sense of joy. I am awestruck that my husband and I could have created such a perfect little being. It takes everything in me to refocus my attention to the streamers and decorations that have yet to be hung throughout the house.

It is already 12:45 p.m. and our guests will begin arriving soon. There is so much left to be done and I secretly pray that everyone will be on Filipino time (late).

I am standing over the dining room table. Snoopy-adorned items lay strewn across our woodgrain table. I pick up a Pigpen-embellished streamer when the doorbell rings.

My ears fill with an excited screech and the sound of tiny footsteps that pound down the hallway. My son sees my parents peek through the window and he propels his body toward them as fast as his little legs can travel. They open the door just in time and he crashes into their arms.

"Lolo! Lola!"

He is thrilled to see his grandparents and giggles loudly as they cover him with kisses and showcase their most recent snack discovery from Costco. His fingers wrap around the crinkly sound of prepackaged snacks and he runs back to the living room, hand in hand with his Lolo. My mother hands me a bag of Lemon Zest Madeleines and sets a clear boundary: "For Kit."

I greet my parents and ask my father to watch my son so my mother and I can finish decorating the house and preparing the serving trays.

"Please don't let him fill up on sweets," I call to my dad over my shoulder, "We are serving *empanada* and *pansit*, and I want him to have a full belly before he eats birthday cake."

He nods a silent acknowledgment and I return to the mindless task of filling goodie bags with stickers, coloring books, and prepackaged crayon sets.

Fifteen minutes pass. I finish placing the last donut on the wooden-pegged dessert board and slide it toward the back of the table, out of reach from my son's curious grasp. The decorations are hung, and the only task left is to change my son into his birthday outfit.

I look across the living room.

He is nowhere to be found.

I stroll across the three seasons room, prepared to see him playing in the backyard.

He is not there.

I begin to feel shaky. Panicked. Did he manage to slip outside in the distracted chaos of party preparation and run into the street? I swallow hard and fight off the anxiety that threatens to engulf me.

I am power walking toward the front door when I hear the tiniest of sounds from around the corner.

A giggle followed by a playful shush.

I slowly make my way around the foyer where I find my father sitting on the floor with my son. He catches my eye and instinctively looks down at my child. My eyes follow his gaze and I force myself to hold back a tight-lipped smile.

"Mama!"

My two-year-old proudly holds up both hands and shows me the donut in each one. His fingers are buried in soft pastry pillows and his cheeks are covered with a sticky white glaze. He smiles up at me triumphantly.

I lock eyes with my father.

"I told you not to let him fill up on sweets!"

My father shrugs and offers a sheepish grin.

"He wanted the donuts, and I wanted him to have them."

Moments like this one, though seemingly inconspicuous to outsiders, are powerful catalysts in healing my inner child. My parents are communicating love to my son in a familiar way—through food.

They stock up on his favorite snacks, make special visits just to drop off fresh fruit, and take great joy in seeing their *apo* (grandchild in Tagalog) fill his belly. I know my son is creating beautiful memories in these moments, too. He feels love, acceptance, joy, and connection. Beyond this familiar form of love, my parents have begun demonstrating care in a newer and more vulnerable way. They get down on the ground to play, chase him around the house, act silly to elicit laughter, and stretch their features into impossible faces that make my sons break out in uncontrollable giggles.

Embracing these intergenerational interactions, and meeting them with gratitude instead of resentment, is one way to heal our inner child. If having children is like watching our hearts run around in different bodies, then witnessing the care our parents bestow to our children can heal our hearts, too.

Within the fields of counseling and psychology, this is often referred to as *parts work*, a modality of counseling that focuses on healing and integrating the wounded parts of ourselves. Engaging in parts work to heal our inner child can include a variety of different strategies. For some, this includes the intentional practicing of activities and interactions that they were denied or did not experience in younger years. For others, these intentional strategies include recreating harmful past experiences in ways that allow closure, healing, and peace.

Many of the storytellers with whom I spoke described how engaging in parts work has represented a powerful strategy to heal their inner child.

Kareena* shares:

To heal my inner child, I try visualization exercises. I reimagine a time where I was so heartbroken, dejected, or depressed. I go back to that moment and imagine my current self sitting next to my child self, giving her a hug and letting her know that things are going to get so much better. I tell her that it's not her fault—that what is happening is not a result of anything she's doing, and unfortunately the adults in the room aren't capable of fulfilling their roles. I remind her that she is strong and powerful and brilliant and her best days are ahead of her. I tell her that she has so many people who love her and I try to envelop her with that energy.

Kimmy Wu shares how she has managed to heal her inner child by implementing radical acceptance and intentionality:

I believe that introducing the concept of self- and other-acceptance can be pivotal because, by definition, acceptance is the literal opposite of rejection. Practicing radical acceptance, which is the acceptance of a whole self through a conscious effort to acknowledge difficult situations and emotions, and honoring and accepting them as they are, can be an extremely powerful way to reparent our inner child. To reparent and heal my inner child, I have been learning to acknowledge, validate, accept, and consistently develop trust between my inner child and adult self.

Shoua Lee expresses how compassionate awareness, radical acceptance, and intentionality have been key to her own healing:

Breaking the harmful patterns we inherited from our childhood is possible with intention, practice, and compassionate awareness. Without compassionate awareness, we can become stuck in the loop of shame or blame. For instance, if we blame or remain resentful at how our parents raised us, our engagement with our parents suffers. Once I started loving myself, I became able to love others authentically. The result of this reciprocity was stronger and deeper connections with others. I have grown much more comfortable with physical touch. I can give tighter and longer embraces. I can look others in their eyes, without fearing they would see something they did not like. I can tell the people in my life, "I love you."

Healing our inner child and resolving our childhood attachment wounds requires a radical acceptance of who we are and an honoring of our journey. It is a daily commitment and practice. When we are fully present for our experience, we can start to forgive ourselves for the actions we have taken to survive. We cannot expect years of muscle memory and deep neural structuring to just change. We must learn new skills and design our lives intentionally. Every morning, I take time to invite the qualities I want to experience and live by. This practice has been profound in my relationships. Throughout the day when I start to find myself too activated or anxious, my intentions ground me and guide my decision making. I also call my parents at least a couple times a week to tell them I love them. Although it may sound robotic, this practice allows me to move with ease and stay aligned with my values and aspirations. Personally, self-forgiveness was

not accessible until I learned to experience my feelings with compassion. I had to
train my nervous system to allow and sit with uncomfortable feelings.

Within each of these narratives, one thing that becomes immediately clear is how emotionally activating this work can be. It is not easy to reflect on our childhood wounds, and it can be even more difficult to listen when our inner child attempts to communicate that which they have craved for so long. My dearest reader, should you decide to pursue your own journey and healing experiences with parts work, I offer the following guidance.

First, engage in journaling. Begin by writing down your thoughts, feelings, hesitations, and ultimate takeaways throughout this process.

Next, leverage a supportive community with whom you can discuss your experiences and lessons. This community may include supportive members from your family of origin, members of your chosen family, as well as your partner, friends, and allies. You may also find community from healing circles.

Inner child work can also include working through our community of voices. Within each of us is an internal dialogue that asserts, "*You are worthy of love and belonging*" or "*You will never be good enough.*" Some of the most profound work I have done with clients is helping them explore the origin of their community of voices. I invite them to reflect on what the voices say as well as the feelings or emotions that arise when the voices are heard. Next, we reflect on *how old* the corresponding feelings or emotions appear to be. Once we have uncovered the ages associated with each voice, we can explore from whom the message may have originated and the extent to which the message continues to serve us, or hold us back, in the present day.

Crab Mentality and Abundance Mindsets

Crab mentality refers to the attitudes and behaviors of individuals who attempt to undermine others whom they believe outperform them. Individuals with crab mentality believe they should be more successful than others, experience envy when others succeed, and hope others will fail.[2] Also referred to as "crab barrel syndrome," this metaphor originated after a fisherman observed how crabs placed in a bucket would keep one another from escaping by pulling each other down. Crab mentality is found within Asian American communities, particularly among the Filipino American diaspora, and occurs when group norms of respect, assistance, and support are believed to be violated.[3]

I spoke with Jay Carlon, a Filipino American contemporary artist and creative visionary from Los Angeles, who shared a powerful reflection about this mentality. According to Jay, colonial mentalities are the analogous buckets that hold

Filipino Americans hostage. However, crabs don't naturally exist in buckets; they are forced into them. Similarly, Filipinos don't naturally exist as a colonized community; oppressive mindsets were instilled into us after we were forced into over 300 years of colonization. Learning to let go of crab mentalities and the internalized scarcity mindsets that drive competition while embracing abundance mindsets can help us reclaim our indigenous values of harmony, gratitude, hospitality, and community.

Asian Americans and children of Asian immigrants can begin challenging the internalization of scarcity mindsets by cultivating worldviews characterized by abundance. Adapting abundance mindsets begins with a recognition that resources can be shared, and that one person's success is not indicative of someone else's failure. This perspective is grounded in community-based worldviews that move away from individualistic and capitalistic narratives that emphasize monetary success as the ultimate goal. Freeing ourselves from scarcity mindsets and limiting cultural scripts such as, *"If I don't take this opportunity I will fail, disappoint my parents, or be left behind"* also buffers burnout in educational and workplace settings by creating opportunities for self-nourishment and restoration. The first step to practicing radical hope and acceptance is knowing *there will always be another opportunity* and *there are more than enough opportunities for everyone to succeed.*

Embodying abundance mindsets also better positions us to advocate for what we need, want, and deserve in romantic relationships. It empowers us to silence that pesky inner critic that screams, *"Nobody else will love me"* and *"What if I can't find another partner?"* Practicing abundance mindsets is one way to honor our inherent value as people, partners, and lovers who do not settle for relationships characterized by abuse, neglect, unhealthy dynamics, and deep unhappiness. When we embody abundance mindsets, we remember that love is a verb and that *to love* represents a conscious action that is practiced with care. Within romantic relationships, embodying abundance mindsets is the key to removing the shackles of attachment wounds that imprison us in beliefs that we must prove our value and worth to partners or that if only we were good enough, smart enough, attractive enough, or successful enough, our partners would love us in the way we deserve. Instead, we allow ourselves to recognize that we are already good enough as we are.

Raising Our Critical Consciousness

We can only achieve abundance mentalities by thinking independently and critically challenging the dominant ethnocentric narrative, which places blame on individuals for their own marginalization.[4] One form of the ethnocentric narrative is the *myth of meritocracy*, a colorblind discourse that posits, *"If you just work hard and pull yourself up by your bootstraps, you will be successful."* The fact of the matter is, not everyone has boots, and not everyone has bootstraps. In reality, systemic forms of oppression persist in ways that limit access to opportunities among communities of color.

We can also overcome scarcity mindsets and raise our critical consciousness by reflecting on the *minority tax*, a societal expectation for minoritized persons to represent their communities, which uniquely impacts Asian Americans. For instance, we are often forced or expected to provide additional forms of emotional labor that are not shared by our white counterparts.[5] How many of us receive invitations to serve on diversity, equity, inclusion, and belonging committees without financial compensation? This is just one example of how the minority tax impacts Asian Americans in the workplace. Ultimately, the dominant ethnocentric narrative expects Asian Americans to work hard and provide emotional labor at the expense of caring for ourselves and can contribute to feelings of shame among Asian Americans and children of Asian immigrants who blame themselves when they struggle to ask for help, feel overwhelmed with responsibilities, and experience workplace burnout.

Raising our critical consciousness by cultivating self-reflection and cultural awareness allows us to externalize experiences of blame. When we begin to identify situations where we are unfairly disadvantaged or privileged and examine the social circumstances that perpetuate these inequities, we learn to stop blaming ourselves for our shortcomings and become emboldened to change the status quo. Let's explore a more modern-day example of how raising critical consciousness benefits our community.

The COVID-19 pandemic awoke many individuals to the realities of racial discrimination. I spoke with countless students, clients, friends, and colleagues who were surprised when news stories that highlighted instances of anti-Asian violence initially began to flash across their screens. The narratives I heard among the Asian American community varied. Whereas some attributed blame to the victims for being at the wrong place at the wrong time, others chalked up these acts of discrimination and violence to the media's tendency to overreport racially and politically charged stories that increased engagement. Others ignored these incidents altogether, believing instead that if they continued to keep their heads down and carry on as normal, their usual demeanor would keep them safe. For countless Asian Americans and children of Asian immigrants, the murder of George Floyd in 2020 led to a collective awakening and increase of racial solidarity. We realized that proximity to whiteness was not sufficient to protect us from racial discrimination and that we had more in common with Black lives than with white ones.[6]

I began to hear more and more Asian Americans and children of Asian immigrants describe symptoms of depression, anxiety, difficulty concentrating, and other somaticized experiences of stress. These individuals also believed that their internalized struggles were somehow their fault—that if only they were stronger and more resilient, or had greater faith in their higher power, their mental health and overall well-being would not be affected. These are some of the narratives that drove me to publish a series of research studies that illuminated how experiencing and witnessing instances of anti-Asian violence (including through the media) resulted in higher rates of depression and anxiety and lower levels of life satisfaction among Asian and Asian American communities.[7] I leveraged my identity as a culturally responsive researcher to raise awareness about the importance of broaching mental health topics among Asian American communities and to give our community members permission to externalize and release notions of self-blame for their struggles.

Unfortunately, experiencing racial discrimination as members of marginalized racial and ethnic communities is as American as apple pie. Understanding the long history of anti-Asian sentiments in America is one way that our community can raise critical consciousness and embody abundance mindsets characterized by feelings of joy, radical hope, and self- and community empowerment. We can do this by recognizing how government policies and media representation of our communities have echoed the yellow peril myth in ways that have enacted centuries of oppression. We can remind ourselves that sexual stereotypes toward Asian American bodies originated from colonial and imperial beliefs that positioned our sexuality as deviant, perverse, and needing to be conquered. Recognizing that we are not to blame for our experiences of oppression empowers us with the knowledge, awareness, and skills required to redirect our energy toward addressing forms of inequity, finding strength in our communities, cultivating resilience, and mitigating the effects of racial discrimination.[8] Ultimately, engaging in critical consciousness and demonstrating curiosity about how our limiting cultural scripts no longer serve us are important strategies for healing among Asian Americans and children of Asian immigrants.

Yub Kim shares how raising critical consciousness facilitated his own healing:

My most significant ah-ha moment came when I accepted that I did not have to prove myself to anyone. My culture and family legacy has helped me grow, and I am not any less than anybody born and raised in this country. I do not have to prove or explain my place in the foreign culture I navigate. This awareness allowed me to focus on my pleasure and enjoyment above all the other noises surrounding my existence. It also allowed me to be kinder and more generous to myself. It is freeing to know that I can be unapologetically me.

Healing Attachment Wounds and Achieving Secure Attachments

If you are reading this book and thinking, "Oh no, I have an insecure attachment style!" rest assured that you are not doomed to face intimate partner challenges forevermore. It seems that, on average, a total of 25 to 30 percent of individuals report changes in their attachment styles throughout their life.[9] Change is possible and within reach!

Think back to the importance of establishing a secure base. This concept was true for infant rhesus monkeys who overcame feelings of fear toward horrifying bear puppets, and it is true for us, too.

Moving toward secure attachments with our partners by healing our own attachment wounds can represent truly challenging yet deeply rewarding endeavors. Many of the thought leaders and community members with whom I spoke describe this difficult and powerful experience.

Dr. Cheung shares:

Healing from an attachment wound is a complex and difficult process, but one worth undergoing. I believe the first step is to understand that our Asian American individual identity is deeply intertwined with our family and cultural identities, for good or bad. Therefore, the healing work should be a two-pronged approach. On the individual side, one needs to work through any trauma and be clear about their own values. On the cultural and family side, one needs to develop an understanding and work on forgiveness, or at the very least, exoneration.

Kimmy Wu explains:

As a recovering disorganized-attached individual, I found new ways of feeling safe by learning to accept myself and allowing others to show me acceptance and love. Since I had no reference for what security looked like in the past, a crucial part of my healing included forming relationships with individuals who are securely attached. These individuals became models for what safety and security can look like and allowed me to experience it directly as an emotionally corrective experience. A conscious effort to allow safety and security, along with insecurity and the fear of rejection, to coexist in harmony has been key to my healing.

In addition to practicing vulnerability and opening ourselves up to both acceptance and the possibility of rejection, there are many strategies we can practice to help us move closer to secure adult relationships. A few examples include:

Increasing awareness of our bodies, feelings, and thoughts when we become
activated and seek closeness

Cultivating stronger communication skills

Engaging in reflective practices to explore the stories we may be creating
around benign events.

Not sure where to start? I've got you covered.

Increasing Self-Awareness

Understanding the thoughts, feelings, and bodily sensations that arise when we
feel like the connection to our romantic partner becomes threatened is a great
place to start when working toward secure attachments. When I work with
clients in counseling settings to strengthen aspects of their attachment, I find
that individuals struggle to connect with their bodies during times of high stress.
In other words, when our attachment system becomes threatened and we believe
our object of affection is going to abandon us, our mind–body connection is the
first thing that flies out the window.

The next time you feel that intense, visceral desire to text your partner multiple times to quell your anxiety or engage in other protest behaviors, try using
this playful intervention I developed.

Stop, Drop, and Roll

Remember when you were a kiddo and the firefighters visited your elemen-
tary school to provide fire safety education? You may have vague memories of
crawling around the classroom carpet, gingerly checking doorknobs for heat,
and practicing the stop, drop, and roll method if you happened to catch fire.

When our attachment system becomes activated, it can certainly *feel* like an
emergency. And in a sense, our brain is figuratively *on fire* because our amygdala
and other areas of the limbic system are lighting up like Christmas trees, giving
us all the indications that something is wrong and that we need to reconnect
with our attachment figure to satisfy our anxieties *right now.*

In these moments, I invite you to take a deep breath and *stop, drop, and roll.*

Stop the protest, distancing, or deactivation behavior before it occurs (or as
soon as you realize that it is happening). Recognize that the emergent and intense feeling you are experiencing (to pursue or to withdraw) is linked to your
activated attachment system.

Drop whatever tool, strategy, thought, or action you were about to use to quiet your activation system. Put down the phone. Step away from the keyboard. Stop packing your bag and planning your escape.

Roll around in your awareness. Roll your attention away from your thoughts and reconnect to your bodily experience. Notice what you notice as you mentally scan your body from the top of your head, down your neck, across your shoulders, and down your arms. Notice the sensations in your hands and in each of your fingers. Next, roll your awareness down your chest and back, across your hips, and down your legs. Finally, move your awareness to your feet and to each toe. Notice what you notice, without judgment about this experience. Did any parts of your body feel tense? Take a few moments to intentionally relax. Perhaps this means unclenching a fist, lowering your shoulders, relaxing the muscles in your face, rolling out your neck, or pulling your tongue off of the roof of your mouth and letting your jaw slacken. Close your eyes and slowly take a few deep breaths in through your nose and out from your mouth. Once you have reconnected with your body, roll your awareness toward your mind, emotions, and desires.

Begin to turn your attention inward and ask yourself the following questions:

What does it feel like to physically be present in my body right now? Perhaps you feel flushed, red, or hot.

Where in my body might I be feeling a sense of tension? To what extent may you notice your fists and/or jaw are clenched? Might there be tension in your neck, shoulders, or back? Roll your attention from head to toe as you scan your body for lingering areas of stress.

Moving from the body toward the mind, begin rolling your awareness toward your emotions.

What emotions feel most intense right now? Perhaps you notice feelings of fear, anger, resentment, or disappointment.

Finally, roll your awareness toward long-term goals. Ask yourself, *What do I want to do, and to what extent will that action bring me closer to the connection I actually desire?*

For avoidantly attached individuals, the desire to run, take flight, or create emotional and psychological distance may be your go-to safety strategy. Among anxiously attached individuals, the desire to engage in checking behaviors ("Are we okay? Are you mad at me? Are you sure you're not going to abandon me?") may be at an all-time high. Remember, these behaviors are coping strategies designed to keep us safe and quell our anxiety. Though these strategies alleviate fears in the short term, if left unchecked, they can stress and overwhelm partners in the long run.

Reframing Secure Love from Boring to Peaceful

Once you understand adult attachment styles, it becomes impossible to interpret the world without these perspectives. We begin to see movies, listen to music, and notice our own relationships in vastly different ways. You may even begin to notice that the film industry has a nasty little habit of romanticizing unhealthy relationship patterns and labeling them "passionate love." From an early age, we witness countless romantic relationships play out where one partner seeks and the other resists, runs, or is unavailable, only to be won over by persistence. This creates narratives in our mind that equate *passion and love* to *unpredictability and unhelpful patterns.*

Moving toward secure attachments is difficult when individuals have become accustomed to the dopamine hits that occur once attachment systems are deactivated. It's easy to become addicted to the high highs and the low lows that characterize more unstable and chaotic relationships while becoming bored with and uninterested in the predictability of emotionally mature and securely attached partners. Without models of secure relationships in childhood, we risk repeating unstable relationships into adulthood. For instance, we interpret those quintessential butterflies as evidence of perfect partnership. We believe true love must be difficult, all-consuming, and unpredictable to be passionate. In reality, the bodily sensations that society colloquially labels *butterflies* are actually representative of anxiety stemming from activated attachment systems. We are testing the waters with this new person and exploring whether a secure attachment forms. For insecurely attached individuals, the challenge isn't finding secure attachment; rather, it's resisting the urge to abandon it.

Love Makes Your Food Cold

What happens in the brain when we fall in love? Let's take a quick look into the science of love to understand how attachment systems play into our relationship patterns and, ultimately, our own healing.

When we see the faces of people we love, the emotional parts of our brain light up. Regions of our brain's reward system become flooded with oxytocin and vasopressin, both of which are linked to attachment and bonding. Our brain also releases a healthy dose of dopamine, which is responsible for the feelings of euphoria associated with early experiences of love and attraction. Interestingly, these dopamine increases trigger a serotonin decrease, a neuromodulator that is linked to appetite and mood.[10] When you combine higher levels of oxytocin, vasopressin, and dopamine with lower levels of serotonin, you are left with the formula for blissful moments and couples who are unshakably captivated by one another. Under this neurobiological spell and with our person, time seems to slip through our fingers. Entrees remain inexplicably untouched, candles have all but burned out, and your entire awareness has been entranced by the conversation. Before you know it, you're the last couple in the restaurant. In the best way possible, love makes your food cold.

These moments of euphoria and excitement can trigger our attachment system. Our brains plead, *More dopamine, please!* and we do everything we can to sustain these exhilarating moments of bliss. When the objects of our affection are reliable, safe, and emotionally available, we develop secure attachments. Conversely, when the person we desire does not satisfy our security-seeking behaviors, does not provide reassurance, or is not accessible, reliable, and emotionally available, our attachment system becomes activated. Consequently, we find ourselves engaging in unhealthy relationship patterns that maintain insecure attachment styles.

Take a moment to reflect on the early moments of dating. Someone has caught your interest and you have already begun exchanging those first tentative messages back and forth. Although you have only just met, your mind races with possibilities for the future and your focus on this new person is all-consuming. You wake up energized and hope they will respond to messages quickly, meeting your eagerness with their own enthusiasm. Your ears fill with the "ding!" of a new notification and your heart begins to race. Seeing their name in your phone elicits euphoria as another small hit of dopamine tickles your brain. Each time your love interest reciprocates your energy, your activated attachment system is satisfied. All is good in the world again, and you continue moving through your day as normal.

Now imagine how it feels when your correspondences are left unanswered. After sending multiple messages back and forth, you decide it's time to extend a little vulnerability. You take a deep breath and carefully type out a new message. You rally the courage and ask to spend a little time together. You read, then re-read, your message, careful to pick words that convey eagerness rather than desperation. You hit *send* and watch your words evolve from a temporary message to a permanent chat bubble. Minutes go by and you are left with radio silence. Those three little dots do not immediately give way to a response. Hours go by and your phone remains silent.

"Ding!" Your ears fill with the melodious sound of your phone's notification. You grab for your phone and glance at the screen.

Jeans are now on sale at Express!

It's an email.

You are filled with disappointment and your mind becomes crowded with thoughts from your community of voices. *You are unlovable. You asked for too much too soon. You are not good enough. Something is wrong with you.*

"Ding!" Another notification. Warily, you reach for your phone. This time, the object of your affection responds. They apologize for the late response and explain that they were caught up in an unexpected meeting. They meet your vulnerability with their own and enthusiastically agree to a date. Relief washes over your body, and the inner critics that populate your community of voices fall silent once more. Your attachment system is satisfied, and you can once again return to your day. When our attachment systems are satisfied over time, we learn our partner is trustworthy and we can count on them to reliably soothe us. Eventually, our attachment system becomes less sensitive, and we experience calm and predictable states. We achieve secure attachment.

Moving away from insecure attachment styles and developing a secure attachment for the first time is tricky. When we are accustomed to the cycles of activation and satisfaction that characterize insecure attachment styles, achieving secure attachment can easily be misinterpreted as *a boring relationship* or *falling out of love*. In reality, we have simply graduated into a more secure and predictable form of love called *companionate love*. Secure love is steady. It is predictable, reliable, and therefore safe. We know when we have achieved secure attachment because our attachment system does not activate like it used to. We know what to expect in our partner and we trust that they are reliable and safe and will honor our emotions. If we want to maintain secure attachments with our partners, we must do the difficult work required to recognize the patterns that remain in our attachment systems and intentionally challenge unhelpful beliefs about how relationships are *supposed* to feel.

Angelika Holleran shares:

Throughout my healing, I have come back to how attachment impacts the relationship with my partner. In my current relationship, my partner is securely attached while I oscillate between secure and anxious-avoidant attachment. There are times I feel that the security my relationship provides is boring, which activates my nervous attachment system. Through my own therapy, and from my work as a therapist, I have learned that the "boringness" represents unfamiliarity to me. I know that some of my needs as a child were not met because my mom was focused on working and creating a better life for me. As a child I did not know this, so feelings of intimacy became associated with feeling unloved which resulted in conditioned independent behavior. In my relationship, this has looked like feeling preoccupied with my partner's ability to reciprocate my love. If he is not successful right away, I would distance myself out of self-preservation.

The more we practice new skills, the stronger our neural pathways become, making us more likely to use them in the future. So, the next time it feels like you are on fire, *stop, drop, and roll.*

Cultivating Stronger Communication Skills

Learning to communicate with your partner in healthy and constructive ways is another powerful tool that can be used to help us move closer toward secure attachments. Asking for what we need, want, and desire is critical to cultivating the safety we need to build healthy and trusting connections.

Tarm shares a beautiful example of how she and her partner have achieved secure attachment by creating spaces for vulnerable and challenging conversations:

Despite historically having an anxious-avoidant attachment style, I am happy to say that I've been able to heal and develop a more secure and healthy attachment in my current partnership. I believe a big contributor to addressing my insecurities and moving toward a mutually healthier relationship was having honest discussions about judgments and being judgmental on both of our ends. Since then, we've been able to unpack how our family upbringing, culture, and experiences impact the way we think about things and the impact of our behaviors.

Ready to practice cultivating stronger communication skills with your partner? Consider taking some of these prompts for a test drive:

I feel safe and connected in our relationship when you _____.
I feel most seen and loved when you _____.
I feel most appreciated when you _____.
I know you are reliable and that I can count on you because _____.

Understanding the Stories We Create

People have an uncanny ability to create meaning out of ambiguity. Though this skill likely developed as a survival mechanism from times where we lived in caves and needed to recognize the threat of saber-toothed tigers, modern relationships tend to benefit from more direct and respectful forms of communication.

In my work as a mental health professional, I have witnessed how individuals with insecure attachment styles struggle to come up with alternative stories when attachment wounds are triggered. When these instances occur, we can fill in the blanks with stories like, "My partner must have found someone more attractive," "They are getting ready to leave me," or "I should have known better than to trust people." One of the most helpful ways to move toward secure attachments is to understand the stories we create and, when they are not working for us, create a new story.

Curious about how this may look? Consider the following vignette.

Carrie is anxiously attached to her partner Jack, who is completing his residency at the hospital. Though Carrie understands that Jack is often busy throughout the workday, she becomes activated when he doesn't respond to her text right away. Upon engaging in self-reflection (and, perhaps, the stop, drop, and roll method), Carrie may notice that she feels flushed in her face and is holding tension in her neck and shoulders. She may identify feelings of anxiety, fear, and concerns of abandonment. She may be able to recognize that her initial thought, "Jack must no longer be interested in me, and he's going to break up with me," is not helpful. She may understand that this story is being created by the fearful part of her brain that hyper-focuses on abandonment.

Most importantly, when she speaks with Jack next, Carrie can communicate her experience with him directly. For example, she may say, "When you didn't respond to my text earlier today, the story I created was that you had lost interest in me and that you were going to end our relationship. To what extent is that story accurate?"

Communicating her fears in a vulnerable, honest, and open way provides her partner with an opportunity to do a few things. First, he can respond honestly to her question, hopefully putting her mind at ease and explaining that it was a busy day at work. Bringing her fears and her story to her partner directly, rather than falling into a trap of perpetuating anxious thoughts, helps to break the feedback loop.

Though this skill is a particularly difficult one to sharpen, it ultimately has the potential to bring partners closer in meaningful and more securely attached ways. A few examples of how you might use this with your partner today:

When _____ happened, the story I created was _____. To what extent might this be true?

I worry about _____ when _____ occurs. What I need in this moment to feel connected is _____ (insert specific behavior request from your partner).

Dr. Sue Johnson, author of *Hold Me Tight: Conversations for Connection*,[11] offers another set of reflections that can determine whether our partner offers a secure base:

Are they there for me?
Can I count on them?

Do they have my back?

Do my feelings matter?

Are they accessible, responsive, and engaged?

When we find ourselves creating narratives fueled by rejection, distress, and abandonment, reflecting on these prompts can help ground an activated attachment system and remind ourselves that there may be a less threatening narrative to consider.

Wait! What If I'm the Secure One?

If you are the secure partner in your relationship, research has identified specific conditions that enable our partners to become their most whole, abundant selves:[12]

1. *Demonstrate emotional availability.* When partners are distressed, give them permission to be vulnerable. Check in on them and provide comfort when things don't go as planned.
2. *Promote autonomy.* Be encouraging of your partner "behind the scenes" by empowering them with the ability to do their own thing while resisting the urge to micromanage, take over the situation, or tell them what is best.
3. *Be encouraging.* Accept your partner for wherever they are in their journey and provide encouragement in ways that boost their self-esteem.

Ultimately, secure partners who are available, sensitive, and responsive to their partners' needs for proximity, safety, and reassurance provide the nurturing base necessary to help them regulate sensitive attachment systems. Over time, individuals with insecure attachment styles become more confident in self-regulation strategies, trust that partners will be reliably responsive, and become more effective at dealing with stress.[13] These interactions reinforce the belief that the world is safe, they are safe, and their partner is safe.

Therapy/Counseling

The importance of engaging in therapy and/or relationship counseling with a licensed mental health professional may also be an important part of our healing journey.

Sharon describes:

Therapy has really helped me uncover the root origin of my behaviors and understand the mechanisms of why I think or act in the way that I do. It has helped me address these things while providing guidance in how to change my behavior, create space, and pause when I initially feel emotionally defensive. I could only go so far on my own to do things differently and to not repeat those same patterns of behavior I experienced from my parents.

Jennifer Alexander* shares:

I cannot expect to get the healing I need from my adoptive parents. To heal from my trauma and attachment wounds, I have gone to therapy and learned to do the work so I can show up for myself in ways no one did for me when I was younger. I am working to love all the parts of myself.

Dr. Band shares:

We can begin to heal by engaging in therapeutic work. That may not look like formal counseling to some, it may be finding a sense of belonging in a chosen community. It is finding a way to express yourself rather than keeping it inside.

Taking these risks and moving toward secure attachments can bring us even closer to the healing orientation described in Chapter 8. Ultimately, when we accept unconditional love from our partner, we can learn to apply the same acceptance to ourselves, without conditions.

To that end, don't be afraid to lean into a deeper exploration of self by reaching out to a licensed mental health professional. Though I wrote this book with the intention that it will serve as a healing guide, it is by no means intended to be a substitute for mental health counseling. In the Resources section at the end of this book, you will find a list of resources that can help you connect with a licensed mental health professional in your area, should you choose to do so.

TLDR: Give yourself a high five: You made it through the heavy chapter on pattern-breaking strategies! In this chapter, we explored narratives that illuminate the value of parts work. Next, we reviewed specific ways to let go of scarcity mentalities and embody abundance mindsets that allow us to cultivate critical consciousness and let go of self-blame when mental health distress occurs. We also explored specific strategies that can help us move closer toward secure attachments. These include increasing self-awareness, my "stop, drop, and roll" method, cultivating stronger communication skills, and understanding the stories we create. If you have been reading this book and wondered, "Wait a minute! What if I'm the secure partner?" I also reviewed a few ways to help support your partner on their healing journey. The chapter ends with an invitation to explore these topics deeper with a licensed mental health professional.

Questions to Ponder

1. What do I need to begin pursuing parts work?
2. How might I begin to let go of scarcity mindsets and embody abundance mentalities?
3. What are some ways I can begin increasing self-awareness to promote my healing?
4. How can I begin implementing stronger communication skills in my relationships?
5. What might be some examples of stories I create when my attachment system becomes activated?

Questions to Bridge the Gap with Parents

1. What parts or qualities of yourself would you like to prioritize more? Which values are most important to you, and why?
2. When do you feel most connected to others? With whom would you like to connect more deeply?
3. When was the last time you felt like a child? What was happening and how did you feel?

10

On Parenting and Healing Diasporic Wounds

I open my eyes to the darkness of our bedroom. As I reach over to my partner's side of the bed, I am greeted by the warmth he has left under the covers. I listen for the sound of footsteps tiptoeing around our home but am only met with silence.

My partner has already left for work, and it is around 6:30 in the morning.

A gentle *coo* fills my ears and I roll onto my side to steal a peek at my youngest son. At only three months old, he is already over 19 lbs. He is *super tabachoy* (Tagalog for chubby).

I take a few moments to appreciate his plump little body and count the rolls on each arm like I always do.

One, two three, four.

He has more rolls than a bakery and he smells just as delicious.

His head is still heavy with sleep, so he turns it to the left, instinctively seeking shelter from the light that streams gently in through the window. His tiny chest rises and falls with a deep sigh that tells me he has drifted back to sleep.

I move silently out of the bedroom and into the kitchen. Reaching into our cabinet, I pull out the Starbucks mug we bought home from our trip to the Philippines last year. As I fill the mug with coffee, I admire the red and yellow designs that capture creative depictions of everything from the Rizal monument to a horse-drawn *kalesa* carriage.

My partner always leaves me a fresh pot of coffee. It is one of the many silent ways he communicates care by anticipating my needs without expecting anything in return. As I bring the mug to my lips and take that first warm sip, I close my eyes and relish this small part of the morning. The house is quiet except for the delicate *tick tick tick* of the kitchen clock.

Seconds later, the sound of our baby monitor jolts me back into the present moment. My two-year-old is awake and ready to start the day. I carefully place my mug onto the counter and the sound of ceramic on granite echoes through the kitchen.

As I make my way upstairs and open the nursery door, my nose fills with the comforting scents of diapers, baby detergent, and lavender. My son's room is always so warm and cozy. I never want to forget the way this room smells.

I approach the crib and find my son, already sitting up, plush blue blanket in hand. His big brown eyes focus on mine through the dimly lit room and I watch his face fall in disappointment.

Bye, mama. Daddy, please!

For as long as I can remember, my son has preferred my husband. Over the last few months, their attachment has only grown stronger as my son begins to grasp at every opportunity for independence. His small voice pulls at my heart, threatening to shatter it into a million pieces.

I reach out to my son, my baby boy, my first-born.

Good morning, anak! Would you like to come downstairs?

He stands up, throwing his blanket onto the crib mattress with all the force his small body can muster.

BYE, mama! Daddy PLEASE!

My heart has dropped into the pit of my stomach and I fight back a lump that has lodged itself deep in my throat.

Anak, Daddy is at work. He will be home soon, and you will be together again. Let's go downstairs and make breakfast.

I extend my arms out and pick him up, struggling to hold him steady as his entire body thrashes in protest.

Daddy, PLEASE!

Tears begin to stream down his face, tracing the lines around his cheeks.

He is adamant and I am heartbroken.

Breaking Inherited Patterns as Parents

In the spirit of transparency, these are the moments when my own attachment wounds become activated as a parent. Although I logically know that I can't take moments like this personally, my emotional brain worries that I have already failed somehow as a mother.

The historical trauma and toxic cultural scripts assert:

Don't burden others with your emotional pain. Be strong and don't talk about your problems. Keep your head down and don't ask for help.

The scarcity mindset voice whispers:

Keep working hard so you can give your children a life filled with cherished memories. Money is the key to keeping your family safe and happy.

The insecure attachment voice coerces:

You have not been as accessible, reliable, and engaged as you could have been. Your son's preference for your husband has occurred because you are not good enough.

I have come to learn that my community of voices are predominantly protective. They developed throughout my childhood and have historically kept me safe by minimizing the painful emotional consequences of abandonment, fear, and rejection. Though they may have served me at one time, I recognize that these cultural scripts are no longer helpful and must be reframed. And perhaps most importantly, I can choose to let them go. Throughout my own healing process, I have intentionally leveraged countless opportunities to repair attachment wounds. I am learning to re-parent myself as I parent my children, and my sons have become my greatest teachers. I embrace each opportunity to reframe the very same cultural scripts that have been passed down in my own family of origin for generations.

I have learned that every little *no* is fueled by autonomy instead of rejection. *We don't talk about our feelings in this family* becomes *Identify and understand the emotions that arise.*

I have recognized that splashing in muddy puddles, pouring out bubble solution, stopping to blow dandelion seeds, and following ants along the sidewalk bring just as much joy as opening gifts on Christmas morning (*Be grateful for opportunities in educational and occupational settings* becomes *Be grateful for opportunities to share special moments with your children*).

I have given myself permission to take up space with little ones who want to make their presence known in the world (*Don't rock the boat or stand out* becomes *Embody all the parts of who you are and exist in a way that is unapologetically authentic*).

I have learned that publications and awards won't keep me warm at night and the drive of productivity will never outweigh the blissful heaviness of a sleeping baby (*Work hard at the expense of my own well-being* becomes *Work hard while balancing what matters*).

I have filled our home and our community with books, toys, and people who represent the beauty of multiculturalism (*Don't become too American* becomes *Being American is an ever-evolving construct*).

The Importance of Awareness

Our scarcity mindset, intergenerational patterns, and internalized cultural scripts have the potential to impact our parenting habits and behaviors. For better or for worse, many of us want so badly to gift our children with the opportunities, experiences, and joys we never had. We work hard with our little ones in mind, hoping they will thrive. We prioritize their happiness because we want to build joyful, comfortable, and loving homes. Because hard work has served us, we hope to instill this same value into our children. However, if we aren't careful, the community of voices we carry can find their way into our parenting patterns.

Promoting awareness is the ultimate first step to healing. We cannot break historical patterns if we don't notice or anticipate them first. Noah* describes how he recognized inherited patterns in his parenting:

> *When I ask my children to do something, I expect them to do it now. It was the same way for me when I was young. I was expected to do it now, and there was no back talk. It was just do it, do it, get it done. Work now, work now, and work hard. Do it the best you can, don't half ass it. So, I try to build that value with my kids. I teach them to pick up after themselves, the basic foundations of hard work, how to take care of themselves, and to have pride in their home. I've always tried hard. I'm always working. I need to sit down and actually enjoy life sometimes.*

Noah* has identified the importance of cultivating awareness in the process of breaking unhelpful parenting patterns—and so can you. A few of these strategies are engaging in mindfulness, reflecting on our own experiences, and incorporating a healing orientation with our children.

Practicing Mindfulness

Parenting is a daily practice in mindfulness. Mindfulness entails the process of noticing—noticing where you are and bringing to mind the thoughts and feelings that arise moment by moment, without judgment. Incorporating mindfulness practices into our role as parents is a helpful way to ensure we are accepting our children wholeheartedly, without conditions. Shoua Lee shares the benefits of engaging in mindfulness and meditation to break parenting patterns:

> *My path to healing started when I was pregnant with my first-born daughter. Recognizing my responsibility as a mother, I started to search for ways I could welcome my daughter into an environment filled with peace and love. This intention led me to practice meditation. Meditation built up my capacity to become aware through breathing and grounding techniques. These skills allowed me to pendulate in and out of my traumatic memories, integrate them, and begin recognizing new pathways for existing. In essence, the practice of meditation trained my nervous system how to modulate stressful events and helped me access the creative parts of myself.*

As evidenced by this passage, awareness is a fundamental component to breaking the patterns that remain as parents. Once we become aware of how historical patterns might impact the relationships we have with our children as well as the extent to which patterns are generationally repeated, we can begin the intentional process of healing.

Ready to begin increasing awareness to your own patterns? Try reflecting on the following prompts:

> *How did my parents and caregivers discipline me as a child? Which strategies did they use, and which emotions did they elicit? To what extent do I discipline my child in similar or different ways?*
>
> *Which parenting strategies did I learn, accept, or inherit from my parents and caregivers? Which of these parenting strategies might be useful and which ones can I choose to let go?*
>
> *How did my parents or caregivers communicate anger, fear, or disappointment? How might their actions have impacted me, both as a child and as an adult?*
>
> *To what extent did I feel safe when my parents or caregivers felt angry, afraid, or disappointed?*
>
> *When I feel anger, fear, or disappointment with my child(ren), how do I typically respond? To what extent might my child(ren) feel safe when I feel angry, afraid, or disappointed?*

Reflecting on these brief prompts can elicit complex emotions, thoughts, and experiences. Take your time as you move through this process with care. Leverage support as needed from your partner, friends, family of origin, and community. Try journaling about these prompts, allowing yourself to write without expectations and judgment. Understanding the origin of our parenting patterns is a powerful first step in cultivating awareness about the extent to which they are harmful or helpful.

As new objects of awareness enter your consciousness, consider deepening your relationships by incorporating the Healing Orientation Model Elements (HOME). I believe breaking the patterns that remain as parents means achieving an orientation with our children that is characterized by full and wholehearted acceptance, without condition. Providing the secure base of this healing orientation allows our children to feel, think, act, and behave in all the ways necessary for them to explore, accept, and embody all the parts of who they are, and who they aspire to be.

We apply the HOME as parents when we:

1. Understand our children.
2. Anticipate their needs.

3. Demonstrate intentionality.
4. Avoid transactional acts.
5. Promote freedom and healing.

Understand Our Children

Who are our children, at their very core? How would you describe their temperament, motivation, desires, and drives? How do they seek connection when faced with distress, and how do they embody feelings such as fear, joy, pain, and peace? What makes them feel most connected, appreciated, and seen? To wholeheartedly accept our children, without conditions, we must first understand them.

Noelle* shares the importance of seeing, accepting, and celebrating our children as unique individuals, all of whom are deserving of dignity, worth, and belonging:

> It's important to me to spend time differently with each of my children because they are unique and need different things. For instance, my daughter values when I help her with schoolwork and my son loves to do more social things. He just got this new Game Boy and all he wants is to sit with me and play the video games I played when I was younger. When he was little, he used to say, "Mommy, my biggest dream is to wake up in the middle of the night and watch a movie." So, we did that. One night I woke him up and said, "It's after midnight, let's watch a movie!" To this day, that's one of his favorite memories. I also have special things with my youngest, like this song that we sing all the time. It's just her song I made for her. I try to do those things because each of my children are different. I know it was hard for my parents to do special things with me when I was growing up because they were working two and three jobs, second and third shift. They weren't able to give me the things I needed when I was little to not feel scared.

Anticipate Their Needs

How can we acknowledge who our children are and better anticipate their needs? What can we do, on a daily, weekly, monthly, and event-specific basis, to set them up for success? How can we proactively let go of historical patterns by anticipating the needs of our children? I.B.* describes her process:

> Since we are trying to have a kid, we think to ourselves about what would set a good example for our future children. We have seen the effects of what our parents did or did not do and how that impacted us. We want to build off their example

and be good examples to our children. It's about catching ourselves and asking ourselves why we are doing something. Is there love and understanding behind our actions or are we doing something as parents out of habit? I think awareness, being able to admit if something was not right, and correcting it are important skills for parents. We need to be able to communicate, apologize, and address issues when they arise with our children.

Demonstrate Intentionality

How can we connect with our children in the ways that matter most to them on a daily, weekly, monthly, and event-specific basis? Shoua Lee shares a wonderful example of how we can intentionally connect with our children through small daily acts:

I have made it a conscious effort to always turn towards my children when they walk into the room and connect with their gaze no matter how busy I am. Whenever I have a meeting at home, I make it a point to tell my audience that they may come in and when they do, I will need a few moments. Of all the things I want in this world, what I want most is to be remembered by my children as a mother who showed them how to make mistakes, how to love themselves, and who always puts them first.

Sharon K. also describes how she intentionally communicates love and demonstrates affection with her children:

My brother and I talk about how we have both intentionally worked on becoming good communicators and becoming openly affectionate and demonstrative with our kids. We make it a point to tell them how much they are loved because our parents did not do those things for us when we were younger.

Avoid Transactional Acts

Believe it or not, it is possible to make sacrifices for our children without reminding them on a regular basis! How can we give to our children without expecting anything in return? First, practice noticing and challenging the emotions that arise when we think children *should* respond in some way. As a mental health clinician, I remind individuals that *should* is practically a four-letter word. Using inflexible terms such as *should*, *must*, and *have to* creates opportunities for resentment because it indicates that something we desire is already not occurring. Instead, we must notice and challenge the "should" statements that lead to resentments and use more flexible language.

A significant part of my own journey to break generational parenting patterns has been learning to accept change and investing in my children's well-being without expectations for reciprocity. I accept that holding space for tantrums, navigating sleepless nights, and turning toward my children to share in moments of excitement are *investments I make* rather than *deposits for withdrawal*. I recognize that starting a family does not make me patient; it simply gives me opportunities to be patient. I give of myself out of love and expect nothing in return.

Finding humor in parenting has also been invaluable to my process. For instance, I accept that having a toddler means I will save his life multiple times a day and the way he will thank me is by eating my snacks. I accept that I used to eat at Michelin-starred restaurants and now I eat whatever falls out of my toddler's mouth. Having children really is a game changer.

When we give to our children from a place of genuine love and care, we are role modeling what it means to receive and accept love. We teach our children they do not have to become somebody who is loveable; they already are somebody worthy of love and belonging. The pattern of bartering acts of service as transactional love tokens ends with us.

Promote Freedom and Healing

When these elements combine over time, we allow our children to experience a greater sense of freedom. This freedom allows them to explore and ultimately construct the people they wish to be in this world. We become the secure base we wished we had as children and, in doing so, we provide experiences of security and healing for our wounded inner child. Ultimately, breaking these patterns as parents helps us move toward wholeness and abundance.

Dr. Valli describes how this healing process looks over time:

> *Transgenerational trauma is not broken overnight. We don't suddenly become a healthy family who can openly talk about intimate partner violence, substance use, infidelity, and other secrets. It involves taking steps whose effects we may never see in our lifetime and trusting that future generations may benefit. When my father ran away from home as a teenager to earn money and support his family, he never thought he would have kids and they would become a college professor and a leading policy researcher on social justice. But he took one step. Which led to another. And another. The pressure to perform our healing in ways that meet the standards of the Western white gaze is itself another indicator of our*

trauma. Our healing is solely ours to claim and name. And we can heal in only one way—our own way.

Embracing Our Mistakes and Ourselves

The commitment to breaking the patterns that remain, as parents and people, represents an evolving process. Some days we may fall back on old habits—and when this happens, I hope you extend a little grace and self-compassion. We are all doing the best we can with what we have, and many of these patterns are carried deep in our bones. They represent longstanding worldviews, practices, and even cultural traditions that have historically served our community well and kept them safe in times of duress. We must therefore learn to hold both dualities simultaneously:

1. These cultural scripts and patterns have historically served a purpose and worked well for our parents, ancestors, and community.
2. Holding onto these cultural scripts and patterns prevents us from achieving secure relationships, greater mental health and well-being, and lives full of abundance.

Mindfulness is a practice I continue to cultivate today. When I am working, I often wish I was with my little ones. When I am with my little ones, I often worry that I should be working. Remembering to shift my focus back into the present has been monumental in my ability to gain the most out of where I am, moment by moment.

How many of us are truly present in these fleeting moments with our kids? In today's fast-paced, capitalistic, and individualistic society, it can be all too easy to become distracted by emails, phone calls, and texts when we could be connecting in meaningful ways with our family. Though I still make mistakes, I am learning to embrace where I am and what I am doing, without judgment. Many storytellers with whom I spoke similarly shared the importance of recognizing mistakes when they arise and committing to doing better next time.

Kareena* shares:

For a long time, I was very nervous about becoming a parent because I didn't want to give my child the type of childhood that I had. When it comes to parenthood, I try to remember that I have a lot of power—I have the power to change things for the next generation and the power to break cycles that came before me. Rather than repeat the same abuse, I have vowed to never, ever go down that route. And it's hard! It is really, really damn hard to choose a different path than the one forged before me, to lean on friends and chosen family to be my compass. It is some of the hardest mental work I've ever done—and there's no scale or thermometer or gauge to clearly see if I'm making any progress. All I can do is set my intention for who I want to be and keep moving toward it. I know I'm going to mess up and I know I'm not perfect. In those moments, I've learned to apologize and to have compassion for myself and this terrifying but gorgeous journey. I try to be the mother I wish I had—one who pays attention, who shows up with patience, who laughs and isn't afraid to be silly, who is available for hugs and loves out loud. There are some days when I actually feel a tinge of jealousy toward the childhood my daughter has, and perhaps that's a sign I'm doing something right.

Dr. Valli describes the realization she feels in her process of motherhood, in a way that I believe will resonate with countless readers and parents:

As a new parent, I know that these values will absolutely leak into my parenting. I know that my son may inadvertently pick up on my patterns. I know that I may have to hear his accusations of not being his fantasy mom—the same accusations I threw at my mom. This is especially true as he grows up as a second-generation Indian American who will face even more pressing and gut-wrenching challenges regarding his racial identity.

We can only break patterns that are objects of our awareness, and new challenges will undoubtedly arise as we grow and become acquainted with deeper parts of ourselves.

Healing Diasporic Wounds

Our complex relationships with our parents and the diasporic wounds we carry are often at the forefront of our healing. As outlined in our earlier chapter on childhood attachment wounds, it's easy for Asian Americans, especially children of Asian immigrants, to struggle with conflicting emotions simultaneously.

We may feel a sense of gratitude for the sacrifice and hard work of our parents while also struggling with feelings of anger, resentment, and disappointment for their shortcomings.

We may express a deep love and compassion for our caregivers while also feeling deeply invalidated, hurt, and rejected.

We may describe feelings of appreciation for our parents' abilities to care for our physical needs while also carrying a deep sense of pain for the emotional and psychological support that was always just out of reach.

Sound familiar?

Cultivating stronger relationships with our parents and healing diasporic wounds can represent a nuanced, emotional, painful, yet ultimately liberating process. Letting go of resentments, learning to forgive without receiving apologies, and understanding the power of perspective are all strategies that transition *hard work* into *heart work*.

Carmel shares the importance of addressing cultural scripts:

It's hard to break these toxic cultural values that have been passed down for years. When we try to talk about them with our elders, we're often gaslit into thinking that we're the problem. But with the courage to continue spreading awareness about them, we're already on the right path to shaping the future generations.

Cathy Park Hong, author of *Minor Feelings*, writes:

For many immigrants, if you move here with trauma, you're going to do what it takes to get by. You cheat. You beat your wife. You gamble. You're a survivor and, like most survivors, you are a god-awful parent.[1]

When it comes to being Asian American and perhaps a child of Asian immigrants in the United States, I've got some bad news and some good news.

The bad news is that we cannot control the extent to which historical trauma, intergenerational patterns, and limiting cultural scripts have been passed down to us. We cannot control the internalized cultural scripts that our wounded inner child has come to believe. We cannot force our parents and caregivers to love us, support us, and show up for us in the ways that we so badly wish they could.

The good news is that we can unlearn the patterns that remain and heal from a lifetime of anger, sadness, resentment, disappointment, and pain. We can identify which cultural scripts serve us and which ones create barriers in our ability to unlock greater psychological well-being and abundance mentalities. And, we can learn strategies to avoid passing unhelpful cultural patterns onto our own children. In this next section, we explore specific and culturally responsive strategies for unlearning internalized scripts and "leveling up" as parents and people. If you've ever played Super Mario Brothers, this next part is full of metaphorical mushrooms to help you grow.

Radically Accepting Our Parents and Ourselves

Grounded in dialectical behavior therapy (DBT), the concept of radical acceptance refers to the process of accepting unchangeable emotions, thoughts, and circumstances.[2] Accepting our parents as they are, rather than as the people we *wish* they could be, represents some of the most challenging, freeing, and deeply healing work in which we can engage. Just as we wish our parents would wholeheartedly accept us as we are, so too do they wish the same from us.

Many of the individuals with whom I spoke described how engaging in radical acceptance represents a complex process that evokes a myriad of emotions. Once we accept our parents as the beautifully flawed people they are, we give ourselves permission to heal our own beautifully flawed selves.

Dr. Valli shares:

My mom has always managed to pull so many powerful emotions for me. I wanted her to be someone very specific: more friendly, relaxed, more "modern," and approving of my personality. She has resisted this fantasy at every opportunity. After almost a decade in the U.S., and away from my parents' home, I got another opportunity to reconnect with my mom. She stayed with me for six months—my third trimester and my fourth. I think very few birthing people get this kind of support. She took over the entire kitchen responsibilities, made specific foods that are healing for postpartum, bathed my son, played with him, and bought him more clothes than he could ever wear! I will always say that she birthed me twice—once on my day of birth, and again when my son was born.

Sharon K. states:

Learning how to radically accept my parents for who they are and letting go of the expectations or wishes of the kind of parent I want them to be has been challenging but helpful. Understanding and accepting that my parents are not able to provide me the kind of relationship and love that I need, and understanding this without attaching judgment, has been both difficult and healing. Acknowledging that I didn't get the kind of love I needed and that even though my parents did the best they could it wasn't enough for me was a hard truth to acknowledge.

Christopher Vo admits:

Even now, I feel that the desire for reconciliation with our parents is somehow hard-wired into our DNA. No matter what I do and no matter how much I accomplish, I find it difficult to shake the ghosts of the past—my ancestors telling me I'm not enough. It took decades for me to find greater security in my own identity, to honor my accomplishments, and shut out the imposter syndrome whispering in my ear. It took me recognizing that validation from my family would never come and that I can be my own mirror to truly thrive.

The hard truth about forgiveness and healing is this: *Our parents cannot heal our childhood wounds. They do not have that power.* Instead, that healing power lies within us. Ultimately, we begin accessing our own healing by radically accepting our parents for who they are and opening ourselves up for corrective emotional experiences. Doing so requires leveraging each of the skills we have explored throughout this book.

Healing from historical trauma narratives and unhelpful cultural scripts requires awareness, understanding, and reflection. We must be aware of their origin, their history, and how they have been passed down generationally. We must understand the purposes they have served both culturally and historically. Finally, we must reflect on the extent to which these patterns serve us or harm us.

Healing from childhood attachment wounds requires intentional movement toward secure relationship patterns. One way we can do this is by going HOME to our partners. We must accept their love and kindness in open-hearted and vulnerable ways. In doing so, we learn to fully love and accept ourselves just as our partners wholeheartedly love and accept us.

Breaking the patterns that remain as parents requires the wholehearted acceptance of our children, without conditions. We can also go HOME to our children by understanding who they are at their core, anticipating their needs, demonstrating intentionality, and avoiding transactional acts to promote freedom and healing.

Understanding Our Parents as a Framework for Healing

An important component of breaking historical patterns as parents requires us to understand our own parents' and ancestors' histories, experiences, and traumas. Ending the conspiracy of silence among our families is a powerful way to begin healing diasporic wounds. This process may include uncovering who our parents are as well as learning about the challenges they faced in childhood. Lisa Factora-Borchers shares:

Healing diasporic wounds takes a lifetime. What I've come to accept is that healing deepens as I deepen. The more that I live, the more profound the work and the more profound the healing can be. It's cyclic. It's nonlinear. Incorporating my parents' wounds into mine was a game changer. I had to learn that being in a close relationship with my parents does not mean that I have to become them. I had to learn that the narrative of who our parents are has to evolve in order to integrate their healing into ours. I had to learn how to see them fully and understand what they had gone through before I could recognize the connective tissue to mine. I have been able to love my parents more authentically as I learned to love myself more authentically. That acceptance came from understanding how traumas and memories influenced how they raised me.

Matthew* describes how self-awareness and reflection can help expand our worldviews and perspectives about our parents' choice:

Taking ethnic studies classes and understanding the sociopolitical dynamics that produced migration patterns have been helpful in my own healing process. We need to contextualize these factors and understand that our parents were oper-ating within a set of systems that produced a limited amount of choices and life chances for them. And so of course they made those choices, and those choices were harmful for you. Knowing that and being able to explain it in terms that extend beyond basic narratives helped me challenge beliefs like, 'Well, they didn't love me enough" or "They didn't want me enough." All of those things helped me to heal and think differently about what it means to have a secure attach-ment to people who love me and whom I love. I think continuing to have ongoing conversations with my parents as an adult have also been healing. I want to know, "Hey, what was life like back then? What choices did you have?"

Across each of these narratives, stories, and reflections, what stands out most is the amount of self- and other-compassion elicited by the storytellers. Radically accepting our parents represents an ongoing and dynamic process, one in which we learn to accept our parents' shortcomings while acknowledging their strengths, celebrating their sacrifices, and recognizing their good intentions.

The Power of Storytelling

As Asian Americans and children of Asian immigrants, achieving a deeper un-derstanding of our parents is often limited by our own inferences about who our parents are and how their experiences may have impacted our upbringing.[3] Therefore, breaking patterns as parents requires us to engage in adaptive inter-generational communication with our parents and caregivers about their his-torical trauma. We must begin acknowledging and embracing the stories of our parents and ancestors while sharing narratives that emphasize our collective re-silience as members of the Asian American community.[4]

Inviting our parents and ancestors to begin sharing their stories can also em-power us to develop stronger cultural identities and ethnic identities. Indeed, connecting with our histories, and the power of our stories, can help Asian Americans and children of Asian immigrants bridge the intergenerational accul-turative gap that often contributes to family conflict and insecure relationships.[5]

I.B.* shares:

I wish that my parents would be able to express how they really feel about certain things or what is going on. As I have grown older, I want to know what my parents are like as people and as adults. What are things that make them really happy? What were the best memories of their life? These are not topics my parents readily bring up; you have to really question them or ask specific questions. I want to know what it was like for them growing up instead of it being used as an example of hardship and reasons why my sisters and I have a better life [than they did]. I know their upbringing was hard, but I imagine they had some fun memories or moments with their family.

Sharon K.* expresses:

When I was growing up, I never thought to ask certain questions because it never occurred to me to ask for more information or that I could even ask. [Now that we are older, my] brother and I have begun asking questions of our parents because we are acutely aware of how little time we have left with them as they are squarely in their senior years. But we are also aware of what kind of emotions and traumas are connected to these memories and we want to be sensitive to that.

As I.B. and Sharon have discovered, we must be sensitive when inviting our parents and ancestors to recount their early experiences. Our parents' stories may include trauma narratives and other stressful experiences that remain un-processed and elicit feelings of discomfort. Specific strategies that have been found to contribute to positive and successful intergenerational communication about historical trauma have been identified in the literature. To achieve the best outcomes, researchers suggest both younger and older members of the genera-tion must be motivated and willing to engage in this discussion, as opposed to the communication being imposed by either party.[6] One way that the younger generation can facilitate this willingness to engage in storytelling is by inviting our parents and ancestors to share their stories at a specific time and date by expressing a personal desire to understand our family histories, struggles, and triumphs. Communicating to our parents and ancestors early on that we *want* to hear their stories can finally afford them the psychological space and time to process their experiences in ways they have not been traditionally given due to a focus on survival and assimilation.

Though timing is critically important when it comes to inviting older gen-erations to share their stories, it does not guarantee the success of this process. Please note that open communication does not necessarily result in positive outcomes, especially when it comes to sharing deeply unprocessed traumatic experiences.[7] Instead, positive outcomes are associated with modulated disclosure as well as communication that is sensitive to the needs of and relationship between generations. Step lightly and explore this opportunity with respect, eagerness, and curiosity.

Cultivating Community Through Storytelling

The healing elements of building community and the power of promoting universality through storytelling cannot be understated. Countless studies, including my own, have evidenced the ways in which leveraging a supportive community, as well as one's ethnic identity, can buffer the impacts of racial discrimination and stress.[8]

Engaging in storytelling represents an important way that Asian Americans engage in meaning making and define who they are, especially as we learn to navigate a bicultural world.[9]

Quan D.* shares how my family's story parallels his own in ways that promoted a deep sense of community and connection:

> Being children of immigrants allows us to learn from one another, share stories, and better understand our own culture and history. Your stories about how your ancestors survived WW2 and had their land taken away hit a soft spot because my parents had gone through similar circumstances. They managed to escape the Vietnam war but were robbed of all their belongings by pirates on their way to Malaysia. The story about how your grandfather changed the family's surname so that his children would not be discriminated against or made fun of in America is the same reason why I didn't give my kids common Asian names. Thank you for sharing that. We may come from different backgrounds but by sharing and having that same connection with one another, I feel we can heal our inner child by knowing that we're not all alone on this journey.

For many of us, connecting with an objective perspective can be one of the most helpful ways to promote healing. Whether this looks like professional mental health counseling, pursuing healing circles, or speaking with trusted friends and family members about your experiences, the value of storytelling while others hold space for us to explore our intrapersonal selves can also be deeply healing.

When it comes to trauma narratives, the more we share our stories, the less power we give to shame. Expressing these bits and pieces of who we are, from where we came, and where we hope to go can empower us to create new meanings and dream about a new future.

So, what is the secret to healing from historical trauma and unhelpful cultural patterns? What is the "secret formula" that we can apply to our hearts and minds in ways that make our pain more palatable and our futures brighter?

Breaking the cultural, social, familial, and intergenerational patterns that limit our ability to unlock our power, access joy, achieve secure relationships, and optimize our well-being is one of the most meaningful journeys we can begin. For many of us, it requires a lifetime of work. We may face moments where it feels as though we are taking two steps forward, only to take three steps back. We may even feel as though moments occur when we are stagnant and are unsure where to go next.

And when these moments undoubtedly occur, I implore you to keep going. Know that you are not alone. Draw from the strengths of your communities, your relationships, and your families.

My dearest reader, thank you for taking the first steps on your healing journey with me. I hope you saw yourself in these pages and recognized similar experiences from the voices of our community. In times when you need strength, gentle reminders, or validation, I hope you circle back to this healing guide.

You are worth investing in your own healing, and reading this book is only the beginning.

TLDR: With a deeper understanding of the ways in which historical trauma, intergenerational patterns, cultural scripts, and scarcity mindsets can create barriers to optimal psychological well-being, secure relationships, and overall well-being, this chapter provides a few specific strategies to take your healing to the next level. In truth, this chapter outlines some of the messiest, most challenging, and heart-space–focused work. We outlined strategies to break inherited patterns as parents and explored narratives that outlined the process of radically accepting our parents. The importance of other adult relationships, such as the ones we cultivate with our friends and community members, is also discussed.

Questions to Ponder

1. What are some examples of inherited parenting patterns that you would like to break in the family that you are creating? How might you begin to do so?
2. How might you begin to radically accept your parents for who they are, rather than who you would like them to have been?
3. To what extent do you feel comfortable engaging in vulnerability with friendships? What might help or hinder the deepening of those relationships?

4. How can the power of storytelling be helpful in your own healing process?
5. What is your story and how would you tell it to your child?

Questions to Bridge the Gap with Parents

1. What do you wish others, including myself, would wholeheartedly accept about you?
2. If your life were captured in a book or a movie, what would be the title? What would be the most important lesson of your story?
3. What are some similarities and differences in the way we were raised?

Conclusion

Final Thoughts and Takeaways

❦

This book is a love letter.

What started out as a reflection of gratitude for my partner quickly evolved to encompass the love I have for my family. Since I began writing this book, our family has grown. We have two sons now, and the six-month-old baby from the introduction is currently running around the house, *sans* pants, well past his third birthday. My husband and I have also welcomed the arrival of another baby boy, whom we have affectionately dubbed "Cheeks." Each of these boys keeps me on my toes, and they provide daily opportunities for reflection and intentionality as I break the patterns that remain as a partner, person, and parent.

This book is also a love letter to our Asian American community.

When I began my own healing journey a few years ago, I started engaging in conversations with other Asian Americans and children of Asian immigrants about their experiences within romantic relationships, friendships, and families of origin. I couldn't believe how much our community had in common. It was in that moment I realized I needed to write this book. It felt impossible to distract myself from the knowledge that our Asian American community was struggling with similar inherited cultural patterns that ultimately deprived us from achieving abundance mindsets, integrated identities, and secure attachments, and yet we lacked the cohesive language and concepts required to facilitate our own collective healing. I hope that this book provides the language needed for ongoing conversations with ourselves, our partners, our parents, and our communities.

If I had a book genie who gave me one wish, I would say, "I want this book to find itself in the hands of readers who need it most." I hope that the messages, stories, and voices that filled these pages also found a way to reach parts of your identity that you never dreamed you would ever revisit.

I am under no fantasy or impression that the entirety of this book will resonate with all readers. Instead, I understand that the relevance of this book will likely differ based on a variety of factors, including readiness and motivation to change, willingness to engage in self-awareness, ability to experience discomfort and vulnerability, and stages of ethnic identity development. In truth, many of the chapters in this book represent emotionally charged, complex, and nuanced topics that many will spend a lifetime untangling.

So where do we go from here? Well, a few guiding considerations come to mind.

To which chapter did you feel the most connected? Were there moments that led to emotional flashbacks? At what point did you experience a sense of excitement? The answers to these questions may give you an idea of where your opportunities for growth may align.

Whether this book opened your eyes to the history of anti-Asian sentiments that have long characterized our collective experience in America, provided the language needed to better equip yourself for cultural conversations, or identified specific pattern-breaking strategies that can help you access greater joy and abundance, I am celebrating you.

Thank you for allowing me to be part of your healing journey.

The cycle of diasporic wounds ends with you.

Acknowledgments

This book was born out of the love I have for my family and community. I am nothing without you all, and I am grateful to contribute to the emerging literature on Asian American mental health, culturally responsive healing, and decolonized frameworks for well-being.

To my editorial team, Dana Bliss and Mary Funchion, thank you for your endless patience as I continued to work and rework each chapter. Thank you for understanding that what I offered my community needed to be grounded in my voice, reflected in the literature, and consistent with Asian American perspectives. To Dana, thank you for encouraging me to rest, meeting at a minute's notice to talk through ideas, and holding me accountable when I fell back into unhelpful patterns. Your kindness and guidance made this process an enjoyable one.

Thank you to my clients and students who have shared their stories and inspired me to reflect on the importance of breaking intergenerational patterns. Your courage to thrive against all odds is forever imprinted on my heart.

To the storytellers who shared their personal anecdotes, thank you. This book would be incomplete without your voices. Thank you for believing in this project and recognizing the value of our stories.

Thank you to my mentors, colleagues, and friends who continue to lift me up, Dr. Lena Salpietro, Dr. Martina Moore, Dr. Madeline Clark, Dr. Letitia Browne-James, Dr. Kathryn MacCluskie, Dr. Elsa Soto-Leggett, Dr. Jillian Jay Watts, Dr. Cat Chang, Dr. Shanice Armstrong, Dr. Charmaine Conner, Dr. Seungbin Oh, Dr. Rick Balkin, Dr. Victoria E. Kress, Angelika Holleran, and so many, many more. Thank you to my ACA, NBCC, and FAHNS families.

A very special thank you to Dr. Kevin Nadal for believing in me and for continuing to pave the way for Filipino American voices. Thank you for inviting my voice to the table and for your endless encouragement in all things, from academia, to publishing, and parenting.

Thank you to my 'Ohana, Dr. Monica P. Band and Dr. Christian D. Chan. To Dr. Band, you are the closest thing I have ever had to a sister. Thank you for uplifting my voice, sharing in your infinite wisdom, and processing the emotional experience of writing this book and being the child of immigrants. Thank you for seeing me, laughing with me, and sitting with me in the difficult moments. I will forever encourage your matcha green tea latte habit and am prepared to walk miles alongside you for ramen. To Dr. Christian D. Chan, thank you for always aligning with me, working with me, and sharing in countless food adventures. *Bao* will forever beat fine dining.

Thank you to my dear friend and colleague, Dr. Clark Ausloos. Thank you for sharing in countless moments of laughter, adventure, and storytelling. My heart fills with joy each time we connect. One day we will get those matching tattoos.

To Dr. Valli Sridharan, thank you for sharing in the joys and the challenges of motherhood. Your presence in my life is a gift and I continue to learn so much from your patience, compassion, and wisdom.

To "The Women Who Eat," Allie Maldonado, Rachel Morrison, and Rachel Kaston Hanawalt, thank you for always listening without judgment and celebrating each of my accomplishments every step of the way. Our friendship has been infinitely healing.

A heartfelt thank you to my parents, Elmie Romana Litam and Patrick "Ducky" Pon Litam. I am nothing without your sacrifices, love, and support. To my amazing, resilient, generous, and radiant mother, thank you for always prioritizing the happiness and care of our family. The selfless way you love our family is a quality I strive to embody each and every day. No matter how old I get, I will always need my mama. I will forever remember how you made *turon* for me every day for a week after Kit was born, and how you rescheduled travel plans to be present for Chaston's arrival into the world. I hope you know that all my very best qualities come from you. To my steadfast, thoughtful, and patient papa, thank you for believing in me and sharing in my excitement about this project. I will always remember the smirk on your face when I recounted the "donut passage" while we waited in line for the Rise of the Resistance.

Thank you to Peggy Marcus ("Busha") and Michael Marcus ("Papa Mike") for the love, tenderness, and care you extend to our family, especially our sons. Your gracious generosity each week made this project, and so many more, possible. Your presence brings me so much peace.

To Maria O. Escuro ("Tita Tata") and Debbie Marcus, thank you for playing with, protecting, and caring for my children at a moment's notice. Without you, this book would not be possible.

Thank you to my brothers, Kuya Patrick ("Cubby"), Mitchell ("Kitters"), and Terrence ("Tiger"), the founding members of the "1392 Club." You are the best brothers and teammates I could have asked for in this life.

Yo, a big ol' shoutout to my "Bro Bro," Christina Eadeh Litam. Our many heartfelt talks, jokes, and moments of true vulnerability resonate more deeply than you know. Thank you for always role modeling graciousness, compassion, and generosity.

To Brittany Litam, thank you for your healing presence and for putting up with my brother. I love you!

To my extended family both near and far, I hope I did our family's story justice.

To my Lolo José, Tito Jesus "Toots" Tibayan Arañez, and Melencia "Mely" Sese, thank you for guiding me from heaven and protecting our family. Until we meet again, I love you.

To my dearest sons, Kit Anthony and Chaston Patrick, may the world never dim your courage, light, and thirst for adventure. I cannot wait to see the amazing people you will grow to become, and I am in awe of you both every day.

And finally, the biggest heartfelt thank you to my greatest love, best friend, and husband, Matthew Anthony Marcus. The way you love me has shown me how to love and accept myself. You are the absolute best father, husband, and person I know. Thank you for reminding me to rest, caring selflessly for our family, anticipating our needs, and forever keeping us healthy and safe. Staying up to enjoy late-night crossword puzzles with you has always been the highlight of my day. Your very presence in my life has been deeply healing. I love you endlessly as I write this, and I love you even more as you read this. You are my favorite mouse.

The Healing Orientation Model Elements (HOME) Assessment

Please respond to each of the items from 1 (Strongly Disagree) to 5 (Strongly Agree).

	Strongly Disagree	Disagree	Undecided	Agree	Strongly Agree
1. My partner is familiar with what I need to feel grounded, relaxed, and peaceful in times of stress.	1	2	3	4	5
2. My partner can easily identify the beliefs, values, and goals that are important to me, even if they do not share them.	1	2	3	4	5
3. My partner understands me.	1	2	3	4	5
4. I have been pleasantly surprised by how well my partner seems to know what I want, need, or desire.	1	2	3	4	5
5. My partner can easily anticipate my feelings, even if I may not explicitly share them.	1	2	3	4	5
6. My partner anticipates my needs.	1	2	3	4	5
7. I can count on my partner.	1	2	3	4	5
8. I can trust my partner to honor my feelings.	1	2	3	4	5
9. My partner is consistently reliable.	1	2	3	4	5
10. I feel free to be myself when I am with my partner.	1	2	3	4	5

(continued)

	Strongly Disagree	Disagree	Undecided	Agree	Strongly Agree
11. My partner engages in thoughtful acts without expecting anything in return.	1	2	3	4	5
12. My partner does not keep score or expect me to repay them for acts of kindness.	1	2	3	4	5
13. I feel at peace with myself because of my partner.	1	2	3	4	5
14. My partner heals wounds from my family of origin.	1	2	3	4	5
15. My inner child feels safe with my partner.	1	2	3	4	5

Score: _____

Results

Planting the Seed (Scores of 1–30)

You may be in the early stages of your relationship or experiencing discomfort around vulnerability. Perhaps your partner, or past partners, have let you down in ways that have led you to believe you are not worthy of love.

Watering the Plant (Scores of 31–45)

You and your partner are on the right track! Though there is plenty of room to grow, it is clear that the foundation for a healing orientation may be in your future.

Trimming the Buds (Scores of 46–60)

You and your partner have all the makings of a successful, healing, and loving orientation. Though every relationship has opportunities for growth, cultivating communication, honesty, and safety may do wonders to fully achieve this healing orientation.

Harvesting the Fruit (Scores of 61–75)

Honey, you're home! You and your partner have achieved a healing orientation in which you feel understood and validated. Your needs are largely anticipated, and your partner is intentional on more days than not. You may even notice that you are able to accept acts of kindness without the intense desire to return the favor right away. You may enjoy a deeper sense of freedom to be yourself; your partner has become a safe place and a safe person.

Note: The HOME assessment is a self-survey designed to provide individuals in romantic relationships with an idea of where they are in their healing orientation. The HOME assessment has not been validated for its psychometric properties nor is it intended to be used as a psychological tool.

Participant Demographics

Name*	Ethnicity	Gender	Sexual Identity	Geographic Location	Generational Status	Age Bracket
Chamari de Silva	Sri Lankan	Woman	-	Texas (South)	1.5 generation	Early 30s
Dr. Ramya Avadhanam	Indian American	Woman	-	Texas (South)	1.5 generation	Early 30s
Dr. Monica Band	Biracial Chinese American	Woman	-	Washington, DC (Mid-Atlantic)	Third generation	Early 30s
Olivia*	Vietnamese American	Woman		Washington, DC (Mid-Atlantic)	First generation	Early 30s
Jai Yang*	Chinese American	Woman	Queer	Ohio (Midwest)	Second generation	Early 30s
Lisa Factora-Borchers	Filipina American	Woman	-	Ohio (Midwest)	First generation	Early 40s
Noah*	Laotian and Thai	Man	-	Ohio (Midwest)	First generation	Early 40s
Christopher Vo	Vietnamese	Man	-	Texas (South)	First generation	Late 30s
Cynthia Siadat	Filipina American	Woman	-	California (West Coast)	First generation	Early 30s
Dr. Christopher Cheung	Chinese and Surinamese	Man	-	Florida (Southeastern)	First generation	Late 30s
Kimmy Wu	Taiwanese American	Woman		Washington DC (Mid-Atlantic)	First generation	Late 20s
Angelika Holleran	Biracial Filipina American	Woman	-	Ohio (Midwest)	Second generation	Early 30s
Sophia*	East Asian and Middle Eastern	Woman	-	Ohio (Midwest)	First generation	Early 30s
Kareena*	Indian American	Woman	-	Washington, DC (Mid-Atlantic)	First generation	Early 30s
Quan D.*	Vietnamese, Chinese, and Malaysian	Man	-	Ohio (Midwest)	Second generation	Early 40s

(continued)

Name*	Ethnicity	Gender	Sexual Identity	Geographic Location	Generational Status	Age Bracket
Dr. Daniela Pila	Filipina American	Woman	-	Connecticut (New England)	1.5 generation	Early 40s
Noelle*	Filipina American	Woman	-	Ohio (Midwest)	First generation	Early 40s
Gabriel K.	Biracial Filipino American	Man	`-	Ohio (Midwest)	Second generation	Early 30s
Le*	Chinese and Vietnamese	Woman	-	California (West Coast)	Second generation	Late 20s
Dr. Valli*	Indian American	Woman	-	Oregon (Pacific Northwest)	First generation	Early 30s
I.B.*	Igorot Filipina and Chinese American	Woman	Pansexual	Hawaii	First generation	Late 20s
Sharon*	Korean American	Woman	-	Ohio (Midwest)	Second generation	Early 40s
Jennifer Alexander*	Chinese American	Woman	-	Michigan (Midwest)	Transracial and transnational adoptee	Late 20s
Carmel*	Filipina American	Woman	-	Illinois (Midwest)	First generation	Mid-20s
Matthew*	Biracial Filipino American	Man	Gay	Wisconsin (Midwest)	First generation	Early 30s
Calypso*	White and Taiwanese	Woman		Ohio (Midwest)	First generation	Mid-30s
Yub Kim	Korean American	Man	Gay	Ohio (Midwest)	First generation	Late 30s
Shoua Lee	Hmong American	Woman	-	California (West Coast)	First generation	Mid-30s
Drake M.*	Biracial Filipino American	Man	Gay	California (West Coast)	First generation	Mid-30s
Bayani*	Filipino American	Man	Gay	California (West Coast)	First generation	Early 30s

Note: *Indicates pseudonym

Notes

Chapter 1

1. Chu Kim-Prieto, Grace S. Kim, Leilani Salvo Crane, Susana Ming Lowe, Phi Loan, and Khanh T. Dinh, "Legacies of War: Asian American Women and War Trauma," *Women & Therapy 41*, no. 3-4 (2018): 203–218. https://doi.org/10.1080/02703149.2018.1425023
2. Gordon Rottman, *World War II Pacific Island Guide: A Geo-Military Study* (Westport, CT: Greenwood Publishing Group, 2002), 318.
3. Yael Danieli, Fran H. Norris, and Brian E. Engdahl, "Multigenerational Legacies of Trauma: Modeling the What and How of Transmission," *American Journal of Orthopsychiatry 86*, no. 6 (2016): 639–651. https://doi.org/10.1037/ort0000145.
4. Donna K. Nagata and Wendy Cheng, "Intergenerational Communication of Race-Related Trauma by Japanese American Former Internees," *American Journal of Orthopsychiatry 73*, no. 3 (2003): 266–278. https://doi.org/10.1037/0002-9432.73.3.266
5. Karen Pyke and Tran Dang, "'FOB and Whitewashed': Identity and Internalized Racism Among Second Generation Asian Americans," *Qualitative Sociology 26* (2003): 147–172.
6. Mental Health America, "Asian American/Pacific Islander Communities and Mental Health" (2023). https://www.mhanational.org/issues/asian-american-pacific-islander-communities-and-mental-health
7. Anneliese A. Singh, Brandee Appling, and Heather Trepal, "Using the Multicultural and Social Justice Counseling Competencies to Decolonize Counseling Practice: The Important Roles of Theory, Power, and Action," *Journal of Counseling and Development 98*, no. 3 (2020): 261–271. https://doi.org/10.1002/jcad.12321
8. Stacey Diane Arañez Litam, Christian S. Chan, Lotes Nelson, and Victor E. Tuazon, "Decolonizing the Interpersonal Theory of Suicide with Filipinx American Clients," *Asian American Journal of Psychology 13*, no. 1 (2022): 73–82. https://doi.org/10.1037/aap0000 255; Walter D. Mignolo, "What Does It Mean to Decolonize?" in *On Decoloniality: Concepts, Analytics, Praxis*, ed. Walter D. Mignolo and Catherine E. Walsh (Durham, NC: Duke University Press, 2018), 105–134.
9. Fang Gong, Sue-Je L. Gage, and Leonardo A. Tacata Jr, "Helpseeking Behavior Among Filipino Americans: A Cultural Analysis of Face and Language," *Journal of Community Psychology 31*, no. 5 (2003): 469–488. https://doi.org/10.1002/jcop.10063
10. Kevin L. Nadal, Kara Mia Vigilia Escobar, Gail T. Prado, E. J. R. David, and Krystal Haynes, "Racial Microaggressions and the Filipino American Experience: Recommendations for Counseling and Development," *Journal of Multicultural Counseling and Development 40*, no. 3 (2012): 156–173. https://doi.org/10.1002/j.2161-1912.2012.00015.x
11. Kevin L. Nadal, Gabriel Corpus, and Alyssa Hufana, "The Forgotten Asian Americans: Filipino Americans' Experiences with Racial Microaggressions and Trauma," *Asian American Journal of Psychology 13*, no. 1 (2022): 51–61. https://doi.org/10.1037/aap0000261
12. Stacey Diane Arañez Litam and Christian Chan, "Experiences of Stress and Help-Seeking Behaviors in Filipino Americans," *Intergenerational Journal for the Advancement of Counselling 44*, no. 4 (2022): 586–603. https://doi.org/10.1007/s10447-022-09485-x
13. Christian D. Chan and Stacey Diane Arañez Litam, "Mental Health Equity of Filipino Communities in COVID-19: A Framework for Practice and Advocacy," *The Professional Counselor 11*, no. 1 (2021): 73–85. https://doi.org/10.15241/cdc.11.1.73
14. Abby Budiman and Neil G. Ruiz, "Key Facts About Asian Americans, a Diverse and Growing Population" (2021). https://www.pewresearch.org/short-reads/2021/04/29/key-facts-about-asian-americans/
15. U.S. Department of Commerce, "U.S. Census Bureau Releases Key Stats in Honor of Asian American, Native Hawaiian, and Pacific Islander Heritage Month" (2022). https://www.comme rce.gov/news/blog/2022/05/us-census-bureau-releases-key-stats-honor-asian-american-nat ive-hawaiian-and

Chapter 2

1. Abby Budiman and Neil G. Ruiz, "Key Facts About Asian Americans, a Diverse and Growing Population" (2021). https://www.pewresearch.org/short-reads/2021/04/29/key-facts-about-asian-americans/.
2. Alexander Saxton, "The Army of Canton in the High Sierra," *Pacific Historical Review 35*, no. 2 (1966): 141–152. https://doi.org/10.2307/3636678
3. William F. Chew, *Nameless Builders of the Transcontinental Railway: The Chinese Workers of the Central Pacific Railroad* (Victoria, BC: Trafford, 2004).
4. Christopher R. B. Merritt, Gary Weisz, and Kelly J. Dixon, "'Verily the Road Was Built with Chinaman's Bones': An Archaeology of Chinese Line Camps in Montana," *International Journal of Historical Archaeology 16*, no. 4 (2012): 666–695. https://doi.org/10.1007/s10761-012-0197-7
5. Iris Chang, *The Chinese in America: A Narrative History* (New York: Viking, 2003); Nancy S. Lee, "Telling Their Own Stories: Chinese Canadian Biography As A Historical Genre," in *The Chinese in America: A History from Gold Mountain to the New Millennium*, ed. Susie Lan Cassel (New York: AltaMira, 2002), 106–121.
6. George Kraus, *High Road to Promontory: Building the Central Pacific (Now the Southern Pacific) Across the High Sierra* (Palo Alto, CA: American West Publishing Co., 1969).
7. Merritt, Weisz, and Dixon, 2012.
8. Lee, 2002.
9. Anna Diamond, "The 1924 Law That Slammed the Door on Immigrants and the Politicians Who Pushed It Back Open," *Smithsonian Magazine,* May 19, 2020. https://www.smithsonian mag.com/history/1924-law-slammed-door-immigrants-and-politicians-who-pushed-it-back-open-180974910/
10. Bill Ong Hing, *Defining America Through Immigration Policy* (Philadelphia: Temple University Press, 2003).
11. John M. Liu and Lucie Cheng, "Pacific Rim Development and the Duality of Post-1965 Asian Immigration to the United States," in *The New Asian Immigration in Los Angeles and Global Restructuring*, ed. Paul M. Ong, Edna Bonacich, and Lucie Cheng (Philadelphia: Temple University Press, 1994), 45–73.
12. Ronald Takaki, *Strangers from a Different Shore: A History of Asian Americans* (Boston: Little, Brown and Company, 1998).
13. Teresa Evans-Campbell, "Historical Trauma in American Indian/Native Alaska Communities: A Multilevel Framework for Exploring Impacts on Individuals, Families, and Communities," *Journal of Interpersonal Violence 23*, no. 3 (2008): 316–338. https://doi.org/10.1177/0886260507312290
14. Peter A. Levine, *Trauma and Memory: Brain and the Body in a Search for the Living Past: A Practical Guide for Understanding and Working with Traumatic Memory* (Berkeley, CA: North Atlantic Books, 2015): 4.
15. Yael Danieli, *International Handbook of Multigenerational Legacies of Trauma* (New York: Springer, 1998).
16. Jieyi Chi and Richard M. Lee, Intergenerational Communication About Historical Trauma in Asian American Families, *Adversity and Resilience Science 3*, no. 33 (2022): 233–511..
17. Takaki, 1998.
18. Chi and Lee, 2022.
19. Chu Kim-Prieto, Grace S. Kim, Leilani Salvo Crane, Susana Ming Lowe, Phi Loan, and Khanh T. Dinh, "Legacies of War: Asian American Women and War Trauma," *Women & Therapy 41*, no. 3-4 (2018): 203–218. https://doi. org/10.1080/02703149.2018.1425023
20. OiYan Poon, "'The Land of Opportunity Doesn't Apply to Everyone': The Immigrant Experience, Race, and Asian American Career Choices," *Journal of College Student Development 55*, no. 6 (2014): 499–514. https://doi.org/10.1353/csd.2014.0056

Chapter 3

1. Diane Hughes, James Rodriguez, Emilie P. Smith, Deborah J. Johnson, Howard C. Stevenson, and John Spicer, "Parents' Ethnic-Racial Socialization Practices: A Review of Research and Directions for Future Study," *Developmental Psychology 42*, no. 5 (2006): 747–770. https://doi.org/10.1037/0012-1649.42.5.747

2. Marcela Raffaelli, Maria I. Iturbide, Miguel Angel Saucedo, and Lorraine Munoz, "You Hear Stories About What They Did and It Makes You Go 'Wow': Adolescents Narrate and Interpret Caregiver Stories About a Difficult Time," *Journal of Adolescent Research 32*, no. 5 (2017): 536–558. https://doi.org/10.1177/0743558416670008

3. Jieyi Cai and Richard T. Lee, "Intergenerational Communication About Historical Trauma in Asian American Families," *Adversity and Resilience Science 3* (2022): 233–245. https://doi.org/10.1007/s42844-022-00064-y

4. Studio ATAO, "Unlearning Scarcity, Cultivating Solidarity." https://www.studioatao.org/unlearning-scarcity-cultivating-solidarity (accessed June 13, 2024).

5. Janany Jeyasundaram, Luisa Yao Dan Cao, and Barry Trentham, "Experiences of Intergenerational Trauma in Second-Generation Refugees: Healing Through Occupation," *Canadian Journal of Occupational Therapy 87*, no. 5 (2020): 412–422. https://doi.org/10.1177/0008417420968684

6. Cai and Lee, 2022.

7. Yael Danieli, Fran H. Norris, and Brian Engdahl, "Multigenerational Legacies of Trauma: Modeling the What and How of Transmission," *American Journal of Orthopsychiatry 86*, no. 6 (2016): 639–651. https:// doi.org/10.1037/ort0000145

8. Cassandra L. Hendrix, Daniel D. Dilks, Brooke G. McKenna, Anne L. Dunlop, Elizabeth J. Corwin, and Patricia A. Brennan, "Maternal Childhood Adversity Associates with Frontoamygdala Connectivity in Neonates," *Biological Psychiatry: Cognitive Neuroscience and Neuroimaging 6*, no. 4 (2021): 470–478. https://doi.org/10.1016/j.bpsc.2020.11.003

Chapter 4

1. Harry F. Harlow, "Love in Infant Monkeys," *Scientific American 200*, no. 6 (1959): 68–74.

2. Harlow, 1959.

3. Harlow, 1959.

4. Harlow, 1959.

5. Harry F. Harlow and Robert Z. Zimmerman, "Affectional Response in the Infant Monkey," *Science 130*, no. 3373 (1959): 421–432. https://doi.org/10.1126/science.130.3373.421

6. Harlow and Zimmerman, 1959.

7. Harlow, 1959.

8. Harlow and Zimmerman, 1959.

9. John Bowlby, *Attachment and Loss* (New York: Basic Books, 1969/1982).

10. Bowlby, 1969/1982.

11. Mary D. Salter Ainsworth, "Attachments Beyond Infancy," *American Psychologist 44* (1989): 709–716. https://doi.org/10.1037//0003-066x.44.4.709; Mary D. Salter Ainsworth, Mary C. Blehar, Everett Walters, and Sally Wall, *Patterns of Attachment: A Psychological Study of the Strange Situation* (Hillsdale, NJ: Erlbaum, 1978); Mary D. Salter Ainsworth and Silvia M. Bell, "Attachment, Exploration, and Separation: Illustrated by Behavior of One-Year-Olds in a Strange Situation," *Child Development 41*, no. 1 (1970): 49–67.

12. Ainsworth and Bell, 1970.

13. Ainsworth and Bell, 1970.

14. Ainsworth and Bell, 1970.

15. Ainsworth and Bell, 1970.

16. Mary Main and Judith Solomon, "Procedures for Identifying Infants as Disorganized-Disoriented During the Ainsworth Strange Situation," in *Attachment in the Preschool Years: Theory, Research and Intervention,* ed. Mark T. Greenberg, Dante Cicchetti, and E. Mark Cummins (Chicago: University of Chicago Press, 1990), 121–160.

17. Ainsworth, Blehar, Walters, and Wall, 1978; Amir Levine and Rachel Heller, *Attached: The New Science of Adult Attachment and How It Can Help You Find—and Keep—Love* (New York: Penguin Random House, 2010).

18. Kim Bartholomew and Leonard M. Horowitz, "Attachment Styles Among Young Adults: A Test of a Four-Category Model," *Journal of Personality and Psychology 61*, no. 2 (1991): 226–244. https://doi.org/10.1037//0022-3514.61.2.226; John Bowlby, *A Secure Base* (New York: Basic Books, 1988); Kay Wilhelm, Inika Gillis, and Gordon Parker, "Parental Bonding and Adult Attachment Style: The Relationship Between Four Category Models," *International Journal Women's Health and Wellness 2*, no. 1 (2016): 1–7. https://doi.org/10.23937/2474-1353/1510016

19. Levine and Heller, 2010.

20. Levine and Heller, 2010.

21. Levine and Heller, 2010.
22. Jeffry A. Simpson and W. Steven Rholes, "Adult Attachment, Stress, and Romantic Relationships," *Current Opinions in Psychology* 13 (2017): 19–24. https://doi.org/10.1016/j.copsyc.2016.04.006
23. Mario Mikulincer and Phillip R. Shaver, *Attachment in Adulthood: Structure, Dynamics, and Change* (New York: Guilford Press, 2010).
24. Ross A. Thompson, "New Directions for Child Development in the Twenty-First Century: The Legacy of Early Attachments," *Child Development 71*, no. 1 (2000): 145–152.
25. Nancy L. Collins, Máire B. Ford, AnaMarie C. Guichard, and Lisa M. Allard, "Working Models of Attachment and Attribution Processes in Intimate Relationships," *Personality and Social Psychology Bulletin 31*, no. 2 (2006): 201–219. https://doi.org/10.1177/0146167205280907
26. Levine and Heller, 2010; Phillip R. Shaver, Dory A. Schachner, and Mario Mikulincer, "Attachment Style, Excessive Reassurance Seeking, Relationship Processes, and Depression," *Personality and Social Psychology Bulletin 31*, no. 3 (2005): 343–359. https://doi.org/10.1177/0146167204271709
27. Levine and Heller, 2010.
28. Shaver, Schachner, and Mikulincer, 2005.
29. Mario Mikulincer and Phillip R. Shaver, "The Attachment Behavioral System in Adulthood: Activation, Psychodynamics, and Interpersonal Processes," in *Advances in Experimental Social Psychology,* edited by Mark Zanna (New York: Elsevier Academic Press, 2003), 53–152.
30. Levine and Heller, 2010; Mikulincer and Shaver, 2003.
31. Mikulincer and Shaver, 2003.
32. Mikulincer and Shaver, 2003.
33. Levine and Heller, 2010.
34. Gabor Maté and Daniel Maté, *The Myth of Normal: Trauma, Illness, and Healing in a Toxic Culture* (New York: Avery, 2022), 16.
35. Meekyung Han, "Relationship Among Perceived Parental Trauma, Parental Attachment, and Sense of Coherence in Southeast Asian American College Students," *Journal of Family Social Work 9*, no. 2 (2005): 25–45. https://doi.org/10.30300/J039v09n02_02
36. Ainsworth, 1989.
37. Michelle Zauner, *Crying in H Mart: A Memoir* (New York: Alfred A. Knopf, 2021), 4.

Chapter 5

1. Meekyung Han, "Relationship Among Perceived Parental Trauma, Parental Attachment, and Sense of Coherence in Southeast Asian American College Students," *Journal of Family Social Work 9*, no. 2 (2005): 25–45. https://doi.org/10.1300/J039v09n02_02
2. Jieyi Cai and Richard T. Lee, "Intergenerational Communication About Historical Trauma in Asian American Families," *Adversity and Resilience Science 3* (2022): 233–245. https://doi.org/10.1007/s42844-022-00064-y; Janany Jeyasundaram, Luisa Yao Dan Cao, and Barry Trentham, "Experiences of Intergenerational Trauma in Second-Generation Refugees: Healing Through Occupation," *Canadian Journal of Occupational Therapy 87*, no. 5 (2020): 412–422. https://doi.org/10.1177/0008417420968684; Ramsay Liem, "Silencing Historical Trauma: The Politics and Psychology of Memory and Voice," *Peace and Conflict: Journal of Peace Psychology 13*, no. 2 (2007): 153–174. https://doi.org/10.1080/10781910701271200; Nancy J. Lin and Karen L. Suyemoto, "So You, My Children, Can Have a Better Life: A Cambodian American Perspective on the Phenomenology of Intergenerational Communication About Trauma," *Journal of Aggression, Maltreatment & Trauma 25*, no. 4 (2016): 400–420. https://doi.org/10.1080/10926771.2015.1133748
3. Harry F. Harlow and Robert Z. Zimmerman, "Affectional Response in the Infant Monkey," *Science 130*, no. 3373 (1959): 421–432. https://doi.org/10.1126/science.130.3373.421
4. Kim Bartholomew and Leonard M. Horowitz, "Attachment Styles Among Young Adults: A Test of a Four-Category Model," *Journal of Personality and Psychology 61*, no. 2 (1991): 226–244. https://doi.org/10.1037//0022-3514.61.2.226; John Bowlby, *A Secure Base* (New York: Basic Books, 1988); Kay Wilhelm, Inika Gillis, and Gordon Parker, "Parental Bonding and Adult Attachment Style: The Relationship Between Four Category Models," *International Journal Women's Health and Wellness 2*, no. 1 (2016): 1–7. https://doi.org/10.23937/2474-1353/1510016
5. Joseph E. Beeney, Aidan G. C. Wright, Stephanie D. Stepp, Michael N. Hallquist, Sophie A. Lazarus, Julie R. S. Beeney, Lori N. Scott, and Paul A. Pilkonis, "Disorganized Attachment and

Personality Functioning in Adults: A Latent Class Analysis," *Personality Disorders: Theory, Research, and Treatment 8*, no. 3 (2017): 206–216. https://doi.org/10.1037/per0000184

6. Jude Cassidy and Jonathan J. Mohr, "Unsolvable Fear, Trauma, and Psychopathology: Theory, Research, and Clinical Considerations Related to Disorganized Attachment Across the Life Span," *Clinical Psychology: Science and Practice 8*, no. 3 (2001): 275–298. https://doi.org/10.1093/clipsy.8.3.275

7. Peter Fonagy, Gyorgy Gergely, Elliot Jurist, and Mary Target, *Affect Regulation, Mentalization, and the Development of the Self* (London: Other Press, 2002).

8. John G. Gunderson and Karlon Lyons-Ruth, "BPD's Interpersonal Hypersensitivity Phenotype: A Gene-Environment-Developmental Model," *Journal of Personality Disorders 22*, no. 1 (2008): 22–41. http://doi.org/10.1521/pedi.2008.22.1.22

Chapter 6

1. https://history.state.gov/milestones/1921-1936/immigration-act (accessed June 15, 2023).

2. Erika Lee, "The 'Yellow Peril' and Asian Exclusion in the Americas," *Pacific Historical Review 76*, no. 4 (2007): 537–562.

3. Chico Herbison and Jerry Schultz, "Quiet Passages: The Japanese-American War Bride Experience." https://kuscholarworks.ku.edu/bitstream/handle/1808/1140/CEAS.1990.n1.pdf?sequence=1 (accessed June 15, 2023).

4. Edward W. Said, *Orientalism: Western Conceptions of the Orient* (Penguin Press, 1978).

5. Rudyard Kipling, *The White Man's Burden* (originally published by Doubleday, 1899). https://www.kiplingsociety.co.uk/poem/poems_burden.htm (accessed June 15, 2023).

6. Traise Yamamoto, "In/visible Difference: Asian American Women and the Politics of Spectacle," *Race, Gender & Class 7*, no. 1 (2000): 43–55.

7. Sameena Azhar, Satarupa Dasgupta, Sunny Sinha, and Sharvari Karandikar, "Diversity in Sex Work in India: Challenging Stereotypes Regarding Sex Workers," *Sexuality & Culture 24* (2020): 1774–1797.

8. Patrick S. Cheng, "'I Am Yellow and Beautiful': Reflections on Queer Asian Spirituality and Gay Male Cyberculture," *Journal of Technology, Theology, and Religion 2*, no. 3 (2011): 1–21.; Y. Joel Wong and Mai-Lin Poon, "Counseling Asian American Men Who Demonstrate Suicidal Behavior," in *Culturally Responsive Counseling with Asian American Men,* ed. William Ming Liu, Derek Kenji Iwamoto, and Mark H. Chae (Routledge/Taylor & Francis Group, 2010), 279–298.

9. Y. Joel Wong, Jesse Owen, Kimberly K. Tran, Dana L. Collins, and Claire E. Higgins, "Asian American Male College Students' Perceptions of People's Stereotypes About Asian American Men," *Psychology of Men & Masculinity 13*, no. 1 (2012): 75–88. https://doi.org/10.1037/a0022800

10. Stewart Chang, "Feminism in Yellowface," *Harvard Journal of Law & Gender 38* (2015): 235–268.

11. William Ming Liu and Tai Chang, "Asian American Men and Masculinity," in *Handbook of Asian American Psychology,* ed. Frederick Leong, Arpana G. Inman, Angela Ebreo, Lawrence Hsin Yang, Lisa Marie Kinoshita, and Michi Fu (Sage Publications, Inc., 2006), 197–212.

12. Rosalind S. Chou, *Asian American Sexual Politics: The Construction of Race, Gender, and Sexuality* (Rowman and Littlefield Publishers, 2012).

13. Azhar, Dasgupta, Sinha, and Karandikar, 2020.

14. Wong, Owen, Tran, Collins, and Higgins, 2012.

15. Cheng, 2011.

16. Russell Leong, *Asian American Sexualities: Dimensions of the Gay and Lesbian Experience* (Routledge, 1995).

17. Jennifer L. Berdahl and Ji-A Min, "Prescriptive Stereotypes and Workplace Consequences for East Asians in North America," *Cultural Diversity and Ethnic Minority Psychology 18*, no. 2 (2012): 141–152. https://doi.org/10.1037/10027692

18. Berdahl and Min, 2012.

19. Diana Burgess and Eugene Borgida, "Who Women Are, Who Women Should Be: Descriptive and Prescriptive Gender Stereotyping in Sex Discrimination," *Psychology, Public Policy, and Law 5*, no. 3 (1999): 665–692. https://doi.org/10.1037/ 1076-8971.5.3.665; Michael J. Gill, "When Information Does Not Deter Stereotyping: Prescriptive Stereotyping Can Bias Judgments Under Conditions That Discourage Descriptive Stereotyping," *Journal of Experimental Social Psychology 40*, no. 5 (2004): 619–632. https://doi.org/10.1016/j.jesp.2003.12.001; Madeline

E. Heilman, Aaron S. Wallen, Daniella Fuchs, and Melinda M. Tamkins, "Penalties for Success: Reactions to Women Who Succeed at Male Gendertyped Tasks," *Journal of Applied Psychology 89*, no. 3 (2004): 416–427. https://doi.org/10.1037/ 0021-9010.89.3.416

20. Berdahl and Min, 2012.
21. Meiko Yoshihama, Chic Dabby, and Shirley Luo, "Facts and Stats Report, Updated and Expanded 2020 Domestic Violence in Asian & Pacific Islander Homes." Asian Pacific Institute on Gender-Based Violence (2020). https://api-gbv.org/wp-content/uploads/2020/10/Facts-stats-rpt-updated-expanded-Oct20201.pdf
22. Mieko Yoshihama, Deborah Bybee, Chic Dabby, and Juliane Blazevski, "Lifecourse Experiences of Intimate Partner Violence and Help-Seeking Among Filipina, Indian, and Pakistani Women." Asian Pacific Institute on Gender-Based Violence (2010). https://www.api-gbv.org/resources/lif ecourse-ipv-help-seeking/
23. Shahmir H. Ali, Sadia Mohaimin, Ritu Dhar, Moltrayee Dhar, Farzana Rahman, Liza Roychowdhury, Tanzeela Islam, and Sahnah Lim, "Sexual Violence Among LGB+ South Asian Americans: Findings from a Community Survey," *PLOS One* (2022). https://doi.org/10.1371/ journal.pone.0264061
24. Yoshihama, Bybee, Dabby, and Blazevski, 2010.
25. Ali, Mohaimin, Dhar, Dhar, Rahman, Roychowdhury, Islam, and Lim, 2022.
26. Jennifer L. Berdahl, "The Sexual Harassment of Uppity Women," *Journal of Applied Psychology 92*, no. 2 (2007): 425–437. https://doi.org/10.1037/0021-9010.92.2.425; Madeline E. Heilman and Tyler G. Okimoto, "Why Are Women Penalized For Success at Male Tasks?: The Implied Communality Deficit," *Journal of Applied Psychology 92*, no. 1 (2007): 81–91. https://doi.org/ 10.1037/0021-9010.92.1.81
27. Stacey Diane Arañez Litam and Megan Speciale, "The Multidimensional Nature of Attraction," in *Handbook for Human Sexuality Counseling: A Sex Positive Approach*, ed. Angela M. Schubert and Mark Pope (Alexandria, VA: American Counseling Association, 2023), 131–144.

Chapter 7

1. Gabor Maté and Daniel Maté, *The Myth of Normal: Trauma, Illness, and Healing in a Toxic Culture* (New York: Avery, 2022), 202.
2. R. Rogers Kobak and Amy Sceery, "Attachment in Late Adolescence: Working Models, Affect Regulation, and Representations of Self and Others," *Child Development 59*, no. 1 (1988): 135–146; Simon Larose and Annie Bernier, "Social Support Processes: Mediators of Attachment State of Mind and Adjustment in Late Adolescence," *Attachment & Human Development 3*, no. 1 (2010): 96–120. https://doi.org/10.1080/14616730010024762
3. Stacey Diane A. Litam, "'Take Your Kung Flu Back to Wuhan': Counseling Asians, Asian Americans, and Pacific Islanders with Race-Based Trauma Related to COVID-19," *The Professional Counselor 10*, no. 2 (2020): 144–156. https://doi.org/10.15241/sdal.10.2.144
4. Annegret Dreher, Eric Hahn, Albert Diefenbacher, Main Huong Nguyen, Kerem Böge, Hannah Burian, Michael Dettling, Ronald Burian, and Thi Minh Tam Ta, "Cultural Differences in Symptom Presentation for Depression and Somatization Measured by the PHQ Between Vietnamese and German Psychiatric Outpatients," *Journal of Psychosomatic Research 102* (2017): 71–77. https://doi.org/10.1016/j.jpsychores.2017.09.010; Sandeep Grover and Abhisek Ghosk, "Somatic Symptoms and Related Disorders in Asians and Asian Americans," *Asian Journal of Psychiatry 7* (2014): 77–79. https://doi.org/10.1016/j.ajp.2013.11.014; Devon E. Hinton, Amie Alley Pollack, Bahr Weiss, and Lam T. Trung, "Culturally Sensitive Assessments of Anxious-Depressive Distress in Vietnam: Avoiding Category Truncation," *Transcultural Psychiatry 55*, no. 3 (2018): 384–404. https://doi.org/10.1177/1363461518764500
5. Stacey Diane A. Litam and Christian D. Chan, "Experiences of Stress and Help-Seeking Behaviors in Filipino Americans," *International Journal for the Advancement of Counselling 44*, no. 4 (2022): 586–603. https://doi.org/10.1007/s10447-022-09485-x
6. Herbert M. Swick, "Toward a Normative Definition of Medical Professionalism," *Academic Medicine 74*, no. 6 (2000): 612–616.
7. Marcia Ines Silvani, Robert Werder, and Claudio Perret, "The Influence of Blue Light on Sleep, Performance, and Wellbeing in Young Adults: A Systematic Review," *Frontiers in Physiology 13* (2022): 1–21. https:./doi.org/10.3389/fphys.2022.943108
8. Jenny Wang, *Permission to Come Home: Reclaiming Mental. Health as Asian Americans* (New York: Balance, 2022), 84–85.

9. Karen Pyke and Tran Dang, "'FOB' and 'Whitewashed': Identity and Internalized Racism Among Second-Generation Asian Americans," *Qualitative Sociology 26* (2003): 147–172.
10. Kevin Leo Yabut Nadal and Stacey Diane A. Litam, "Colorism," in *SAGE Encyclopedia of Filipina/x/o American Studies*, ed. Kevin Leo Yabut Nadal, Allyson Tintiangco-Cubales, and E. J. R. David (Thousand Oaks, CA: SAGE Publications, Inc., 2022), 181–185.
11. E. J. R. David and Sumie Okazaki, "The Colonial Mentality Scale (CMS) for Filipino Americans: Scale Construction and Psychological Implications," *Journal of Counseling Psychology 53*, no. 2 (2006): 241–252. https://doi.org/10.1037/0022-0167.53.2.241
12. Jean Kim, "Asian American Identity Development Theory," in *New Perspectives on Racial Identity Development: A Theoretical and Practical Anthology*, ed. Charmaine L. Wijeyesinghe and Bailey W. Jackson (New York: NYU Press, 2001), 67–90.

Chapter 8

1. Chapman, Gary D. *The Five Love Languages* (Farmington Hills, MI: Walker Large Print, 2010).
2. Laurie L. Meschke and Linda P. Juang, "Obstacles to Parent–Adolescent Communication in Hmong American Families: Exploring Pathways to Adolescent Mental Health Promotion," *Ethnicity and Health 19*, no. 2 (2014): 144–159. https://doi.org/10.1080/13557858.2013.814765
3. Victoria Kress and Matthew Paylo, *Treating Those with Mental Disorders: A Comprehensive Approach to Case Conceptualization and Treatment* (Chicago: Pearson, 2018).
4. Carl R. Rogers, *A Way of Being* (Boston: Houghton Mifflin, 1995).
5. Kress and Paylo, 2018.
6. Carl R. Rogers, "The Necessary and Sufficient Conditions of Therapeutic Personality Change," *Journal of Consulting Psychology 21*, no. 2 (1957): 95–103. https://doi.org/10.1037/0033-3204.44.3.240
7. Rogers, 1957.
8. Rogers, 1957.
9. Rogers, 1957.
10. Rogers, 1957, 101.
11. Michelle Zauner, *Crying in H Mart: A Memoir* (New York: Alfred A. Knopf, 2021), 142–143.

Chapter 9

1. Jenny T. Wang, *Permission to Come Home: Reclaiming Mental Health as Asian Americans* (New York: Balance, 2022), 4.
2. Burcu Uzum and Yasemin Ozdemir, "Crab Syndrome 'If I Can't Do It, You Can't Do It': Scale Development Study," *Journal of Organizational Behavior Research 5*, no. 2 (2020): 241–252.
3. Carliss D. Miller, "The Crabs in a Barrel Syndrome: Structural Influence on Competitive Behavior," *Academy of Management Proceedings 2014* (2014): 155–156.
4. Roderick J. Watts, Jaleel K. Abdul-Adil, and Terrance Pratt, "Enhancing Critical Consciousness in Young African American Men: A Psychoeducational Approach," *Psychology of Men & Masculinity 3*, no. 1 (2002): 41–50. https://doi.org/10.1037/1524-9220.3.1.41
5. Stacey Diane A. Litam and Christian D. Chan, "Breaking the Bamboo Ceiling: Practical Strategies for Asian American and Pacific Islander Counselor Educators," *Counselor Education and Supervision 60*, no. 3 (2021): 174–189. https://doi.org/10.1002/ceas.12210
6. Stacey Diane A. Litam and Christian D. Chan, "Grounded Theory of AAPI for #BlackLivesMatter," *The Professional Counselor 11*, no. 4 (2021): 400–442. https://doi.org/10.15241/sdal.11.4.400
7. Stacey Diane A. Litam and Christian D. Chan, "Experiences of Stress and Help-Seeking Behaviors in Filipino Americans," *Journal for the Advancement of Counselling 44*, no. 4 (2022): 586–603. https://doi.org/10.1007/s10447-022-09485-x; Stacey Diane A. Litam and Seungbin Oh, "Ethnic Identity and Coping Strategy as Moderators of COVID-19 Racial Discrimination Experiences Among Chinese Americans," *Counseling Outcome Research and Evaluation 13*, no. 2 (2020): 101–115. https://doi.org/10.1080/21501378.2020.1814138; Stacey Diane A. Litam and Seungbin Oh, "Coping Strategies as Moderators of COVID-19 Racial Discrimination in Filipinos," *Asian American Journal of Psychology 13*, no. 1 (2022): 18–29. https://doi.org/10.1037/aap0000253; Seungbin Oh and Stacey Diane A. Litam, "COVID-19 Racial Discrimination on Emotional Distress and Life Satisfaction Among Asian Americans: Examining a Moderated Mediation Model," *Asian American Journal of Psychology*

13, no. 3 (2022): 270–282. https://doi.org/10.1037/aap0000267; Seungbin Oh, Stacey Diane A. Litam, and Catharina Y. Chang, "Racism and Stress-Related Growth Among Asian Internationals: Ethnic Identity, Resilience, and Coping During COVID-19," *International Journal for the Advancement of Counselling 45*, no. 2 (2022): 226–248. https://doi.org/10.1007/s10447-022-09494-w; Seungbin Oh, Stacey Diane A. Litam, and Catharina Y. Chang, "COVID-19 Racial Discrimination and Mental Health of Korean Americans: Role of Ethnic Identity and Coping Strategy," *Stigma and Health 7*, no. 4 (2022): 461–470. https://doi.org/10.1037/sah0000407

8. Elan C. Hope and Robert J. Jagers, "The Role of Sociopolitical Attitudes and Civic Education in the Civic Engagement of Black Youth," *Journal of Research on Adolescence 24*, no. 3 (2014): 460–470. https://doi.org/10.1111/jora.12117

9. Amir Levine and Rachel Heller, *Attached: The New Science of Adult Attachment and How It Can Help You Find—and Keep—Love* (New York: Penguin Random House, 2010).

10. Semir Zeki, "The Neurobiology of Love," *FEBS Letters 581* (2007): 2576–2579.

11. Johnson, Susan M., *Hold Me Tight: Seven Conversations for a Lifetime of Love* (New York: Little, Brown & Co., 2008).

12. Brooke C. Feeney and Roxanne L. Thrush, "Relationship Influences on Exploration in Adulthood: The Characteristics and Function of a Secure Base," *Journal of Personality and Social Psychology 98*, no. 1 (2010): 57–76. https://doi.org/10.1037/a0016961

13. Mario Mikulincer and Phillip R. Shaver, "The Attachment Behavioral System in Adulthood: Activation, Psychodynamics, and Interpersonal Processes," *Advances in Experimental Social Psychology 35* (2003): 53–152.

Chapter 10

1. Cathy Park Hong, *Minor Feelings: An Asian American Reckoning* (One World, 2020), 34.

2. Marsha M. Linehan, *DBT Skills Training Manual*, 2nd edition (New York: Guilford Press, 2015).

3. Janany Jeyasundaram, Luisa Yao Dan Cao, and Barry Trentham, "Experiences of Intergenerational Trauma in Second-Generation Refugees: Healing Through Occupation," *Canadian Journal of Occupational Therapy 87*, no. 5 (2020): 412–422. https://doi.org/10.1177/0008417420968684; Nancy J. Lin and Karen L. Suyemoto, "So You, My Children, Can Have a Better Life: A Cambodian American Perspective on the Phenomenology of Intergenerational Communication About Trauma," *Journal of Aggression, Maltreatment & Trauma 25*, no. 4 (2016): 400–420. https://doi.org/10.1080/10926771.2015.1133748

4. Jieyi Cai and Richard T. Lee, "Intergenerational Communication About Historical Trauma in Asian American Families," *Adversity and Resilience Science 3* (2022): 233–245. https://doi.org/10.1007/s42844-022-00064-y; Stacey Diane A. Litam, "'Take Your Kung Flu Back to Wuhan': Counseling Asians, Asian Americans, and Pacific Islanders with Race-Based Trauma Related to COVID-19," *The Professional Counselor 10*, no. 2 (2020): 144–156. https://doi.org/10.15241/sdal.10.2.144

5. P. Priscilla Lui, "Intergenerational Cultural Conflict, Mental Health, and Educational Outcomes Among Asian and Latino/a Americans: Qualitative and Meta-analytic Review," *Psychological Bulletin 141*, no. 2 (2015): 404–446. https://doi.org/10.1037/a0038449

6. Nancy J. Lin and Karen L. Suyemoto, "So You, My Children, Can Have a Better Life: A Cambodian American Perspective on the Phenomenology of Intergenerational Communication About Trauma," *Journal of Aggression, Maltreatment & Trauma 25*, no. 4 (2016): 400–420. https://doi.org/10.1080/10926771.2015.1133748

7. Nina Thorup Dalgaard and Edith Montgomery, "Disclosure and Silencing: A Systematic Review of the Literature on Patterns of Trauma Communication in Refugee Families," *Transcultural Psychiatry 52*, no. 5 (2015): 579–593. https://doi.org/10.1177/1363461514568442

8. Stacey Diane A. Litam and Christian D. Chan, "Experiences of Stress and Help-Seeking Behaviors in Filipino Americans," *Journal for the Advancement of Counselling 44*, no. 4 (2022): 586–603. https://doi.org/10.1007/s10447-022-09485-x; Seungbin Oh, Stacey Diane A. Litam, and Catharina Y. Chang, "Racism and Stress-Related Growth Among Asian Internationals: Ethnic Identity, Resilience, and Coping During COVID-19," *International Journal for the Advancement of Counselling 45*, no. 2 (2022): 226–248. https://doi.org/10.1007/s10447-022-09494-w

9. Qi Wang, Jessie Bee Kim Koh, and Qingfang Song, "Meaning Making Through Personal Storytelling: Narrative Research in the Asian American Context," *Asian American Journal of Psychology 6*, no. 1 (2015): 88–96. https://doi.org/10.1037/a0037317

Resources

Asian American Health Initiative
https://aahiinfo.org

Asian Mental Health Collective
https://www.asianmhc.org

Asian Mental Health Project
https://www.asianmentalhealthproject.com

National Asian American Pacific Islander Mental Health Association
https://www.naapimha.org/aanhpi-service-providers

National Queer Asian Pacific Islander Alliance
https://www.nqapia.org

South Asian Mental Health Initiative & Network
https://samhin.org

Bibliography

Ainsworth, Mary D. Salter. "Attachments Beyond Infancy." *American Psychologist* 44 (1989): 709–716. https://doi.org/10.1037//0003-066x.44.4.709

Ainsworth, Mary D. Salter, and Silvia M. Bell. "Attachment, Exploration, and Separation: Illustrated by Behavior of One-Year-Olds in a Strange Situation." *Child Development 41*, no. 1 (1970): 49–67.

Ainsworth, Mary D. Salter, Mary C. Blehar, Everett Walters, and Sally Wall. *Patterns of Attachment: A Psychological Study of the Strange Situation*. Hillsdale, NJ: Erlbaum, 1978.

Ali, Shahmir H., Sadia Mohaimin, Ritu Dhar, Moltrayee Dhar, Farzana Rahman, Liza Roychowdhury, Tanzeela Islam, and Sahnah Lim. "Sexual Violence Among LGB+ South Asian Americans: Findings from a Community Survey." *PLOS One* (2022). https://doi.org/10.1371/journal.pone.0264061

Azhar, Sameena, Satarupa Dasgupta, Sunny Sinha, and Sharvari Karandikar. "Diversity in Sex Work in India: Challenging Stereotypes Regarding Sex Workers." *Sexuality & Culture 24* (2020): 1774–1797.

Bartholomew, Kim, and Leonard M. Horowitz. "Attachment Styles Among Young Adults: A Test of a Four-Category Model." *Journal of Personality and Psychology 61*, no. 2 (1991): 226–244. https://doi.org/10.1037//0022-3514.61.2.226

Beeney, Joseph E., Aidan G. C. Wright, Stephanie D. Stepp, Michael N. Hallquist, Sophie A. Lazarus, Julie R. S. Beeney, Lori N. Scott, and Paul A. Pilkonis. "Disorganized Attachment and Personality Functioning in Adults: A Latent Class Analysis." *Personality Disorders: Theory, Research, and Treatment 8*, no. 3 (2017): 206–216. https://doi.org/10.1037/per0000184

Berdahl, Jennifer L. "The Sexual Harassment of Uppity Women." *Journal of Applied Psychology 92*, no. 2 (2007): 425–437. https://doi.org/10.1037/0021-9010.92.2.425

Berdahl, Jennifer L., and Ji-A Min. "Prescriptive Stereotypes and Workplace Consequences for East Asians in North America." *Cultural Diversity and Ethnic Minority Psychology 18*, no. 2 (2012): 141–152. https://doi.org/10.1037/10027692

Bowlby, John. *Attachment and Loss*. New York: Basic Books, 1969/1982.

Bowlby, John. *A Secure Base*. New York: Basic Books, 1988.

Budiman, Abby, and Neil G. Ruiz. "Key Facts About Asian Americans, A Diverse and Growing Population." Pew Research Center. (2021). https://www.pewresearch.org/short-reads/2021/04/29/key-facts-about-asian-americans/

Burgess, Diana, and Eugene Borgida. "Who Women Are, Who Women Should Be: Descriptive and Prescriptive Gender Stereotyping in Sex Discrimination." *Psychology, Public Policy, and Law 5*, no. 3 (1999): 665–692. https://doi.org/10.1037/ 1076-8971.5.3.665

Cai, Jieyi, and Richard T. Lee. "Intergenerational Communication About Historical Trauma in Asian American Families." *Adversity and Resilience Science 3* (2022): 233–245. https://doi.org/10.1007/s42844-022-00064-y

Cassidy, Jude, and Jonathan J. Mohr. "Unsolvable Fear, Trauma, and Psychopathology: Theory, Research, and Clinical Considerations Related to Disorganized Attachment Across the Life Span." *Clinical Psychology: Science and Practice 8*, no. 3 (2001): 275–298. https://doi.org/10.1093/clipsy.8.3.275

Chan, Christian D., and Stacey Diane Arañez Litam. "Mental Health Equity of Filipino Communities in COVID-19: A Framework for Practice and Advocacy." *The Professional Counselor 11*, no. 1 (2021): 73–85. https://doi.org/10.15241/cdc.11.1.73

Chang, Iris. *The Chinese in America: A Narrative History*. New York: Viking, 2003.

Chang, Stewart. "Feminism in Yellowface." *Harvard Journal of Law & Gender 38* (2015): 235–268.

Chapman, Gary D. *The Five Love Languages*. Farmington Hills, MI: Walker Large Print, 2010.

Cheng, Patrick S. "'I Am Yellow and Beautiful': Reflections on Queer Asian Spirituality and Gay Male Cyberculture." *Journal of Technology, Theology, and Religion 2*, no. 3 (2011): 1–21.

Chew, William F. *Nameless Builders of the Transcontinental Railway: The Chinese Workers of the Central Pacific Railroad*. Victoria, BC: Trafford, 2004.

Chi, Jieyi, and Richard M. Lee, "Intergenerational Communication About Historical Trauma in Asian American Families." *Adversity and Resilience Science 3*, no. 33 (2022), 233–511.

Chou, Rosalind S. *Asian American Sexual Politics: The Construction of Race, Gender, and Sexuality*. Chicago: Rowman and Littlefield Publishers, 2012.

Collins, Nancy L., Máire B. Ford, AnaMarie C. Guichard, and Lisa M. Allard. "Working Models of Attachment and Attribution Processes in Intimate Relationships." *Personality and Social Psychology Bulletin 31*, no. 2 (2006): 201–219. https://doi.org/10.1177/0146167205280907

Dalgaard, Nina Thorup, and Edith Montgomery. "Disclosure and Silencing: A Systematic Review of the Literature on Patterns of Trauma Communication in Refugee Families." *Transcultural Psychiatry 52*, no. 5 (2015): 579–593. https:// doi.org/10.1177/1363461514568442.

Danieli, Yael. *International Handbook of Multigenerational Legacies of Trauma*. New York: Springer, 1998.

Danieli, Yael, Fran H. Norris, and Brian Engdahl. "Multigenerational Legacies of Trauma: Modeling the What and How of Transmission." *American Journal of Orthopsychiatry 86*, no. 6 (2016): 639–651. https:// doi.org/10.1037/ort0000145

David, E. J. R., and Sumie Okazaki. "The Colonial Mentality Scale (CMS) for Filipino Americans: Scale Construction and Psychological Implications." *Journal of Counseling Psychology 53*, no. 2 (2006): 241–252. https://doi.org/10.1037/0022-0167.53.2.241

Diamond, Anna. "The 1924 Law That Slammed the Door on Immigrants and the Politicians Who Pushed It Back Open." *Smithsonian Magazine*, May 19, 2020. https://www.smithso nianmag.com/history/1924-law-slammed-door-immigrants-and-politicians-who-pushed-it-back-open-180974910/

Dreher, Annegret, Eric Hahn, Albert Diefenbacher, Main Huong Nguyen, Kerem Böge, Hannah Burian, Michael Dettling, Ronald Burian, and Thi Minh Tam Ta. "Cultural Differences in Symptom Presentation for Depression and Somatization Measured by the PHQ Between Vietnamese and German Psychiatric Outpatients." *Journal of Psychosomatic Research 102* (2017): 71–77. https://doi.org/10.1016/j.jpsychores.2017.09.010

Evans-Campbell, Teresa. "Historical Trauma in American Indian/Native Alaska Communities: A Multilevel Framework for Exploring Impacts on Individuals, Families, and Communities." *Journal of Interpersonal Violence 23*, no. 3 (2008): 316–338. https://doi.org/ 10.1177/0886260507312290

Feeney, Brooke C., and Roxanne L. Thrush. "Relationship Influences on Exploration in Adulthood: The Characteristics and Function of a Secure Base." *Journal of Personality and Social Psychology 98*, no. 1 (2010): 57–76. https://doi.org/10.1037/a0016961

Fonagy, Peter, Gyorgy Gergely, Elliot Jurist, and Mary Target. *Affect Regulation, Mentalization, and the Development of the Self*. London: Other Press, 2002.

Gill, Michael J. "When Information Does Not Deter Stereotyping: Prescriptive Stereotyping Can Bias Judgments Under Conditions That Discourage Descriptive Stereotyping." *Journal of Experimental Social Psychology 40*, no. 5 (2004): 619–632. https://doi.org/10.1016/ j.jesp.2003.12.001

Gong, Fang, Sue-Je L. Gage, and Leonardo A. Tacata Jr. "Help-Seeking Behavior Among Filipino Americans: A Cultural Analysis of Face and Language." *Journal of Community Psychology 31*, no. 5 (2003): 469–488. https://doi.org/10.1002/jcop.10063

Grover, Sandeep, and Abhisek Ghosk. "Somatic Symptoms and Related Disorders in Asians and Asian Americans." *Asian Journal of Psychiatry 7* (2014): 77–79. https://doi.org/10.1016/j.ajp.2013.11.014

Gunderson, John G., and Karlon Lyons-Ruth. "BPD's Interpersonal Hypersensitivity Phenotype: A Gene-Environment-Developmental Model." *Journal of Personality Disorders 22*, no. 1 (2008): 22–41. http://doi.org/10.1521/pedi.2008.22.1.22

Han, Meekyung. "Relationship Among Perceived Parental Trauma, Parental Attachment, and Sense of Coherence in Southeast Asian American College Students." *Journal of Family Social Work 9*, no. 2 (2005): 25–45. https://doi.org/10.1300/J039v09n02_02

Harlow, Harry F. "Love in Infant Monkeys." *Scientific American 200*, no. 6 (1959): 68–74.

Harlow, Harry F., and Robert Z. Zimmerman. "Affectional Response in the Infant Monkey." *Science 130*, no. 3373 (1959): 421–432. https://doi.org/10.1126/science.130.3373.421

Heilman, Madeline E., and Tyler G. Okimoto. "Why Are Women Penalized For Success at Male Tasks?: The Implied Communality Deficit." *Journal of Applied Psychology 92*, no. 1 (2007): 81–91. https://doi.org/10.1037/0021-9010.92.1.81

Heilman, Madeline E., Aaron S. Wallen, Daniella Fuchs, and Melinda M. Tamkins. "Penalties for Success: Reactions to Women Who Succeed at Male Gendertyped Tasks." *Journal of Applied Psychology 89*, no. 3 (2004): 416–427. https://doi.org/10.1037/ 0021-9010.89.3.416

Hendrix, Cassandra L., Daniel D. Dilks, Brooke G. McKenna, Anne L. Dunlop, Elizabeth J. Corwin, and Patricia A. Brennan. "Maternal Childhood Adversity Associates with Frontoamygdala Connectivity in Neonates." *Biological Psychiatry: Cognitive Neuroscience and Neuroimaging 6*, no. 4 (2021): 470–478. https://doi.org/10.1016/j.bpsc.2020.11.003

Herbison, Chico, and Jerry Schultz. "Quiet Passages: The Japanese-American War Bride Experience." https://kuscholarworks.ku.edu/bitstream/handle/1808/1140/CEAS.1990. n1.pdf?sequence=1 (accessed June 15, 2023).

Hing, Bill Ong. *Defining America Through Immigration Policy.* Philadelphia: Temple University Press, 2003.

Hinton, Devon E., Amie Alley Pollack, Bahr Weiss, and Lam T. Trung. "Culturally Sensitive Assessments of Anxious-Depressive Distress in Vietnam: Avoiding Category Truncation." *Transcultural Psychiatry 55*, no. 3 (2018): 384–404. https://doi.org/10.1177/136346151 8764500

https://history.state.gov/milestones/1921-1936/immigration-act (accessed June 15, 2023).

Hong, Cathy Park. *Minor Feelings: An Asian American Reckoning.* One World, 2020.

Hope, Elan C., and Robert J. Jagers. "The Role of Sociopolitical Attitudes and Civic Education in the Civic Engagement of Black Youth." *Journal of Research on Adolescence 24*, no. 3 (2014): 460–470. https://doi.org/10.1111/jora.12117

Hughes, Diane, James Rodriguez, Emilie P. Smith, Deborah J. Johnson, Howard C. Stevenson, and John Spicer. "Parents' Ethnic-Racial Socialization Practices: A Review of Research and Directions for Future Study." *Developmental Psychology 42*, no. 5 (2006): 747–770. https://doi.org/10.1037/0012-1649.42.5.747

Jeyasundaram, Janany, Luisa Yao Dan Cao, and Barry Trentham. "Experiences of Intergenerational Trauma in Second-Generation Refugees: Healing Through Occupation." *Canadian Journal of Occupational Therapy 87*, no. 5 (2020): 412–422. https://doi.org/ 10.1177/0008417420968684

Johnson, Susan M. *Hold Me Tight: Seven Conversations for a Lifetime of Love.* New York: Little, Brown & Co., 2008.

Kim, Jean. "Asian American Identity Development Theory." In *New Perspectives on Racial Identity Development: A Theoretical and Practical Anthology*, edited by Charmaine L. Wijeyesinghe and Bailey W. Jackson, 67–90. New York: NYU Press, 2001.

Kim-Prieto, Chu, Grace S. Kim, Leilani Salvo Crane, Susana Ming Lowe, Phi Loan, and Khanh T. Dinh. "Legacies of War: Asian American Women and War Trauma." *Women & Therapy 41*, no. 3-4 (2018): 203–218. https://doi.org/10.1080/02703149.2018.1425023

Kipling, Rudyard. *The White Man's Burden* (originally published by Doubleday, 1899). https://www.kiplingsociety.co.uk/poem/poems_burden.htm (accessed June 15, 2023).

Kobak, R. Rogers, and Amy Sceery. "Attachment in Late Adolescence: Working Models, Affect Regulation, and Representations of Self and Others." *Child Development 59*, no. 1 (1988): 135–146.

Kraus, George. *High Road to Promontory: Building the Central Pacific (Now the Southern Pacific) Across the High Sierra.* Palo Alto, CA: American West Publishing Co., 1969.

Kress, Victoria, and Matthew Paylo. *Treating Those with Mental Disorders: A Comprehensive Approach to Case Conceptualization and Treatment.* Upper Saddle River, NJ: Pearson, 2018.

Larose, Simon, and Annie Bernier. "Social Support Processes: Mediators of Attachment State of Mind and Adjustment in Late Adolescence." *Attachment & Human Development 3*, no. 1 (2010): 96–120. https://doi.org/10.1080/14616730010024762

Lee, Erika. "The 'Yellow Peril' and Asian Exclusion in the Americas." *Pacific Historical Review 76*, no. 4 (2007): 537–562.

Lee, Nancy S. "Telling Their Own Stories: Chinese Canadian Biography As A Historical Genre." In *The Chinese in America: A History from Gold Mountain to the New Millennium*, edited by Susie Lan Cassel, 106–121. New York: AltaMira, 2002.

Leong, Russell. *Asian American Sexualities: Dimensions of the Gay and Lesbian Experience.* New York: Routledge, 1995.

Levine, Amir, and Rachel Heller. *Attached: The New Science of Adult Attachment and How It Can Help You Find—and Keep—Love.* New York: Penguin Random House, 2010.

Levine, Peter A. *Trauma and Memory: Brain and the Body in a Search for the Living Past: A Practical Guide for Understanding and Working with Traumatic Memory.* Berkeley, CA: North Atlantic Books, 2015.

Liem, Ramsay. "Silencing Historical Trauma: The Politics and Psychology of Memory and Voice." *Peace and Conflict: Journal of Peace Psychology 13*, no. 2 (2007): 153–174. https://doi.org/10.1080/10781910701271200

Lin, Nancy J., and Karen L. Suyemoto. "So You, My Children, Can Have a Better Life: A Cambodian American Perspective on the Phenomenology of Intergenerational Communication About Trauma." *Journal of Aggression, Maltreatment & Trauma 25*, no. 4 (2016): 400–420. https://doi.org/10.1080/10926771.2015.1133748

Linehan, Marsha M. *DBT Skills Training Manual* (2nd ed.). New York: Guilford Publications, 2015.

Litam, Stacey Diane A. "'Take Your Kung Flu Back to Wuhan': Counseling Asians, Asian Americans, and Pacific Islanders with Race-Based Trauma Related to COVID-19." *The Professional Counselor 10*, no. 2 (2020): 144–156. https://doi.org/10.15241/sdal.10.2.144

Litam, Stacey Diane Arañez, and Christian D. Chan. "Breaking the Bamboo Ceiling: Practical Strategies for Asian American and Pacific Islander Counselor Educators." *Counselor Education and Supervision 60*, no. 3 (2021): 174–189. https://doi.org/10.1002/ceas.12210

Litam, Stacey Diane Arañez, and Christian D. Chan. "Experiences of Stress and Help-Seeking Behaviors in Filipino Americans." *Intergenerational Journal for the Advancement of Counselling 44*, no. 4 (2022): 586–603. https://doi.org/10.1007/s10447-022-09485-x

Litam, Stacey Diane Arañez, and Christian D. Chan. "Grounded Theory of AAPI for #BlackLivesMatter." *The Professional Counselor 11*, no. 4 (2021): 400–442. https://doi.org/10.15241/sdal.11.4.400

Litam, Stacey Diane Arañez, Christian S. Chan, Lotes Nelson, and Victor E. Tuazon. "Decolonizing the Interpersonal Theory of Suicide with Filipinx American Clients." *Asian American Journal of Psychology 13*, no. 1 (2022): 73–82. https://doi.org/10.1037/aap0000255

Litam, Stacey Diane Arañez, & Seungbin Oh. "Coping Strategies as Moderators of COVID-19 Racial Discrimination in Filipinos." *Asian American Journal of Psychology 13*, no. 1 (2022): 18–29. https://doi.org/10.1037/aap0000253

Litam, Stacey Diane Arañez, & Seungbin Oh. "Ethnic Identity and Coping Strategy as Moderators of COVID-19 Racial Discrimination Experiences Among Chinese Americans." *Counseling Outcome Research and Evaluation 13*, no. 2 (2020): 101–115. https://doi.org/10.1080/21501378.2020.1814138

Litam, Stacey Diane Arañez, and Megan Speciale. "The Multidimensional Nature of Attraction." In *Handbook for Human Sexuality Counseling: A Sex Positive Approach*, edited by Angela M. Schubert and Mark Pope, 131–144. Alexandria, VA: American Counseling Association, 2023.

Liu, John M., and Lucie Cheng. "Pacific Rim Development and the Duality of Post-1965 Asian Immigration to the United States." In *The New Asian Immigration in Los Angeles and Global Restructuring*, edited by Paul M. Ong, Edna Bonacich, and Lucie Cheng, 45–73. Philadelphia: Temple University Press, 1994.

Liu, William Ming, and Tai Chang. "Asian American Men and Masculinity." In *Handbook of Asian American Psychology*, edited by Frederick Leong, Arpana G. Inman, Angela Ebreo, Lawrence Hsin Yang, Lisa Marie Kinoshita, and Michi Fu, 197–212. Thousand Oaks, CA: Sage Publications, Inc., 2006.

Lui, P. Priscilla. "Intergenerational Cultural Conflict, Mental Health, and Educational Outcomes Among Asian and Latino/a Americans: Qualitative and Meta-analytic Review." *Psychological Bulletin 141*, no. 2 (2015): 404–446. https://doi.org/10.1037/a0038449

Main, Mary, and Judith Solomon. "Procedures for Identifying Infants as Disorganized-Disoriented During the Ainsworth Strange Situation." In *Attachment in the Preschool Years: Theory, Research and Intervention*, edited by Mark T. Greenberg, Dante Cicchetti, and E. Mark Cummins, 121–160. Chicago: University of Chicago Press, 1990.

Maté, Gabor, and Daniel Maté. *The Myth of Normal: Trauma, Illness, and Healing in a Toxic Culture*. New York: Avery, 2022.

Mental Health America. "Asian American/Pacific Islander Communities and Mental Health." 2023. https://www.mhanational.org/issues/asian-american-pacific-islander-communities-and-mental-health

Merritt, Christopher R. B., Gary Weisz, and Kelly J. Dixon. "'Verily the Road Was Built with Chinaman's Bones': An Archaeology of Chinese Line Camps in Montana." *International Journal of Historical Archaeology 16*, no. 4 (2012): 666–695. https://doi.org/10.1007/s10 761-012-0197-7

Meschke, Laurie L., and Linda P. Juang. "Obstacles to Parent–Adolescent Communication in Hmong American Families: Exploring Pathways to Adolescent Mental Health Promotion." *Ethnicity and Health 19*, no. 2 (2014): 144–159. https://doi.org/10.1080/13557 858.2013.814765

Mignolo, Walter D. "What Does It Mean to Decolonize?" In *On Decoloniality: Concepts, Analytics, Praxis*, edited by Walter D. Mignolo and Catherine E. Walsh, 105–134. Durham, NC: Duke University Press, 2018.

Mikulincer, Mario, and Phillip R. Shaver. *Attachment in Adulthood: Structure, Dynamics, and Change*. New York: Guilford Press, 2010.

Mikulincer, Mario, and Phillip R. Shaver. "The Attachment Behavioral System in Adulthood: Activation, Psychodynamics, and Interpersonal Processes." In *Advances in Experimental Social Psychology*, edited by Mark Zanna, 53–152. New York: Elsevier Academic Press, 2003.

Miller, Carliss D. "The Crabs in a Barrel Syndrome: Structural Influence on Competitive Behavior." *Academy of Management Proceedings* 2014 (2014): 155–156.

Nadal, Kevin L., Gabriel Corpus, and Alyssa Hufana. "The Forgotten Asian Americans: Filipino Americans' Experiences with Racial Microaggressions and Trauma." *Asian American Journal of Psychology 13*, no. 1 (2022): 51–61. https://doi.org/10.1037/aap0000261

Nadal, Kevin L., Kara Mia Vigilia Escobar, Gail T. Prado, E. J. R. David, and Krystal Haynes. "Racial Microaggressions and the Filipino American Experience: Recommendations for

Counseling and Development." *Journal of Multicultural Counseling and Development 40*, no. 3 (2012): 156–173. https://doi.org/10.1002/j.2161-1912.2012.00015.x

Nadal, Kevin Leo Yabut, and Stacey Diane A. Litam. "Colorism." In *SAGE Encyclopedia of Filipina/x/o American Studies*, edited by Kevin Leo Yabut Nadal, Allyson Tintiangco-Cubales, and E. J. R. David, 181–185. Thousand Oaks, CA: SAGE Publications, Inc., 2022.

Nagata, Donna K., and Wendy Cheng. "Intergenerational Communication of Race-Related Trauma by Japanese American Former Internees." *American Journal of Orthopsychiatry 73*, no. 3 (2003): 266–278. https://doi.org/10.1037/0002-9432.73.3.266

Oh, Seungbin, and Stacey Diane A. Litam. "COVID-19 Racial Discrimination on Emotional Distress and Life Satisfaction Among Asian Americans: Examining a Moderated Mediation Model." *Asian American Journal of Psychology 13*, no. 3 (2022): 270–282. https://doi.org/10.1037/aap0000267

Oh, Seungbin, Stacey Diane A. Litam, and Catharina Y. Chang. "COVID-19 Racial Discrimination and Mental Health of Korean Americans: Role of Ethnic Identity and Coping Strategy." *Stigma and Health 7*, no. 4 (2022): 461–470. https://doi.org/10.1037/sah0000407

Oh, Seungbin, Stacy Diane A. Litam, and Catharina Y. Chang. "Racism and Stress-Related Growth Among Asian Internationals: Ethnic Identity, Resilience, and Coping During COVID-19." *International Journal for the Advancement of Counselling 45*, no. 2 (2022): 226–248. https://doi.org/10.1007/s10447-022-09494-w

Poon, OiYan. "'The Land of Opportunity Doesn't Apply to Everyone': The Immigrant Experience, Race, and Asian American Career Choices." *Journal of College Student Development 55*, no. 6 (2014): 499–514. https://doi.org/10.1353/csd.2014.0056

Pyke, Karen, and Tran Dang. "'FOB and Whitewashed': Identity and Internalized Racism Among Second Generation Asian Americans." *Qualitative Sociology 26* (2003): 147–172.

Raffaelli, Marcela, Maria I. Iturbide, Miguel Angel Saucedo, and Lorraine Munoz. "You Hear Stories About What They Did and It Makes You Go 'Wow': Adolescents Narrate and Interpret Caregiver Stories About a Difficult Time." *Journal of Adolescent Research 32*, no. 5 (2017): 536–558. https://doi.org/10.1177/0743558416670008

Rogers, Carl R. "The Necessary and Sufficient Conditions of Therapeutic Personality Change." *Journal of Consulting Psychology 21*, no. 2 (1957): 95–103. https://doi.org/10.1037/0033-3204.44.3.240

Rogers, Carl R. *A Way of Being*. Boston: Houghton Mifflin, 1995.

Rottman, Gordon. *World War II Pacific Island Guide: A Geo-Military Study*. Westport, CT: Greenwood Publishing Group, 2002.

Ryan, Joanne, Isabelle Chaudieu, Marie-Laure Ancein, and Richard Saffery. "Biological Underpinnings of Trauma and Post-traumatic Stress Disorder: Focusing on Genetics and Epigenetics." *Epigenetics 8*, no. 11 (2016): 1553–1569.

Said, Edward W. *Orientalism: Western Conceptions of the Orient*. New York: Pantheon Books, 1978.

Saxton, Alexander. "The Army of Canton in the High Sierra." *Pacific Historical Review 35*, no. 2 (1966): 141–152. https://doi.org/10.2307/3636678

Shaver, Phillip R., Dory A. Schachner, and Mario Mikulincer. "Attachment Style, Excessive Reassurance Seeking, Relationship Processes, and Depression." *Personality and Social Psychology Bulletin 31*, no. 3 (2005): 343–359. https://doi.org/10.1177/0146167204271709

Silvani, Marcia Ines, Robert Werder, and Claudio Perret. "The Influence of Blue Light on Sleep, Performance, and Wellbeing in Young Adults: A Systematic Review." *Frontiers in Physiology 13* (2022): 1–21. https:./doi.org/10.3389/fphys.2022.943108

Simpson, Jeffry A., and W. Steven Rholes. "Adult Attachment, Stress, and Romantic Relationships." *Current Opinions in Psychology 13* (2017): 19–24. https://doi.org/10.1016/j.copsyc.2016.04.006

Simpson, Jeffry A., W. Steven Rholes, Lorne Campbell, and Carol L. Wilson. "Changes in Attachment Orientations Across the Transitions to Parenthood." *Journal of Experimental Social Psychology* 39, no. 4 (2003): 317–331. https://doi.org/10.1016/S0022-1031(03)00030-1

Singh, Anneliese A., Brandee Appling, and Heather Trepal. "Using the Multicultural and Social Justice Counseling Competencies to Decolonize Counseling Practice: The Important Roles of Theory, Power, and Action." *Journal of Counseling and Development* 98, no. 3 (2020): 261–271. https://doi.org/10.1002/jcad.12321

Studio ATAO. "Unlearning Scarcity, Cultivating Solidarity." https://www.studioatao.org/unlearning-scarcity-cultivating-solidarity (accessed June 13, 2024).

Swick, Herbert M. "Toward a Normative Definition of Medical Professionalism." *Academic Medicine* 74, no. 6 (2000): 612–616.

Takaki, Ronald. *Strangers from a Different Shore: A History of Asian Americans*. Boston: Little, Brown and Company, 1998.

Thompson, Ross A. "New Directions for Child Development in the Twenty-First Century: The Legacy of Early Attachments." *Child Development* 71, no. 1 (2000): 145–152.

U.S. Department of Commerce. "U.S. Census Bureau Releases Key Stats in Honor of Asian American, Native Hawaiian, and Pacific Islander Heritage Month" (2022). https://www.commerce.gov/news/blog/2022/05/us-census-bureau-releases-key-stats-honor-asian-american-native-hawaiian-and

U.S. House of Representatives History, Art & Archives. (n.d.). *Immigration and Nationality Act of 1965*. https://history.house.gov/Historical-Highlights/1951-2000/Immigration-and-Nationality-Act-of-1965/

Uzum, Burcu, and Yasemin Ozdemir. "Crab Syndrome 'If I Can't Do It, You Can't Do It': Scale Development Study." *Journal of Organizational Behavior Research* 5, no. 2 (2020): 241–252.

Wang, Jenny. *Permission to Come Home: Reclaiming Mental Health as Asian Americans*. New York: Balance, 2022.

Wang, Qi, Jessie Bee Kim Koh, and Qingfang Song. "Meaning Making Through Personal Storytelling: Narrative Research in the Asian American Context." *Asian American Journal of Psychology* 6, no. 1 (2015): 88–96. https://doi.org/10.1037/a0037317

Watts, Roderick J., Jaleel K. Abdul-Adil, and Terrance Pratt. "Enhancing Critical Consciousness in Young African American Men: A Psychoeducational Approach." *Psychology of Men & Masculinity* 3, no. 1 (2002): 41–50. https://doi.org/10.1037/1524-9220.3.1.41

Wilhelm, Kay, Inika Gillis, and Gordon Parker. "Parental Bonding and Adult Attachment Style: The Relationship Between Four Category Models." *International Journal Women's Health and Wellness* 2, no. 1 (2016): 1–7. https://doi.org/10.23937/2474-1353/1510016

Wong, Y. Joel, Jesse Owen, Kimberly K. Tran, Dana L. Collins, and Claire E. Higgins. "Asian American Male College Students' Perceptions of People's Stereotypes About Asian American Men." *Psychology of Men & Masculinity* 13, no. 1 (2012): 75–88. https://doi.org/10.1037/a0022800

Wong, Y. Joel, and Mai-Lin Poon. "Counseling Asian American Men Who Demonstrate Suicidal Behavior." In *Culturally Responsive Counseling with Asian American Men*, edited by William Ming Liu, Derek Kenji Iwamoto, and Mark H. Chae, 279–298. New York: Routledge/Taylor & Francis Group, 2010.

Yamamoto, Traise. "In/visible Difference: Asian American Women and the Politics of Spectacle." *Race, Gender & Class* 7, no. 1 (2000): 43–55.

Yoshihama, Meiko, Deborah Bybee, Chic Dabby, and Juliane Blazevski. "Lifecourse Experiences of Intimate Partner Violence and Help-Seeking Among Filipina, Indian, and Pakistani Women." Asian Pacific Institute on Gender-Based Violence (2010). https://www.api-gbv.org/resources/lifecourse-ipv-help-seeking/

Yoshihama, Meiko, Chic Dabby, and Shirley Luo. "Facts and Stats Report, Updated and Expanded 2020 Domestic Violence in Asian & Pacific Islander Homes." Asian Pacific Institute on Gender-Based Violence (2020). https://api-gbv.org/wp-content/uploads/2020/10/Facts-stats-rpt-updated-expanded-Oct20201.pdf

Zauner, Michelle. *Crying in H Mart: A Memoir.* New York: Alfred A. Knopf, 2021.

Zeki, Semir. "The Neurobiology of Love." *FEBS Letters 581* (2007): 2576–2579.

Index

For the benefit of digital users, indexed terms that span two pages (e.g., 52–53) may, on occasion, appear on only one of those pages.

abandonment. *See* rejection and abandonment
Abercrombie & Fitch, 33, 94–95
abundance mindsets, xv, 12, 35, 38, 86, 94, 102, 122–23, 124, 146, 155
Acts of Service love language, 101
Ainsworth, Mary, 43
Alexander, Jennifer
  attachment style, 56
  demographics, 165
  identity and sense of belonging, 98
  therapy and counseling, 134
  work-life balance, 84, 88
anti-miscegenation laws, 62, 63–64
Antoun, Sophia, 56–57, 103, 165
anxious attachment style
  adult attachment, 45–46
  inherited from parents, 55–56
anxious-resistant/avoidant attachment style
  adult attachment, 45, 56, 130, 131
  infant–caregiver attachment, 43, 44
Asian Americans
  barriers to access to emotional/mental health care, 9–11
  growth of population, 11
  historical waves of immigration, 17
  identity development model, 97
  income and education disparities, 7
  language barriers, 9–10
  model minority myth, 7–8
  overlapping commonalities of subgroups, x–xi, 1
  percentage who are immigrants, 16
  somaticizing psychological distress, 79–80
Asian Exclusion Act of 1924, 62
Asianized attribution, 64
assimilation and fitting in, 6, 24, 25
  becoming too American, 33–34
  conflict avoidance, 31–32
  cultural tightrope, 34
  disconnect between parents and children, 33–35
  hiding ethnic/racial identity, 94–97

parental/ancestral focus on, xiv, 5, 30, 33, 48, 150
pejoratives and intragroup othering, 33, 95
attachment and attachment styles, 40–49, 51–57
  adult attachment styles, 44–47
  anxious, 45–46, 55–56
  anxious-resistant/avoidant, 43, 44, 45
  attachment system, 45
  attachment wounds, 47–49, 125–26
  avoidant, 43, 44, 45, 46–47, 53–54
  disorganized-disoriented, 44, 56–57
  emphasis on food and physical caregiving, 48–49
  healing and achieving secure attachments, 125–26
  history of attachment theory, 41–44
  infant–caregiver attachment styles, 43–44
  inheriting parental attachment styles, 51–57, 137–38
  insecurity driving need to prove self-worth, 79
  parenting and parenthood, 137–38
  reframing secure love from boring to peaceful, 126–27
  science of love, 128–30
  secure, 43–44, 45, 125–26
  shock of birth, and need for comfort and soothing, 40–41
  stop, drop, and roll exercise, 126–27, 130
attention, not drawing to oneself, 3, 4
autonomy, 46, 57, 133, 138
Avadhanam, Ramya
  demographics, 165
  family historical patterns, 19
  fitting in, 34
  self-sacrifice, 90
  silence and conflict avoidance, 92
  wholehearted acceptance, 103
  working twice as hard to get half as far, 25
avoidant attachment style
  adult attachment, 45, 46–47
  infant–caregiver attachment, 43, 44
  inherited from parents, 53–54
  See also anxious-resistant/avoidant attachment style

awakening to social political consciousness
     stage, 97
awareness, 117
     compassionate awareness, 120
     embracing identity, 97
     importance of for breaking inherited
          patterns, 138–39
     self-awareness, xvi–xvii, 88, 126–30
     See also HOME Assessment

balance
     childhood trauma and, 78
     struggle for, 24
     work–life balance, 79, 83, 88
     See also productivity and hard work
Band, Monica P.
     attachment style, 53–54
     attachment wounds, 47
     conspiracy of silence, 30
     demographics, 165
     hard work and productivity, 84
     therapy and counseling, 134
     wholehearted acceptance, 107, 115
Bataan Death March, 2–3, 4
Battle of Mactan, 33
Bayani
     demographics, 165
     hard work and productivity, 80
     self-sacrifice, 89
     sexual liberation, 70
     sexual stereotypes, 67
     wholehearted acceptance, 111
     work-life balance, 84–85
Bowlby, John, 43

Calypso
     attachment style, 57
     hard work and productivity, 84
     need for approval, 80–81
     scarcity mindset, 21
     sexual stereotypes, 65–66
     wholehearted acceptance, 111
Carlon, Jay, 121–22
Carmel, 93, 96, 97–98, 146, 165
Cecilio (author's great-uncle), 2–3, 4
centering pleasure, 75
Chapman, Gary, 101
Charlie's Angels (film), 94–95
Cheung, Christopher
     attachment style, 54
     conflict avoidance, 92
     conspiracy of silence, 29–30
     demographics, 165

healing attachment wounds, 125
     wholehearted acceptance, 114–15
Chinese Exclusion Act of 1882, 17, 63–64
collectivism, 1–2, 52, 92, 93
     defined, 1
     descriptive stereotypes, 71
     indebtedness to ancestors, 1–2
     intersectionality with career, 6–7
     sexuality and, 69
colonial mentalities, 95, 96, 121–22
colorism, 94–95
comfort women, 61
commitments, honoring, 4, 91
communication skills, cultivating stronger, 131
community of voices, 79, 81, 82–83, 86, 92, 121,
     129–30, 138–39
companionate love, 130
comparisons
     children's accomplishments, xiv, 21–22
     children's versus parents' challenges, 8
     invalidating children's emotional distress, 8
competition, 20–21, 25, 27–28, 85, 121–22
conditions of worth, 105, 110–11
conflict avoidance, 7, 28–29, 79–80
     attachment styles, 45, 46, 57
     avoiding rocking the boat, 31–32
     communicating emotional consequences
          after conflict, 91
     conspiracies of silence, 30–31, 92–94, 108
     people-pleasing behaviors, 31, 89
     promoting interpersonal harmony, 1, 26–27,
          52, 102
     vulnerability, 8, 9, 52, 102–3
conspiracies of silence, 4–5, 7, 8, 9, 11, 13
     children's internalized beliefs regarding, 5–6
     conflict avoidance, 30–31, 79, 92–94, 108
     dangers of, 5
     defined, 4–5
     emotional and mental health challenges, 8
     emotional distance in relationships, 9
     healing from, 35–38
     talking about emotions, 28–31
     unlocking trauma narratives, 36
constructive personality change, 105–6
contact comfort drive, 43
Coolidge, Calvin, 17
coping skills and strategies
     assimilation as, 33
     avoidant attachment styles, 127
     contact comfort drive, 43
     hyperactive forms of coping, 46
     identity development process, 97
     lack of, 29

orientation with romantic partner, 102–3
  problematic, xviii, 54, 79–80, 81
  protest behaviors, 45–46
COVID-19 pandemic, 123
crab mentality, 121–22
critical consciousness, raising, 122–24
Crying in H Mart (Zauner), 48–49, 110
Cultural Revolution, 19

deactivation strategies, 46–47, 126
descriptive sexual stereotypes, 71, 75–76
De Silva, Chamari, 27–28, 32, 109, 165
dialectical behavior therapy (DBT), 146–47
disappointment
  fear of disappointing others, 15–16, 28,
    79, 122
  increasing awareness, 140
  insecure attachment styles, 79
discrimination
  critical consciousness, 124
  deviation from behavioral expectations, 6
  efforts to avoid, 25, 31–32, 33, 96, 97
  intragroup othering, 6, 33, 95
  legislation, 17, 64
  pandemic-era awakening to, 123–24
  See also trauma
disorganized-disoriented attachment style
  infant–caregiver attachment, 44
  inherited from parents, 56–57
distancing strategies, 30–31, 46–47, 126
dopamine, 128–29
Dory (author's Lola (grandmother)), 2, 3, 4

emotional availability, 46–47, 53, 54, 129, 133
emotional flashbacks, xviii, 9, 156
empathy
  constructive personality change and, 105
  toward parents/ancestors, xvii, 5, 35
encouragement, providing for partner, 133
epigenetics, 20
ethnic allegiance, 24, 25
ethnic awareness stage, 97
ethnic/racial identity, 12, 33, 145, 151
  hiding, 94–97
  learning to embrace, 97–99
Everything Everywhere All At Once
    (film), 51, 68

Factora-Borchers, Lisa, 112–13, 148–49, 165
fearful avoidant attachment style. *See*
    disorganized-disoriented attachment style
fetishization, 63, 73, 74
filial piety, 1–2, 26, 52

fitting in. *See* assimilation and fitting in
Five Love Languages, The (Chapman), 101
flexible boundary setting, 9, 83, 90–91, 99
Floyd, George, 123

Gabriel K., 26, 37, 165
gratitude, 6, 8, 9, 27–29, 80, 91, 138, 145

Haldeman, Michelle Hisako, 165
hard work. *See* productivity and hard work
Harlow, Harry, 41, 42–43
Hart-Cellar Act (Immigration and Nationality
    Act) of 1965, 17–18, 20–21, 22
heads down, keeping, xv, 3, 9, 15, 79, 82, 85,
    123, 137
heart work, 146
Heller, Rachel S. F., 45
historical trauma. *See* trauma
Hold Me Tight (Johnson), 132–33
Holleran, Angelika, 109, 130, 165
HOME (Healing Orientation Model Elements)
    Assessment, xi, 104–16, 161–63
  anticipating needs, wants, and desires,
    108–11, 141–42
  avoiding transactional acts, 142–43
  freedom, growth, and healing, 111–14,
    143–44
  intentionality, 142
  parenting and parenthood, 141–44
  understanding, 106–8, 141
Hong, Cathy Park, 146
Hsu, Stephanie, 51
Hukbalahap, 36
human sex trafficking, 61, 82

I.B.
  attachment style, 54
  demographics, 165
  gratitude for parental sacrifices, 27
  hard work and productivity, 84
  parenting and parenthood, 141–42
  understanding parents' experiences, 37, 150
  work-life balance, 88
identity, x, 2
  ethnic/racial identity, 12, 33, 94–99,
    145, 151
  hiding, 94–97
  identity development model, 97
  leveraged as social capital for parents, xiv
  minimizing, 9
  recreating new sense of, xv
  sexual identity, 12, 69–70
  storytellers and story collection, 12

Immigration Act of 1924, 17, 62
incorporation stage, 97
infant–caregiver attachment styles, 43–44
inner child
    communities of voices, 81
    defined, 79
    disconnect between knowing and
        understanding and sensing and feeling, 79
    healing, 102–3, 104, 112, 117–21, 143, 151
    invalidating, 26, 82
internal working model (IWM), 43
interpersonal harmony, 1, 26–27, 52, 92, 102
intraethnic and intragroup othering, 6, 33, 95

Jackson, 73
Jeanine, 66, 67, 69
John Carroll University, 81
Johnson, Sue, 132–33
José (author's Lolo (grandfather)), 2–3, 4
journaling, 121, 140

karaoke, 115–16
Kareena
    attachment style, 52, 54
    conspiracy of silence, 89
    demographics, 165
    healing inner child, 119–20
    parenting and parenthood, 144–45
    wholehearted acceptance, 107
    working twice as hard to get half as far, 26
Khmer Rouge, 18
Kim, Jean, 97
Kim, Yub, 38, 67–68, 70–71, 124, 165
Kipling, Rudyard, 63
Korean War, 18–19

Lapu-Lapu, 33
Le, 93, 165
Lee, Shoua
    attachment style, 53
    cultural messages and internalized values, 32
    demographics, 165
    hard work and productivity, 80
    healing inner child, 120–21
    intentionally connecting with children, 142
    mindfulness in parenting, 139
    sexual stigma, 69
    wholehearted acceptance, 113
Levine, Amir, 45
Litam, Stacey Diane Arañez, xiii
    ancestors' obedience and rule following, 3
    ancestors' sacrifices, 2, 3–5
    ancestors' trauma, 2–3

    background of, xvi–xvii
    early morning with sons, 136–37
    father's absence, 77–78
    first day at new school, 59–60
    humor in parenting, 143
    intergenerational interactions at son's
        birthday, 117–19
    internalizing cultural scripts, 25
    naming second child, 33
    need to prove self-worth through
        productivity, 81–83
    objectives in writing book, xvi
    origin of values, 2–4
    scarcity mindset, xiii–xv
    wasting food, 15–16
    wholehearted acceptance, 100–1
    windows of productivity, 86–87
    working twice as hard to get half as far, 24
Liu, Lucy, 94–95
Long, John Luther, 62
Loti, Pierre, 62
loud, not being, 3, 4. See also attention, not
        drawing to oneself
love languages theory, 101–2
    Acts of Service, 101
    Physical Touch, 101
    Quality Time, 101
    Receiving Gifts, 101
    Words of Affirmation, 101

Madame Butterfly (Long), 62
Madame Chrysanthème (Loti), 62
Magellan, Ferdinand, 33
Manolo, Drake, 67, 165
Maté, Daniel, 47
Maté, Gabor, 35, 47, 78
Matthew, 106–7, 109–10, 149, 165
Mean Girls (film), 96
Mental Health America, 9–10
microaggressions, ix, 10–11
mindfulness, xv, 139–40, 144. See also
        awareness
minority tax, 123
model minority myth, 7–8, 11, 25, 31–32, 71, 95
myth of meritocracy, 122–23
Myth of Normal, The (Maté and Maté), 35, 47,
        78

National Origins Formula, 62
Nguyen, Claudia, 165
1917 Act, 17
90-Day Fiancé (TV show), 63
Noah, 37, 139, 165

Noelle, Dr.
  demographics, 165
  parenting and parenthood, 141
  patterns, 33–34
  self-sacrifice, 90
  wholehearted acceptance, 113–14

obedience and rule following, 2, 3, 4, 6, 7, 24, 25
Olivia, 19–20, 55, 107
Orientalism, 63
oxytocin, 128–29

Page Act of 1875, 60–61
parenthood, healing diasporic wounds during
  anticipating children's needs, 141–42
  avoiding transactional acts, 142–43
  awareness, 138–39
  breaking inherited patterns, 137–38
  freedom and healing, 143–44
  HOME Assessment, 139–44
  intentionality, 142
  mindfulness, 139–44
  radical acceptance, 146–48
  self-compassion, 144–45
  sense of humor, 143
  storytelling, 149–52
  understanding children, 141
  understanding parents, 148–49
parts work, 119–21
pattern-breaking strategies, 117–34
  abundance mindset, 122–23
  crab mentality, 121–22
  cultivating stronger communication skills,
    131
  healing attachment wounds and achieving
    secure attachments, 125–26
  healing the inner child, 117–21
  increasing self-awareness, 126–30
  parenthood, 136–53
  raising critical consciousness, 122–24
  responsiveness of secure partners to other's
    needs, 133
  therapy and counseling, 133–34
  understanding the stories we
    create, 131–33
people-pleasing behaviors, 9, 31, 55, 89
permission giving, 75
Permission to Come Home (Wang), 89, 117
person-centered theory, 105–14, 116
Petersen, William, 7
Pew Research Center, 11, 16
Physical Touch love language, 101
Pila, Daniela, 34, 113, 165

prescriptive sexual stereotypes, 71, 75–76
problem minorities, 7
productivity and hard work, xvii, 2, 5, 6, 8, 22,
    24, 36
  driving need to prove self-worth through,
    78–85
  focus on, leading to burnout, 83–86
  milestones, 6, 21, 22, 83
  minority tax, 123
  myth of meritocracy, 122–23
  realities afforded by ancestors' sacrifice, 35
  reasons for overvaluing, 85–86
  sacrificing desires for career, 26
  windows of productivity, 86–88
  working twice as hard to get half as far, xvii, 6,
    24, 25–27, 79
protest behaviors, 45–46

Quality Time love language, 101
Quan D., 19, 26, 98, 151, 165
queer Asians, 65

radical acceptance, 120–21, 146–48
Rape of Nanking, 61
Receiving Gifts love language, 101
redirection stage, 97
rejection and abandonment
  absent working parents, 78
  conspiracies of silence, 79, 92, 93–94
  entrusting baby to strangers for survival, 78
  fear of, 9, 45–46, 55, 56, 57, 85, 125
  inability to embrace whole self for fear
    of, 114
  insecure attachment styles, 44, 45–46, 53, 55,
    56, 79, 126
  opening up to possibility of, 125
  protection of community of voices, 138
  relationship with work versus with people, 85
  sexuality and, 65, 66–67, 68, 70
  understanding the stories we create, 132, 133
rhesus monkey experiments, 42–43, 125
rocking the boat/standing out, avoiding, xiv, 9,
    25, 31–32, 33
Rogers, Carl Ransom, 105–14, 116
rule following. See obedience and rule following

sacrifice, xiv, 1–2, 3–5, 11, 28, 30, 77–78, 80
  author's ancestors, 2, 3–5
  at expense of well-being, 89–90
  gratitude and indebtedness for, 6, 27, 108, 145
  parental reminders of, 102–3, 108, 142–43
  realities afforded by, 35, 37, 38
saving face, 1–2, 32, 92

scarcity mindset, xiii–xiv, xv, 2, 15–23
  avoiding rocking the boat, 32
  competition, 20–21, 25, 27–28, 121–22
  –defined, 20
  driving need to prove self-worth, 79
  effects of, 21
  freeing self from, 122
  gratitude for opportunities, 27–28
  origin of, 17
  parenting and parenthood, 137
  resource hoarding, 21
  wasting food, 15–16
secure attachment style
  adult attachment, 45
  freedom to grow and, 111–12, 116
  freedom to heal and, 112–14, 116
  infant–caregiver attachment, 43–44
secure base concept, 43, 54, 125, 132–33
self-awareness, xvi–xvii, 88, 126–30
  reframing secure love from boring to
      peaceful, 128
  science of love, 128–30
  stop, drop, and roll exercise, 126–27, 130
self-compassion, xvi, 88, 91, 144–45
self-reflection, 123
self-worth
  attachment styles, 57
  conditions of worth, 105
  driving need to prove through productivity,
      78–85
  internal working model, 43
  measuring by achievements, 83
serotonin, 128–29
sexual identity, 12, 69–70
sexual objectification, 66, 74
sexual scripts and stereotypes, xv, 11, 12
  avoiding fetishization, 74
  breaking stigma around, 68–71
  challenging, 71–73
  challenging potential partners, 74–75
  descriptive stereotypes, 71
  impact of, 65–68
  men, 63–64, 66–68
  prescriptive stereotypes, 71
  queer Asians, 65
  regaining sense of power by centering
      pleasure, 75–76
  sexual violence, 72
  women, 60–63, 65–66
sexual stigma, 69
shame
  avoiding rocking the boat, 32
  driving need to prove self-worth through
      productivity, 78–83

ethnic, 95–96
  internalizing, xv
  talking about emotions, 8, 79
  See also conspiracies of silence; saving face
Sharon K.
  attachment style, 53, 54
  demographics, 165
  historical trauma, 18–19
  intentionality with children, 142
  radical acceptance, 147
  sexual stereotypes, 66
  storytelling, 150
  therapy and counseling, 134
Shirley (author's *yaya* (nanny)), 77
Siadat, Cynthia, 36, 55, 165
skin-whitening, 95
Sok, Monica, 18
Sophia, 56–57, 103
status obsession, 21, 25, 73
stop, drop, and roll exercise, 126–27, 130
storytelling, 12–13
  cultivating community through, 151–52
  parental, 26–27
  power of, 149–51
  trauma narratives, 149–51
  understanding the stories we create, 131–33
strange situation procedure, 43
substance abuse, 9–10, 72
Substance Abuse and Mental Health Services
      Administration (SAMHSA), 9–10
supportive community, 121, 151

Tarm, 30, 110, 131
Thalia, 73
Time magazine, 7
Toll of the Sea, The (film), 62
transactional actions and relationships, 104,
      108, 110–11, 116, 141, 142–43, 148
Transcontinental Railroad, 17, 20–21
trauma, 4, 6, 10–11, 15–23, 28–29
  attachment styles and childhood trauma, 52
  attachment wounds, 47–49
  author's ancestors, 2–3
  conspiracies of silence, 4–5, 30
  impact of childhood trauma, 78
  intergenerational, 20, 47
  origin of historical trauma, 18
  parenting and parenthood, 137
  regaining sense of power by centering
      pleasure, 75–76
  storytelling, 12, 149–51
  traumatic shocks associated with
      immigration, 18–20
  unlocking, 36

unconditional positive regard, 105
University of Cincinnati, 81

Valli, Dr.
  acculturation, 34
  Asian American identity, 98
  career and collectivism, 6–7
  challenge of seeking mental health care, 10
  demographics, 165
  healing diasporic wounds, 143–44
  parenting and parenthood, 145
  radical acceptance, 147
vasopressin, 128–29
Vietnam war, 30
Vo, Christopher, 29, 32, 147, 165
vulnerability, xviii, 8, 11, 48, 49, 52, 53
  expressing emotions, 28–30, 36, 102–3
  leading to conflict, 8
  wholehearted acceptance, 107–8, 115–16

Wang, Jenny T., 89, 117
War Brides Act of 1945, 62
white identification stage, 97
white proximity, 6, 25, 95, 96
wholehearted acceptance
  anticipating needs, wants, and desires, 104, 108–11

freedom to grow and heal, 104, 111–16
  HOME Assessment, 104, 106–16
  love languages, 101–4
  person-centered theory, 105–14
  understanding, 104, 106–8
Wong Liu Tsong (Anna May
    Wong), 61–62
Words of Affirmation love language, 101
workaholism. See productivity
    and hard work
Wu, Kimmy
  attachment style, 57
  conflict avoidance, 92–93
  demographics, 165
  radical acceptance, 120
  secure attachments, 125
  work-life balance, 88

Xuan, Tessa, 165

Yang, Jai, 19
YanYan, 66–67, 69
"yellow fever," 74
Yeoh, Michelle, 51

Zauner, Michelle, 49, 110

About the Author

Stacey Diane Arañez Litam (she/her/siya) is a Filipina and Chinese American mother, wife, daughter, sister, and friend. Beyond these central personal identities, Dr. Litam is a professor in counselor education, licensed professional clinical counselor, and clinical sexologist. She is a keynote speaker and consultant on topics related to mental health and sexual well-being, Asian American issues, and diversity, equity, inclusion, and belonging. She is passionate about decolonizing mental health perspectives, centering Filipino American stories, and creating spaces where individuals who hold multiple intersecting marginalized identities feel seen, heard, and worthy of compassion and healing. Dr. Litam received a bachelor's degree in psychology and a master's degree in clinical mental health counseling from John Carroll University. She earned her PhD in counselor education and supervision from Kent State University and has published extensively on Filipino American and Asian American mental health, social justice counseling, human sexuality, and human sex trafficking. She spends her free time with family and enjoys traveling the world in search of the most delicious foods and the perfect cake donut.